INDIA BOOKVARSITY

LOTUS CHOICES

Editor: Mahendra Kulasrestha

Classics Revived
for an
Ultramodern World

The Golden Book of BUDDHISM

Humanity's Oldest Religion of Peace

Life of the Buddha
Dhammachakka Pavattana-Sutta
Dhammapada
Prajna-paramita Hridaya Sutra
Vajrachchhedika
Sukhavati Vyuha, and
Mahaparinibbana Sutta

Lotus PRESS

4735/22, Prakash Deep Building,
Ansari Road, Darya Ganj,
New Delhi- 110002

THE GOLDEN BOOK OF BUDDHISM

Selected Suttas of
both Hinayana and
Mahayana Buddhism,
with Ashvaghosha's
Buddha-Charita, translated
into easy-to-understand English by

F. MAX MULLER
T.W. RHYS DAVIDS
and
SAMUEL BEAL

Lotus Press : Publishers & Distributors
Unit No. 220, 2nd Floor, 4735/22, Prakash Deep Building,
Ansari Road, Darya Ganj, New Delhi- 110002
Ph.: 41325510, 98118-38000
• E-mail : lotuspress1984@gmail.com
www.lotuspress.co.in

Source:
Sacred Books of the East
Edited by F. Max Muller
and published by
Clarendon Press, Oxford, UK
in the 1880s

The Golden Book of Buddhism

ISBN: 81-8382-143-X

Printed & Published by : **Lotus Press Publisher & Distributors,** New Delhi-02

Editorspeak

Revive Buddhism in India

I am a lover of Buddhism and regard it as a possible saviour of humanity in the present terror-stricken world. The great regard given to Dalai Lama in the West is a shining example of the general acceptance of his message of peace. The establishment of Peace Pagodas worldwide by the followers of Fuji Guruji—the famous Japanese monk well known as the person who gave the three monkeys to Mahatma Gandhi—and also participated in his movement—and their peace marches in many countries in the last two decades, is another example of its success—as well as future potential and possibilities.

I am also of the definite view that Hinduism made a very great mistake by pushing out Buddhism from their/our country, and without going into a discussion, would like to emphasise the urgent need of rectification, in moral and cultural, as well as political interests. Dr. Syama Prasad Mukherji, the Hindu Mahasabha-Jan Sangh (now BJP) leader, had this vision—which should be honestly followed by the present-day Hindus. The following article culled from the speeches and writings of Swami Vivekananda also underlines the good things of Buddhism in an effective manner.

The significance of Buddhism in modern times cannot be under-rated. If religion is a basic necessity for human beings, perhaps Buddhism, with certain pluses and minuses, can be promoted as the global religion of the fast globalising world. Since I am not a scholar of this great religion, I take the liberty of presenting the views of an authority on the subject, Dr. N.K. Devaraja, who retired as the Head of the Dept. of Philosophy at the Benares Hindu University, now late, in some detail. He was also a well-known litterateur, and a friend of the present writer; his works on philosophy are well known. In a contribution to the Silver Jubilee

Commemorative Volume of the Sikkim Research Institute of Tibetology and other Buddhistic studies, published by Vision Books, with which the present writer has been associated. He writes:

"During the recent decades Buddhism has been steadily gaining in popularity particularly among the intellectuals. Unlike the pundits belonging to the times of Kumarila and Sankara who felt intense hostility towards Buddhism, modern Indian scholars, most of whom are Hindus and some Jains, have been inclined to be as sympathetic and painstaking in their studies of Buddhist thinkers as in those of their own philosophers. An important factor here, no doubt, has been the growth of the nationalistic sentiment which makes people anxious to recover and preserve all that is valuable in their common heritage. Another factor, not unrelated to the first, has been the desire to preserve our cultural identity vis-a-vis the cultures of the West, and to reassert, through redefinition and renewed emphasis, the values, intellectual, moral and religious, that characterise that identity. Hindu and Jain scholars have also been struck by the identity of spirit underlying the surface differences between the major spiritual traditions developed in this country. Thus, scholars like late Prof. S. Radhakrishnan, and Prof. T.R.V. Murty have emphasized the similarities of attitude and outlook, as also of spiritual vision, informing such divergent looking systems as the Advaita of Sankara and the Sunyavada of the Madhyamikas.

"In the West, however, the reasons for the increasing popularity of Buddhism have been entirely different. A characteristic development in the West during the past three centuries has been the growth and diffusion of the scientific outlook. The conflict between science and religion during the last several centuries having been settled in favour of science, Western man has been suffering from deeply felt alienation from his ethico-religious heritage. Unable to reconcile Christianity with science, the Western intellectual is faced with the unpleasant choice between disregarding the testimony of science on the one hand and the guidance of religion and the optimism of faith on the other. In the circumstances discerning intellectuals, unable to endure the vacuum created by loss of faith in the traditional religion and its wisdom, felt drawn towards the rationalist gospel of the Buddha with its pronounced aversion to belief in a creator God and the dogma of creation. The empirical or experiential temper of Buddhist teaching is another factor that appeals to the minds of modern men and women. For the Buddha's teaching is based, not on the authority of any scriptures, but on the testimony of experience, the existential situation of man endowed with sensitive self awareness.

"A provocative verse of Dharmakiriti enumerates five marks of a fool. These include belief in scriptures, belief in the dogma of creation, and pride born of belief in caste hierarchy. The verse empitomises the revolutionary content of the Buddha's teachings. The Buddhist denial of an enduring self and enduring objects, and their distrust of language as the vehicle of objective knowledge so poignantly expressed by Nagarjuna are other aspects of the Buddhist doctrine that appear intriguing to the modern mind.

"Modern science has progressed by refusing to base itself on authority, religious or personal. Nor does the scientific world-view, insisting as it does on the prevalence of inviolable laws in nature, countenance belief in a creator lord of nature. Science has also dealt a blow to the category of substance, so dear to metaphysicians of all brands. It is no mean achievement of Buddhist thinkers to have questioned that belief centuries before the rise of modern science. And the Buddha's repudiation of caste and of the cult of animal sacrifice, were equally daring feats in the peculiar historical circumstances in which he found himself.

"The peculiar charm of Buddhism for the modern man consists in the fact that, with all its rationalist and experiential bias, it claims to embody a world-view and a philosophy of life that centres mainly around ethico-religious values. In contradistinction to other world religions, Buddhism provides man with a system of religious values without putting him in conflict with science; it thus tends to fill the void produced by the breakdown of traditional religious beliefs, brought about by the impact of science. For, unlike Buddhism, most of the religious traditions require their followers, when faced with the disconcerting consequences of science, to take shelter in uncritical faith—faith in this or that scripture, in this or that Saviour, and so forth. This insistence on faith, on uncritical acceptance of dogmas in conflict with science or reason, produces traumatic disturbances in sensitive minds.

"Buddhism is of interest to the modern man as a creed or philosophy that centres its attention on man and teaches a wisdom that can elevate him spiritually in his life here on earth. This need not imply that Buddhism has said the last word as to the wisdom of living. Nor is it necessary for us today either to accept Buddhism in its entirety or to reject it completely. All that can be claimed on behalf of Buddhism is that, as a religious philosophy and a way of life, it is more suited to our scientific age with its humanistic temper than most other religions of the world."

Our knowledge of Buddhism is limited to the name of Buddha, the words Suffering, Nirvana, and perhaps the maxim *'Bhaujana Hitaya, Bahujana Sukhaya'* also. It is a pity, to say the least. I have always wanted to know more about it; the books simply do not exist. The present work tries to provide a sampler from the many scriptures, representing the two main segments, Hinayana and Mahayana, with selections from his life penned by the famous Sanskrit poet Ashvaghosa, *Buddha-Charit,* though not from its original in Sanskrit but from its Chinese translation—because Buddhist scriptures were relatively easily available in those languages. The concept of heaven in Buddhism, which sounds strong in the background of its basic ideology, is also presented in a separate chapter; it is known as Sukhavati—the land or city of bliss—and has a much larger and elaborate version also. Buddhism, as it spread in other countries, acquired various shapes and forms, perhaps to suit their levels and requirements.

Vivekananda on Buddha and His Religion

Buddhism is historically the most important religion because it was the most tremendous movement that the world ever saw, the most gigantic spiritual wave ever to burst upon human society. There is no civilization on which its effect has not been felt in some way or other.

The followers of Buddha were most enthusiastic and very missionary in spirit. They were the first among the adherents of various religions not to remain content with the limited sphere of their Mother Church. They spread far and wide. They travelled east and west, north and south. They reached into darkest Tibet; they went into Persia, Asia Minor; they went into Russia, Poland, and many other countries of the Western world. They went into China, Korea, Japan; they went into Burma, Siam, the East Indies, and beyond.

To understand this movement properly one should know what conditions prevailed in India at the time Buddha came, just as to understand Christianity you have to grasp the state of Jewish society at the time of Christ.

When you study the civilization of India, you find that it has died and revived several times; this is its peculiarity. Most races rise once and then decline for ever. The peaceful nations, India and China, fall down, yet rise again; but the others, once they go down, do not come up—they die. Blessed are the peacemakers, for they shall enjoy the earth.

At the time Buddha was born, India was in need of a great spiritual leader, a prophet. There was already a most powerful body of priests. One will understand the situation better if he remembers the history of the Jews—how they had two types of religious leaders, priests and prophets, the priests keeping the people in ignorance and grinding superstition into their minds. All through the Old Testament, you find the prophets challenging the superstitions of the priests.

The priests in India, the Brahmins, possessed great intellectual and psychic powers. It was they who began the spiritual development of India, and they accomplished wonderful things. But the time came when the free spirit of development that had at first actuated the Brahmins disappeared. They began to arrogate powers and privileges to themselves. If a Brahmin killed a man, he would not be punished. Even the most wicked Brahmin must be worshipped!

But while the priests were flourishing, there existed also the poet-prophets called Sannyasins. The Sannyasins have nothing to do with the two thousand ceremonies that the priests have invented. India was full of it in Buddha's day. There were the masses of people, and they were debarred from all knowledge. If just a word of the Vedas entered the ears of a man, terrible punishment was visited upon him. The priests had made a secret of the Vedas.

At last one man could bear it no more. He

had the brain, the power, and the heart—a heart as infinite as the broad sky. This man had the brain to discover the means of breaking the bondages of souls. He learnt why men suffer, and he found the way out of suffering. He taught one and all without distinction and made them realize the peace of enlightenment. This was the man Buddha.

Buddha was the triumph in the struggle that had been going on between the priests and the prophets in India. One of his great messages was the equality of man. Buddha was the great preacher of equality. Every man and woman has the same right to attain spirituality. The difference between the priests and the other castes he abolished. Even the lowest were entitled to the highest attainments; he opened the door of Nirvana to one and all. His teaching was bold even for India; it was hard for India to swallow Buddha's doctrine.

The religion of Buddha spread fast. It was because of the marvellous love which, for the first time in the history of humanity, overflowed a large heart and devoted itself to the service not only of all men but of all living things—a love which did not care for anything except to find a way of release from suffering for all beings.

Buddha's idea is that there is no God, only man himself. He repudiated the mentality which underlies the prevalent ideas of God. He found it made men weak and superstitious. Everything independent is happy; everything dependent is miserable.

The life of Buddha has an especial appeal. All my life I have been very fond of Buddha. I have more veneration for that character than for any other—that boldness, that fearlessness, and that tremendous love! He was born for the good of men. Others may seek God, others may seek truth for themselves; he did not even care to know truth for himself. He sought truth because people were in misery. How to help them, that was his only concern.

And consider his marvellous brain! No emotionalism. That giant brain never was superstitious. Believe not because an old manuscript has been produced, because it has been handed down to you from your forefathers, but think for yourself; search truth for yourself; realize it yourself. Then if you find it beneficial to one and many, give it to people.

People were able to appreciate and embrace his teachings, so revolutionary, so different from what they had been taught by the priests through the ages!

And consider his death. If he was great in life, he was also great in death. He ate food offered to him by an outcaste, a *chandal*. Hindus do not touch them, because they eat everything indiscriminately. He told his disciples, 'Do not eat this food, but I cannot refuse it. Go to the man and tell him he has done me one of the greatest services of my life—he has released me from the body.'

Buddhistic India

There have been great religions before Buddhism arose, in India and elsewhere, but, more or less, they are confined within their own races. With Buddhism first begins that peculiar phenomenon of religion boldly starting out to conquer the world. Within a few centuries of its birth, the barefooted, shaven-headed missionaries of Buddha had spread over all the then known civilized world, and they penetrated even further—from Lapland on the one side to the Philippine Islands on the other. In India itself, the religion of Buddha had at one time nearly swallowed up two-thirds of the population.

Still, it has the largest number of followers of any religion, and it has indirectly modified the teachings of all the other religions. A good deal of Buddhism entered into Asia Minor. It was a constant fight at one time whether the Buddhists would prevail or the later sects of Christians.

His method of work and organization was quite striking. The idea that we have today of Church is his creation. He organized these monks and made them into a body. Even the voting by ballot is there five hundred and sixty years before Christ. The Church became a tremendous power, and did great missionary work. Then came, three hundred years after, two hundred years before Christ, the great emperor Asoka, as he has been called by Western historians, the divinest of monarchs, and that man became entirely converted to the idea of Buddha, and he spread the religion worldwide. He sent his own children as well as others to propagate the ideology and set up inscriptions all over.

The first inscription describes the terror and misery of war, and how he became converted to religion. Then said he: "Henceforth let none of my descendants think of acquiring glory by conquering other races. If they want glory, let them help other races; let them send teachers of sciences and teachers of religion." And next you find how he is sending missionaries even to Alexandria. You wonder that you find all over that part of the country sects rising immediately, called Theraputae, Essenes, and all those—extreme vegetarians, and so on. Asoka built hospitals for men and for animals.

Buddhism was the foundation of the

Christian religion; the Catholic Church came from Buddhism.

He was the only man who was ever ready to give up his life for animals to stop a sacrifice. He once said to a king, 'If the sacrifice of a lamb helps you to go to heaven, sacrificing a man will help you better; so sacrifice me.' The king was astonished.

To many the path becomes easier if they believe in God. But the life of Buddha shows that even a man who does not believe in God, has no metaphysics, belongs to no sect, and goes not to any church, or temple, and is a confessed materialist, even he can attain to the highest.

It was the great Buddha, who never cared for the dualist gods, and who has been called an atheist and materialist, who yet was ready to give up his body for a poor goat. That Man set in motion the highest moral ideas any nation can have. Wherever there is a moral code it is a ray of light from that Man.

Contents

Latest

The first Indian Buddhist temple in modern times is planned to be built in Lnoyang, in the place where the first Buddhists from India arrived in China in ancient times. The Chinese government has given India a very large plot of land in the old temple complex to build the temple. It will be built along the times of the famous Sanchi Stupa in a modern setting. It will mark the return of Buddhism in China.

The spot, known as Baima Temple Complex, is regarded as the cradle of Chinese Buddhism, and was built after Emperor Ming of the Eastern Handynasty welcomed the first Buddhist monks from India, she Mong and Zhu Falan, and a white horse which carried the Sutra and the image of Lord Buddha.

(Nov. 2005)

1

Buddha
Glimpses of a Great Life

There was a descendant of the Ikshvaku family, an invincible Sakya monarch, pure in mind and of unspotted virtue, called Suddhodana. Joyously reverenced by all men, as the new moon is welcomed by the world, the king indeed was like the heaven-ruler Sakra, his queen like the divine Sachi. Strong and calm of purpose as the earth, pure in mind as the water-lily, her name, figuratively assumed, Maya, she was in truth incapable of class-comparison.

On her in likeness as the heavenly queen descended the spirit and entered her womb. A mother, but free from a grief or pain, she was without any false or illusory mind. Disliking the clamorous ways of the world, she remembered the excellent garden of Lumbini, a pleasant spot, a quiet forest retreat, with its trickling fountains, and blooming flowers and fruits.

Quiet and peaceful, delighting in meditation, respectfully she asked the king for liberty to roam therein; the king, understanding her earnest desire, was seized with a seldom-felt anxiety to grant her request. He commanded his kinsfolk, within and without the palace, to repair with her to that garden shade; and now the queen Maya knew that her time for child-bearing was come. She rested calmly on a beautiful couch, surrounded by a hundred thousand female attendants; it was the eighth day of the fourth moon, a season of serene and agreeable character.

Whilst she thus religiously observed the rules of a pure discipline, Bodhisattva was born from her right side, come to deliver the world, constrained by great pity, without causing his mother pain or anguish.

Gradually emerging from the womb, he shed in every direction the rays of his glory. As one born from recumbent space, and not through the gates of life, through countless kalpas, practising virtue, self-conscious he came forth to life, without confusion. Calm and collected, not falling headlong was he born, gloriously manifested, perfectly adorned, sparkling with light he came from the womb, as when the sun first rises from the East.

His body was effulgent with light, and like the sun which eclipses the shining of the lamp, so the true gold-like beauty of Bodhisattva shone forth, and was diffused everywhere. Upright and firm and unconfused in mind, he deliberately took seven steps, the soles of his feet resting evenly upon the ground as he went, his footmarks remained bright as seven stars.

Moving like the lion, king of beasts, and looking earnestly towards the four quarters, penetrating to the centre the principles of truth, he spake thus with the fullest assurance: "This birth is in the condition of a Buddha; after this I have done with renewed birth; now only am I born this once, for the purpose of saving all the world."

And now from the midst of heaven there descended two streams of pure water, one warm, the other cold, and baptized his head, causing refreshment to his body. And now he is placed in the precious palace hall, a jewelled couch for him to sleep upon, and the heavenly kings with their golden flowery hands hold fast the four feet of the bed.

In the garden of Lumbini, filling the spaces between the trees, rare and special flowers, in great abundance, bloomed out of season. All cruel and malevolent kinds of beings, together conceived a loving heart; all diseases and afflictions among men without a cure applied, of themselves were healed. The various cries and confused sounds of beasts were hushed and silence reigned; the stagnant water of the river-courses flowed apace, whilst the polluted streams became clear and pure.

Mara, the heavenly monarch, alone was grieved and rejoiced not. The Royal Father Suddhodana, beholding his son, strange and miraculous, as to his birth, though self-possessed and assured in his soul, was yet moved with astonishment and his countenance changed, whilst he alternately weighed with himself the meaning of such an event, now rejoiced and now distressed.

The queen-mother beholding her child, born thus contrary to laws of nature, her timorous woman's heart was doubtful; her mind, through fear, swayed between extremes: Not distinguishing the happy from the sad portents, again and again she gave way to grief; and now the aged women of the world, in a confused way supplicating heavenly guidance, implored the gods to whom their rites were paid to bless the child; to cause peace to rest upon the royal child.

Now there was at this time in the grove, a certain soothsayer, a Brahmin, of dignified mien and widespread renown, famed for his skill and scholarship: beholding the signs, his heart rejoiced, and he exulted at the miraculous event. Knowing the king's mind to be somewhat perplexed, he addressed him with truth and earnestness: "Men born in the world chiefly desire to have a son the most renowned; but now the king, like the moon when full, should feel in himself a perfect joy, having begotten an unequalled son, for by this the king will become illustrious among his race; the spiritual omens that are everywhere manifested indicate for your house and dominion a course of continued prosperity. The most excellently endowed child now born will bring deliverance to the entire world: none but a heavenly teacher has a body such as this, golden-coloured, gloriously resplendent.

"One endowed with such transcendent marks must reach the state of Samyak-Sambodhi, or, if he be induced to engage in worldly delights, then he must become a universal monarch; mighty in his righteous government. But if he seek a dwelling among the mountain forests, with single heart searching for deliverance, having arrived at the perfection of true wisdom, he will become illustrious throughout the world; as the sun is brightest of all luminaries, so Tathagata, born in the world, is the most eminent of men; his eyes clear and expanding, the lashes both above and below moving with the lid, the iris of the eye of a clear blue colour, in shape like the moon when half full, such characteristics as these, without contradiction, foreshadow the most excellent condition of perfect wisdom."

The king hearing the words of the seer, was glad, and offered him gifts.

"Now have I begotton a valiant son," he said, "who will establish a wheel authority, whilst I, when old and gray-headed, will go forth to lead a hermit's life, so that my holy, king-like son may not give up the world and wander through mountain forests."

Suddhodana seeing the excellent marks, predictive signs, of his son, was greatly affected with reverence to the child: he redoubled measures for its protection, and was filled with constant thought; moreover, he issued decrees through the empire, to liberate all captives in prison, extending his gifts to all.

When the child was ten days old, his father's mind being now quite tranquil, he announced a sacrifice to all the gods, and prepared to give liberal offerings to all the religious bodies; Sramanas and Brahmins invoked by their prayers a blessing from the gods, whilst he bestowed gifts on the royal kinspeople and the ministers and the poor within the country. Then, selecting by divination a lucky-time, they took the child back to his own palace, with a double-feeding white-pure-tooth, carried in a richly-adorned chariot cradle, with ornaments of every kind and colour round his neck; shining with beauty, exceedingly resplendent with unguents. The queen embracing him in her arms, going around, worshipped the heavenly spirits.

Life in the palace

And now in the household of Suddhodana, because of the birth of the royal prince, his clansmen and younger brethren, with his ministers, were all generously disposed, whilst elephants, horses and chariots, and the wealth of the country, and precious vessels, daily increased and abounded, being produced wherever requisite; so, too, countless hidden treasures came of themselves from the earth. Enmity and envy gave way to peace; content and rest prevailed on every side; whilst there was closer union amongst the true of heart, discord and variance were entirely appeased; the gentle air distilled a seasonable rain, no crash of storm or tempest was heard, the springing seeds, not waiting for their time, grew up apace and yielded abundant increase.

The king having begotten a royal prince, these marks of prosperity were seen; and because of such a concourse of propitious signs, the child was named Siddhartha. And now his royal mother, the queen Maya, beholding her son born under such circumstances, beautiful as a child of heaven, adorned with every excellent distinction, from excessive joy which could not be controlled, died, and was born in heaven. Then Prajapati Gautami, beholding the prince, like an angel, with beauty seldom seen on earth, seeing him thus born and now his mother dead, loved and nourished him as her own child; and the child regarded her as his mother.

So as the light of the sun or the moon, little by little increases, the royal child also increased each day in every mental excellence and beauty of person. And he was brought to learn the useful arts, when lo! once instructed he surpassed his teacher. His father, the king, seeing his exceeding talent, and his deep purpose to have done with the world and its allurements, began to inquire as to the names of those in his tribe who were renowned for elegance and refinement. Elegant and graceful, and a lovely maiden, was she whom they called Yasodhara; in every way fitting to become a consort for the prince, and to allure by pleasant wiles his heart. The prince with a mind so far removed from the world, with qualities so distinguished, and with so charming an appearance, the virtuous damsel, lovely and refined, gentle and subdued in manner; majestic like the queen of heaven, choosing a proper dwelling according to the year, surrounded by singing women, Boddhisattva dwelt in his lofty palace, with music. The king, his father, for the prince's sake, dwelt purely in his palace, practising every virtue. He also attended to his religious duties, sacrificing by fire to all the spirits, with clasped hands adorning the moon, bathing his body in the waters of the Ganges; cleansing his heart in the waters of religion.

And now the son of Suddhodana, and his virtuous wife Yasodhara, as time went on, growing to full estate, their child Rahula was born; and then Suddhodana considered thus: "My son, the prince, having a son born to him, the affairs of the empire will be handed down in succession, the prince having begotten a son, will love his son as I love him, and no longer think about leaving his home as an ascetic, I now have found complete rest of heart."

Now the king, having begotten a royal son, indulged him in every sort of pleasure; desiring that he might enjoy these worldly delights, and not wish to wander from his home in search of wisdom.

Reacting to disease and death

There are pleasant garden glades, flowing fountains, pure refreshing lakes, with every kind of flower, and trees with fruit, deep shade beneath. There, too, are various kinds of wondrous birds, flying and sporting in the midst, bright coloured, giving out their floating scent; minstrel maidens cause their songs and chorded music, to invite the prince. He, hearing the sounds of singing, sighs for the pleasures of the garden shades, and cherishing within these happy thoughts, he dwelt upon the joys of an outside excursion; even as the chained elephant ever longs for the free desert wilds.

The royal father, hearing that the prince would enjoy to wander through the gardens, first ordered all his attendant officers to adorn and arrange them. To make level and smooth the king's highway, to remove from the path all offensive matter, all old persons, diseased or deformed, all those suffering through poverty or great grief, so that his son in his present humour might see nothing likely to afflict his heart. The adornments being duly made, the prince was invited to an audience.

Now see the jewel-fronted gaudy chariot; the four equally pacing, stately horses; good-tempered and well trained; perfectly pure and white, and draped with flowery coverings. In the same chariot stands the stately driver; the streets were scattered over with flowers; precious drapery fixed on either side of the way.

So the country-folk and the town-folk, hearing that the prince was coming forth, the well-to-do not waiting for their servants, those asleep and awake not mutually calling to one another, all went pouring along the way on foot; the towers were filled, the mounds by the trees, the windows and the terraces along the streets. And now beautiful as the opening lily, he advances towards the garden glades, wishing to accomplish the words of the Rishi. The prince, seeing the ways prepared and watered and the joyous holiday appearance of the people; seeing too the drapery and chariot, pure, bright, shining, his heart exulted greatly and rejoiced.

And now a Devaraja of the Pure abode, suddenly appeared by the side of the road; his form changed into that of an old man, struggling for life, his heart weak and oppressed. The prince seeing the old man, filled with apprehension, asked his charioteer, "What kind of man is this?—his head white and his shoulders bent, his eyes bleared and his body withered, holding a stick to support him along the way. Is his body suddenly dried up by the heat, or has he been born in this way?"

The charioteer, his heart much embarrased, scarcely dared to answer truly, till the pure-born (Deva) added his spiritual power, and caused him to frame a reply in true words: "These are the indications of what is called 'old age.' This man was once a sucking child, brought up and nourished at his mother's breast, and as a youth full of sportive life, handsome, and in enjoyment of the five pleasures; as years passed on his frame decaying, he is brought now to the waste of age."

The prince, greatly agitated and moved, asked his charioteer this question and said, "Is man the only one afflicted with age, or shall I, and others also, be such as he?"

The charioteer again replied and said, "Your highness also inherits this lot: as time goes on, the form itself is changed, and this must doubtless come, beyond all hindrance. The youthful form must wear the garb of age, throughout the world, this is the common lot."

Bodhisattva, who had long prepared the foundation of pure and spotless wisdom, broadly setting the root of every high quality, with a view to gather large fruit in his present life, hearing these words respecting the sorrow of age, was afflicted in mind, and his hair stood upright. Shaking with apprehension, he deeply sighed; constrained at heart because of the pain of age; with shaking head and constant gaze, he thought upon this misery of decay; Bodhisattva then addressed his charioteer:

"Quickly turn your chariot and go back. Ever thinking on this subject of old age approaching, what pleasures now can these gardens afford, the years of my life like the fast-flying wind; turn your chariot, and with speedy wheels take me to my palace."

And so his heart keeping in the same sad tone, he was as one who returned to a place of entombment; unaffected by any engagement or employment, so he found no rest in anything with in his home.

The king hearing of his son's sadness urged his companions to induce him again to go abroad, and forthwith incited his ministers and attendants to decorate the gardens even more then before. The Deva then caused himself to appear as a sick man; struggling for life, he stood by the wayside, his body swollen and disfigured, sighing with deep-drawn groans; his hands and knees contracted and sore with disease, his tears flowing as he piteously muttered his petition. The prince asked his charioteer, "What sort of man, again, is this?"

Replying, he said, "This is a sick man. The four elements all confused and disordered, worn and feeble, with no remaining strength, bent down with weakness, looking to his fellow-men for help."

The prince hearing the words thus spoken, immediately became sad and depressed in heart, and asked, "Is this the only man afflicted thus, or are others liable to the same calamity?"

In reply he said, "Through all the world, men are subject to the same condition; those who have bodies must endure affliction, the poor and ignorant, as well as the rich and great."

The prince, when these words met his ears, was oppressed with anxious thought and grief; his body and his mind were moved throughout, just as the moon upon the ruffled tide. "Placed thus in the great furnace of affliction, say! what rest or quiet can there be! Alas! that worldly men, blinded by ignorance and oppressed with dark delusion, though the robber sickness may appear at any time, yet live with blithe and joyous hearts!"

On this, turning his chariot back again, he grieved to think upon the pain of sickness. As a man beaten and wounded sore, with body weakened, leans upon his staff, so dwelt he in the seclusion of his palace, lone-seeking, hating worldly pleasures.

The king, hearing once more of his son's return, asked anxiously the reason why, and in reply was told—"He saw the pain of sickness."

The king, in fear, like one beside himself, roundly blamed

the keepers of the way; his heart constrained, his lips spoke not; again he increased the crowd of music-women, the sounds of merriment twice louder than aforetime, if by these sounds and sights the prince might be gratified; and indulging worldly feelings, might not hate his home. Night and day the charm of melody increased, but his heart was still unmoved by it.

The king himself then went forth to observe everything successively, and to make the gardens even yet more attractive, selecting with care the attendant women, that they might excel in every point of personal beauty; quick in wit and able to arrange matters well, fit to ensnare men by their winning looks; he placed additional keepers along the king's way, he strictly ordered every offensive sight to be removed, and earnestly exhorted the illustrious coachman, to look well and pick out the road as he went.

And now that Deva of the Pure Abode, again caused the appearance of a dead man; four persons carrying the corpse lifted it on high, and appeared to be going on in front of Bodhisattva; the surrounding people saw it not, but only Bodhisattva and the charioteer.

Once more he asked, "What is this they carry?—with streamers and flowers of every choice description, whilst the followers are overwhelmed with grief, tearing their hair wailing piteously."

And now the gods instructing the coachman, he replied and said, "This is a dead man: all his powers of body destroyed, life departed; his heart without thought, his intellect dispersed; his spirit gone, his form withered and decayed; stretched out as a dead log; family ties broken—all his friends who once loved him, clad in white cerements, now no longer delighting to behold him, remove him to lie in some hollow ditch tomb."

The prince hearing the name of Death, his heart constrained by painful thoughts, he asked, "Is this the only dead man, or does the world contain like instances?"

Replying thus he said, "All, everywhere, the same; he who begins his life must end it likewise; the strong and lusty and the middle-aged, having a body, cannot but decay and die."

The prince was now harassed and perplexed in mind: his body bent upon the chariot leaning-board, with bated breath and struggling accents, stammered thus, "Oh worldly men! How fatally deluded! beholding everywhere the body brought to dust, yet everywhere the more carelessly living; the heart is neither lifeless wood nor stone, and yet it thinks not 'all is vanishing!'"

Then turning, he directed his chariot to go back, and no longer waste his time in wandering.

Renouncing the world

The king then sent his chief ministers, and the most distinguished of his family, young in years and eminent for beauty, as well as for wisdom and dignity of manners, to accompany and rest with him, both night and day, in order to influence the prince's mind. And now within a little interval, the prince again requested the king that he might go out.

Once more the chariot and the well-paced horses were prepared, adorned with precious substances and every gem; and then with all the nobles, his associates, surrounding him, he left the city gates.

Now by the roadside, as he beheld the ploughmen, plodding along the furrows, and the writhing worms, his heart again was moved with piteous feeling, and anguish pierced his soul afresh; to see those labourers at their toil, struggling with painful work, their bodies bent, their hair dishevelled, the dripping sweat upon their faces, their persons fouled with mud and dust; the ploughing oxen, too, bent by the yokes, their lolling tongues and gaping mouths. The nature of the prince, loving, compasionate, his mind conceived most poignant sorrow, and nobly moved to sympathy, he groaned with pain; then stooping down he sat upon the ground, and watched this painful scene of suffering; reflecting on the ways of birth and death! "Alas!" he cried, "for all the world! How dark and ignorant, void of understanding!"

And then to give his followers chance of rest, he bade them each repose where'er they list, whilst he beneath the shadow of a Jambu tree, gracefully seated, gave himself to thought. He pondered on the fact of life and death, inconstancy, and endless progress to decay. His heart thus fixed without confusion, the five senses covered and clouded over, lost in possession of enlightenment and insight, he entered on the first pure state of ecstasy.

All low desire removed, most perfect peace ensued; and fully now in Samadhi he saw the misery and utter sorrow of the world; the ruin wrought by age, disease, and death; the great misery following on the body's death; and yet men not awakened to the truth! oppressed with others' suffering age, disease, and death, this load of sorrow weighed his mind. "I now will seek," he said, "a noble law, unlike the worldly methods known to men. I will oppose disease and age and death, and strive against the mischief wrought by these on men."

At this time a Deva of the Pure Abode, transforming himself into the shape of a Bhikshu, came to the place where the prince was seated; the prince with due consideration rose to meet him, and asked him who he was. In reply he said,

"I am a Shraman, depressed and sad at thought of age, disease, and death; I have left my home to seek some way of rescue, but everywhere I find old age, disease, and death; all things hasten to decay and there is no permanence. Therefore I search for the happiness of something that decays not, that never perishes, that never knows beginning, that looks with equal mind on enemy and friend, that heeds not wealth nor beauty; the happiness of one who finds repose alone in solitude, in some unfrequented dell, free from molestation, all thoughts about the world destroyed; dwelling in some lonely hermitage, untouched by any worldly source of pollution, begging for food sufficient for the body."

And forthwith as he stood before the prince, gradually rising up he disappeared in space.

The prince, with joyful mind, considering, recollected former Buddhas, established thus in perfect dignity of manner; with noble mien and presence, as this visitor. Thus calling things to mind with perfect self-possession, he reached the thought of righteousness, and by what means it can be gained. Indulging thus for some time in thoughts of religious solitude, he now suppressed his feelings and controlled his members, and rising turned again towards the city.

The prince entering the city, there met him men and women, earnest for their several ends; the old besought him for their children, the young sought something for the wife, others sought something for their brethren; all those allied by kinship or by family, aimed to obtain their several suits, all of them joined in relationship dreading the pain of separation. And now the prince's heart was filled with joy, as he suddenly heard those words "separation and association." "These are joyful sounds to me," he said, "they assure me that my vow shall be accomplished."

Then deeply pondering the joy of "snapped relationship," the idea of Nirvana, deepened and widened in him, his body as a peak of the Golden Mount, his shoulder like the elephant's, his voice like the spring-thunder, his deep-blue eyes like that of the king of oxen; his mind full of religious thoughts, his face bright as the full moon, his step like that of the lion king, thus he entered his palace; even as the son of Lord Sakra, or Sakra-putra, his mind reverential, his person dignified, he went straight to his father's presence, and with head inclined, inquired, "Is the king well?" Then he explained his dread of age, disease, and death, and sought respectfully permission to become a hermit. "For all things in the world," he said, "though now united, tend to separation." Therefore, he prayed to leave the world; desiring to find "true deliverance."

His royal father hearing the words "leave the world," was forthwith seized with great heart-trembling, even as the strong wild elephant shakes with his weight the boughs fo some young sapling; going forward, seizing the prince's hands, with falling tears, he spake as follows:

"Stop! nor speak such words, the time is not yet come for 'a religious life;' you are young and strong, your heart beats full, to lead a religious life frequently involves trouble; it is rarely possible to hold the desires in check, the heart not yet estranged from their enjoyment; to leave your home and lead a painful ascetic life, your heart can hardly yet resolve on such a course. To dwell amidst the desert wilds or lonely dells, this heart of yours would not be perfectly at rest, for though you love religious matters, you are not yet like me in years; you should undertake the kingdom's government, and let me first adopt ascetic life; but to give up your father and your sacred duties, this is not to act religiously; you should suppress this thought of 'leaving home,' and undertake your worldly duties, find your delight in getting an illustrious name, and after this give up your home and family."

The prince, with proper reverence and respectful feelings, again besought his royal father; but promised if he could be saved from four calamities, that he would give up the thought of "leaving home." If he would grant him life without end, no disease, nor undesirable old age, and no decay of earthly possessions, then be would obey and give up the thought of "leaving home."

The royal father then addressed the prince, "Speak not such words as these, for with respect to these four things, who is there able to prevent them or say nay to their approach; asking such things as these, you would provoke men's laughter! But put away this thought of 'leaving home' and once more take yourself to pleasure."

The prince again besought his father, "If you may not grant me these four prayers, then let me go I pray, and leave my home. O! place no difficulties in my path; your son is dwelling in a burning house, would you indeed prevent his leaving it!"

The prince, beholding his royal father bathed with tears and o'erwhelmed with grief, forthwith returned to his abode, and sat himself in silence to consider; all the women of the palace, coming towards him, waited as they circled him, and gazed in silence on his beauteous form.

"And now," he said, "I have awakened to the truth! Resolved am I to leave such false society."

At this time the Deva of the Pure Abode descended and approached, unfastening the doors. The prince, too, at this time rose and walked along, amid the prostrate forms of all the women; with difficulty reaching the inner hall, he called to Chhandaka, in these words, "My mind is now athirst and longing for the draught of the fountain of sweet dew; saddle then my horse, and quickly bring it here. I wish to reach the deathless city; my heart is fixed beyond all change, resolved I am and bound by sacred oath; these women, once so charming and enticing, now behold I altogether loathsome; the gates, which were before fast-barred and locked, now stand free and open! these evidences of something supernatural, point to a climax of my life."

Chhandaka stood reflecting inwardly, whether to obey or not the prince's order, without informing his royal father of it, and so incur the heaviest punishment.

The Devas then gave spiritual strength; and unperceived the horse equipped came round, with even pace; a gallant steed, with all his jewelled trappings for a rider; high-maned, with flowing tail, broad-backed, short-haired and eared, with belly like the deer's, head like the king of parrots, wide forehead, round and claw-shaped nostrils, breath like the dragon's, with breast and shoulders square, true and sufficient marks of his high breed.

The royal prince, stroking the horse's neck, and rubbing down his body, said, "My royal father ever rode on thee, and found thee brave in fight and fearless of the foe; now I desire to rely on thee alike! to carry me far off to the stream of endless life, to fight against and overcome the opposing force of men, the men who associate in search of pleasure, the men who engaged in the search after wealth, the crowds who follow and flatter such persons; in opposing sorrow, friendly help is difficult to find, in seeking religious truth there must be rare enlightenment, let us then be knit together thus as friends; then, at last, there will be rest from sorrow. But now I wish to go abroad, to give deliverance from pain; now then, for your own sake it is, and for the sake of all your kind, that you should exert your strength, with noble pace, without lagging or weariness."

Having thus exhorted him, he bestrode his horse, and grasping the reins proceeded forth; the man like the sun shining forth from his tabernacle, the horse like the white floating cloud, exerting himself but without exciting haste, his breath concealed and without snorting; four spirits (Devas) accompanying him, held up his feet, heedfully concealing his advance, silently and without noise; the heavy gates fastened and barred, the heavenly spirits of themselves caused to open.

Thus man and horse, both strong of heart, went onwards, lost to sight like streaming stars, but ere the eastern quarter flashed with light, they had advanced three yojanas.

Explorations

The royal prince, keeping along the stream, then crossing the Ganges, he took the road towards the Vulture Peak, hidden among the five mountains, standing alone a lovely peak as a roof amid the others. The trees and shrubs and flowers in bloom, the flowing fountains, and the cooling rills; all these he gazed upon—then passing on, he entered the city of the five peaks, calm and peaceful, as one come down from heaven. The country folk, seeing the royal prince, his comeliness and his excessive grace, though young in years, yet glorious in his person, incomparable as the appearance of a great master, seeing him thus, strange thoughts affected them, as if they gazed upon the banner of Isvara.

Now the men and women of Rajagriha, the old and young alike, were moved, and cried, "This man so noble as a recluse, what common joy is this for us!" At this time Bimbisara Raja, placed upon a high tower of observation, seeing all those men and women, in different ways exhibiting one mark of scuprise, calling before him some man outside, inquired at once the cause of it; this one bending his knee below the tower, told fully what he had seen and heard, "That one of the Sakya race, renowned of old, a prince most excellent and wonderful, divinely wise, beyond the way of this world, a fitting king to rule the eight regions, now without home, is here, and all men are paying homage to him."

The king on hearing this was deeply moved at heart, and though his body was restrained, his soul had gone. Calling his ministers speedily before him, and all his nobles and attendants, he bade them follow secretly the prince's steps, to observe what charity was given. So, in obedience to the command, they followed and watched him steadfastly, as with even gait and unmoved presence he entered the town and begged his food, according to the rule of all great hermits, with joyful mien and undisturbed mind, not anxious whether much or little alms were given; whatever he received, costly or poor, he placed within his bowl, then turned back to the wood, and having eaten it and drunk of the flowing stream, he joyous sat upon the immaculate mountain.

With every outward form of courtesy and reverence the king approached and asked him respectfully of his welfare. Bodhisattva, answering as he was moved, in his turn made similar inquiries. Then the king, the questioning over, sat down with dignity upon a clean-faced rock. And so he steadfastly beheld the divine appearance of the prince, the sweetness and complacency of his features revealing what his station was and high estate, his family renown, received by inheritance; the king, who for a time restrained his feelings, now wishful to get rid of doubts, inquired why one descended from the royal family of the sun-brightness having attended to religious sacrifices through ten thousand generations, whereof the virtue had descended as his full inheritance, increasing and accumulating until now, why he so excellent in wisdom, so young in years, had now become a recluse, rejecting the position of a Chakravartin's son, begging his food, despising family fame, his beauteous form, fit for perfumes and anointings, why clothed with coarse garments; the hand which ought to grasp the reins of empire, instead thereof, taking its little stint of food.

Bimbisara used every kind of winning expedient in argument. The royal prince, unmoved and fixed, remained firm as Mount Sumeru. The prince on his part respectfully replied, in the following words, deep and heart-stirring:

"Illustrious and world-renowned! Your words are not opposed to reason, descendant of a distinguished family—an Aryan—amongst men a true friend indeed, righteous and sincere to the bottom of your heart, it is proper for religion's sake to speak thus. In all the world, in its different sections, there is no chartered place for solid virtue, for it virtue flags and folly rules, what reverence can there be, or honour paid, to a high name or boast of prowess, inherited from former generations! And so there may be in the midst of great distress, large goodness, these are not mutually opposed.This then is so with the world in the connection of true worth and friendship.

"A true friend who makes good use of wealth—is rightly called a fast and firm treasure, but he who guards and stints the profit he has made, his wealth will soon be spent and lost; the wealth of a country is no constant treasure, but that which is given in charity is rich in returns, therefore charity is a true friend: although it scatters, yet it brings no repentance; you indeed are known as liberal and kind, I make no reply in opposition to you, but simply as we meet, so with agreeable purpose we talk.

"I fear birth, old age, disease, and death, and so I seek to find a sure mode of deliverance; I have put away thought of relatives and family affection, how is it possible then for me to return to the world and not to fear to revive the poisonous snake, and after the hail to be burned in the fierce fire; indeed, I fear the objects of these several desires, this whirling in the stream of life troubles my heart, these five desires, the inconstant thieves—stealing from men their choicest treasures, making them unreal, false, and fickle—are like the man called up as an apparition; for a time the beholders are affected by it, but it has no lasting hold upon the mind; so these five desires are the great obstacles, forever disarranging the way of peace; if the joys of heaven are not worth having, how much less the desires common to men, begetting the thirst of wild love, and then lost in the enjoyment, as the fierce wind fans the fire, till the fuel be spent and the fire expires; of all unrighteous things in the world, there is nothing worse than the domain of the five desires; for all men maddened by the power of lust, giving themselves to pleasure, are dead to reason.

"You say that while young a man should be gay, and when old then religious, but I regard the feebleness of age as bringing with it loss of power to be religious, unlike the firmness and power of youth, the will determined and the heart established; but death as a robber with a drawn sword follows us all, desiring to catch his prey; how then should we wait for old age, ere we bring our mind to a religious life? Inconstancy is the great hunter, age his bow, disease his arrows, in the fields of life and death he hunts for living things as for the deer; when he can get his opportunity, he takes our life; who then would wait for age? And what the teachers say and do, with reference to matters connected with life and death, exhorting the young, mature, or middle-aged, all to contrive by any means, to prepare vast meetings for sacrifices, this they do indeed of their own ignorance; better far to reverence the true law, and put an end to sacrifice to appease the gods! Destroying life to gain religious merit, what love can such a man possess? Even if the reward of such sacrifices were lasting, even for this, slaughter would be unseemly; how much more, when the reward is transient! Shall we, in search of this, slay that which lives, in worship?

this is like those who practise wisdom, and the way of religious abstraction, but neglect the rules of moral conduct.

"Slaughter and peaceful homes are enemies! those who would have peace hate slaughter, and if those who slaughter are so hateful, then put an end, O king, to those who practise it! And bid these find release, as those who drink and yet are parched with thirst."

Then the king, clasping together his hands, with greatest reverence and joyful heart, said. "That which you now seek, may you obtain quickly the fruit thereof: having obtained the perfect fruit, return I pray and graciously receive me!"

Bodhisattva, his heart inwardly acquiescing, purposing to accomplish his prayer, departing, pursued his road, going to the place where Arada Kalama dwelt; whilst the king with all his retinue, their hands clasped, themselves followed a little space, then with thoughtful and mindful heart, returned once more to Rajagriha!

The child of the glorious sun of the Ikshvaku race, going to that quiet peaceful grove, reverently stood before the Muni, the great Rishi Arada Rama; the dark-clad followers of the Kalam (Sangharama) seeing afar-off Bodhisattva approaching, with loud voice raised a joyful chant, and with suppressed breath muttered "Welcome," as with clasped hands they reverenced him. Approaching one another, they made mutual inquiries; and this being done, with the usual apologies, according to their precedence in age they sat down; the Brahmacharins observing the prince, beheld his personal beauty and carefully considered his appearance; respectfully they satisfied themselves of his high qualities, like those who, thirsty, drink the "pure dew."

Then with raised hands they addressed the prince: "Have you been long an ascetic, divided from your family and broken from the bonds of love, like the elephant who has cast off restraint? Full of wisdom, completely enlightened, you seem well able to excape the poisonous fruit of this world.

"We see that your will is strong and fixed, capable of

becoming a vessel of the true law, able to embark in the boat of wisdom, and to cross over the sea of life and death. The common class, enticed to come to learn, their talents first are tested, then they are taught; but as I understand your case, your mind is already fixed and your will firm; and now you have undertaken the purpose of learning. I am persuaded you will not in the end shrink from it."

The prince hearing this exhortation, with gladness made reply: "You have with equal intention, illustrious! cautioned me with impartial mind: with humble heart I accept the advice, and pray that it may be so with me as you anticipate; that I may in my night-journey obtain a torch, to guide me safely through treacherous places; a handy boat to cross over the sea;—may it be so even now with me! But as I am somewhat in doubt and anxious to learn, I will venture to make known my doubts, and ask, with respect to old age, disease, and death, how are these things to be escaped?"

At this time Arada hearing the question asked by the prince, briefly from the various Sutras and Sastras quoted passages in explanation of a way of deliverance. "But thou," he said, "illustrious youth! so highly gifted, and eminent among the wise! hear what I have to say, as I discourse upon the mode of ending birth and death; nature, and change, birth, old age, and death, these five attributes belong to all; nature is in itself pure and without fault; the involution of this with the five elements, causes an awakening and power of perception, which, according to its exercise, is the cause of change; form, sound, order, taste, touch, these are called the five objects of sense; as the hand and foot are called the two ways, so these are called the roots of action (the five Skandhas); the eye, the ear, the nose, the tongue, the body these are named the roots of understanding.

"The root of mind is twofold, being both material, and also intelligent; nature by its involutions is the cause, the knower of the cause is I; Kapila the Rishi and his numerous followers, on this deep principle of soul, practising wisdom, found deliverance. Kapila and now Vachaspati, by the power of Buddhi perceiving the character of birth, old age, and death, declare that on this is founded true philosophy; whilst all opposed to this, they say, is false. Ignorance and passion, causing constant transmigration, abiding in the midst of these, they say, is the lot of all that lives. Doubting the truth of soul is called excessive doubt, and without distinguishing aright, there can be no method of escape. Deep speculation as to the limits of perception is but to involve the soul; thus unbelief leads to confusion, and ends in differences of thought and conduct.

"Again, the various speculations on soul, such as 'I know and perceive,' 'I come' and 'I go,' or 'I remain fixed,' these are called the intricacies of soul. And then the fancies raised in different natures, some saying 'this is so,' others denying it, and this condition of uncertainty is called the state of darkness. Then there are those who say that outward things are one with soul, who say that the objective is the same as mind, who confuse intelligence with instruments, who say that number is the soul. Thus not distinguishing aright, these are called excessive quibbles, marks of folly, nature changes, and so on."

"To worship and recite religious books, to slaughter living things in sacrifice, to render pure by fire and water, and thus awake the thought of final rescue, all these ways of thinking are called without right expedient, the result of ignorance and doubt, by means of word or thought or deed; involving outward relationships, this is called depending on means; making the material world the ground of soul, this is called depending on the senses. By these eight sorts of speculation are we involved in birth and death. The foolish masters of the world make their classifications in these five ways: Darkness, folly, and great folly, angry passion, with timid fear. Indolent coldness is called darkness; birth and death are called folly; lustful desire is great folly; because of great men subjected to error, cherishing angry feelings, passion results; trepidation of the heart is called fear.

"Thus these foolish men dilate upon the five desires;

but the root of the great sorrow of birth and death, the life destined to be spent in the five ways, the cause of the whirl of life, I clearly perceive, is to be placed in the existence of 'I'; because of the influence of this cause, result the consequences of repeated birth and death; this cause is without any nature of its own, and its fruits have no nature; rightly considering what has been said, there are four matters which have to do with escape, kindling wisdom—opposed to dark ignorance—making manifest—opposed to concealment and obscurity—if these four matters be understood, then we may escape birth, old age, and death. Birth, old age, and death being over, then we attain a final place; the Brahmins all depending on this principle, practising themselves in a pure life, have also largely dilated on it, for the good of the world."

The prince hearing these words again inquired of Arada: "Tell me what are the expendients you name, and what is the final place to which they lead, and what is the character of that pure Brahman life; and again what are the stated periods during which such life must be practised, and during which such life is lawful; all these are principles to be inquired into; and on them I pray you discourse for my sake."

Then that Arada, according to the Sutras and Sastras, spoke: "Yourself using wisdom is the expedient; but I will further dilate on this a little; first by removing from the crowd and leading a hermit's life, depending entirely on alms for food, extensively practising rules of decorum, religiously adhering to right rules of conduct; desiring little and knowing when to abstain, receiving whatever is given in food, whether pleasant or otherwise, delighting to practise a quiet life, diligently studying all the Sutras and Sastras; observing the character of covetous longing and fear, without remnant of desire to live in purity, to govern well the organs of life, the mind quieted and silently at rest; removing desire, and hating vice, all the sorrows of life put away, then there is happiness; and we obtain the enjoyment of the first Dhyana.

"Having obtained this first Dhyana, then with the illumination thus obtained, by inward meditation is born reliance on thought alone, and the entanglements of folly are put away; the mind depending on this, then after death, born in the Brahma heavens, the enlightened are able to know themselves; by the use of means is produced further inward illumination; diligently persevering, seeking higher advance, accomplishing the second Dhyana, tasting of that great joy, we are born in the Kwong-yin heaven; then by the use of means putting away this delight, practising the third Dhyana, resting in such delight and wishing no further excellence, there is a birth in the Subhakritsna heaven; leaving the thought of such delight, straightway we reach the fourth Dhyana, all joys and sorrows done away, the thought of escape produced; we dwell in this fourth Dhyana, and are born in the Vrihat-phala (extensive-fruit) heaven; because of its long enduring years, it is thus called Vrihat-phala; whilst in that state of abstraction rising higher, perceiving there is a place beyond any bodily condition, adding still and persevering further in practising wisdom, rejecting this fourth Dhyana, firmly resolved to persevere in the search, still contriving to put away every desire after form, gradually from every pore of the body there is perceived a feeling of empty release, and in the end this extends to every solid part, so that the whole is perfected in an apprehension of emptiness. In brief, perceiving no limits to this emptiness, there is opened to the view boundless knowledge. Endowed with inward rest and peace, the idea of 'I' departs, and the object of 'I'—clearly discriminating the non-existence of matter, this is the condition of immaterial life. As the Munja (grass) when freed from its horny case, or as the wild bird which escapes from its prison trap, so, getting away from all material limitations, we thus find perfect release. Thus ascending above the Brahmans, deprived of every vestige of bodily existence, we still endure. Endued with wisdom! let it be known this is real and true deliverance. You ask what are the expedients for obtaining this escape; even as I have before detailed, those who have deep faith will learn. The Rishis Jaigishavya, Janaka, Vriddha Parasara, and other searchers after truth, all by the way I have explained, have reached true deliverance."

The prince hearing these words, deeply pondering on the outline of these principles, and reaching back to the influences produced by our former lives, again asked with further words:

"I have heard your very excellent system of wisdom, the principles very subtle and deep-reaching, from which I learn that because of not 'letting go' (by knowledge as a cause), we do not reach the end of the religious life; but by understanding nature in its involutions, then, you say, we obtain deliverance; I perceive this law of birth has also concealed in it another law as a germ; you say that the 'I' (i.e., the soul of Kapila) being rendered pure, forthwith there is true deliverance; but if we encounter a union of cause and effect, then there is a return to the trammels of birth; just as the germ in the seed, when earth, fire, water, and wind seem to have destroyed in it the principle of life, meeting with favourable concomitant circumstances will yet revive, without any evident cause, but because of desire; so those who have gained this supposed release, likewise keeping the idea of 'I' and living things, have in fact gained no final deliverance; in every condition, letting go the three classes and again reaching the three excellent qualities, because of the eternal existence of soul, by the subtle influences of that, influences resulting from the past, the heart lets go the idea of expedients, and obtains an almost endless duration of years.

"This, you say, is true release; you say 'letting go the ground on which the idea of soul rests,' that this frees us from 'limited existence,' and that the mass of people have not yet removed the idea of soul, and are therefore still in bondage. But what is this letting go Gunas (cords fettering the soul); if one is fettered by these Gunas, how can there be release? For Guni (the object) and Guna (the quality) in idea are different, but in substance one; if you say that you can remove the properties of a thing and leave the thing by arguing it to the end, this is not so. If you remove heat from fire, then there is no such thing as fire, or if you remove surface from body, what body can remain? Thus Guna is as it were surface, remove this and there can be no Guni. So that this deliverance, spoken of before, must leave a body yet in bonds.

"Again, you say that by clear knowledge you get rid of body; there is then such a thing as knowledge or the contrary; if you affirm the existence of clear knowledge, then there should be someone who possesses it; if there be a possessor, how can there be deliverance from this personal 'I'? If you say there is no 'knower,' then who is it that is spoken of as 'knowing'? If there is knowledge and no person, then the subject of knowledge may be a stone or a log; moreover, to have clear knowledge of these minute causes of contamination and reject them thoroughly, these being so rejected, there must be an end, then, of the 'doer.' What Arada has declared cannot satisfy my heart. This clear knowledge is not universal wisdom, I must go on and seek a better explanation."

Going to then to the place of Udra Rishi, he also expatiated on this question of "I." But although he refined the matter to the utmost, laying down a term of "thought" and "no thought" taking the position of removing "thought" and "no thought," yet even so he came not out of the mire; for supposing creatures attained that state, still, he said, there is a possibility of returning to the coil, whilst Bodhisattva sought a method of getting out of it.

So once more leaving Udra Rishi, he went on in search of a better system, and came at last to Mount Kia-ke (the forest of mortification), where was a town called pain-suffering forest. Here the five Bhikshus had gone before. When then he beheld these five, virtuously keeping in check their senses, holding to the rules of moral conduct, practising mortification, dwelling in that grove of mortification; occupying a spot beside the Nairanjana river, perfectly composed and filled with contentment, Bodhisattva forthwith by them selecting one spot, quietly gave himself to thought. The five Bhikshus knowing him with earnest heart to be seeking escape, offered him their services with devotion, as if reverencing Isvara Deva.

Having finished their attentions and dutiful services, then going on he took his seat not far off, as one about to enter on a course of religious practice, composing all his members as he desired. Bodhisattva diligently applied himself to "means," as one about to cross over old age, disease, and death. With full purpose of heart he set himself to endure mortification, to restrain every bodily passion, and give up thought about sustenance, with purity of heart to observe the fast-rules, which no worldly man can bear; silent and still, lost in thoughtful meditation; and so for six years he continued, each day eating one hemp grain, his bodily form shrunken and attenuated, seeking how to cross the sea of birth and death, exercising himself still deeper and advancing further; making his way perfect by the disentanglement of true wisdom, not eating, and yet not looking to that as a cause of emancipation, his four members although exceedingly weak, his heart of wisdom increasing yet more and more in light; his spirit free, his body light and refined, his name spreading far and wide, as "highly gifted," even as the moon when first produced, or as the Kumuda flower spreading out its sweetness.

Everywhere through the country his excellent fame extended; the daughters of the lord of the place both coming to see him, his mortified body like a withered branch, just completing the period of six years, fearing the sorrow of birth and death, seeking earnestly the method of true wisdom, he came to the conviction that these were not the means to extinguish desire and produce ecstatic contemplation; nor yet the means by which in former time, seated underneath the Jambu tree, he arrived at that miraculous condition, that surely was the proper way, he thought, the way opposed to this of "withered body."

"I should therefore rather seek strength of body, by drink and food refresh my members, and with contentment cause my mind to rest. My mind at rest, I shall enjoy silent composure; composure is the trap for getting Dhyana; while in ecstasy perceiving the true law, then the force of truth obtained, disentanglement will follow. And thus composed, enjoying perfect quiet, old age and death are put away; and then defilement is escaped by this first means; thus then by equal steps the excellent law results from life restored by food and drink."

Enlightenment

Having carefully considered this principle, bathing in the Nairanjana river, he desired afterwards to leave the water but owing to extreme exhaustion was unable to rise; then a heavenly spirit holding out a branch, taking this in his hand he raised himself and came forth. At this time on the opposite side of the grove there was a certain chief herdsman, whose eldest daughter was called Nanda. One of the Suddhavasa Devas addressing her said, "Budhisattva dwells in the grove, go you then, and present to him a religious offering."

Nanda Balada (or Balaga or Baladhya) with joy came to the spot, above her hands, i.e. on her wrists, white chalcedony bracelets, her clothing of a gray colour; the gray and the white together contrasted in the light, as the colours of the rounded river bubble; with simple heart and quickened step she came, and, bowing down at Bodhisattva's feet, she reverently offered him perfumed rice milk, begging him of his condescension to accept it.

Bodhisattva taking it, partook of it at once, whilst she received, even then, the fruits of her religious act. Having eaten it, all his members refreshed, he became capable of receiving Bodhi; his body and limbs glistening with renewed strength, and his energies swelling higher still, as the hundred streams swell the sea, or the first quartered moon daily increases in brightness. The five Bhikshus having witnessed this, perturbed, were filled with suspicious reflection; they supposed that his religious zeal was flagging, and that he was leaving and looking for a better abode, as though he had obtained deliverance, the five elements entirely removed.

Bodhisattva wandered on alone, directing his course to that "fortunate" tree, beneath whose shade he might accomplish his search after complete enlightenment. Over the ground wide and level, producing soft and pliant grass, easily he advanced with lion step, pace by pace, whilst the earth shook withal; and as it shook, Kalanaga aroused, was filled with joy, as his eyes were opened to the light. Forthwith he exclaimed: "When formerly I saw the Buddhas of old, there was the sign of an earthquake as now; the virtues of a Muni are so great in majesty, that the great earth cannot endure them; as step by step his foot treads upon the ground, so is there heard the sound of the rumbling earth-shaking; a brilliant light now illumines the world, as the shining of the rising sun; five hundred bluish-tinted birds I see, wheeling round to the right, flying through space; a gentle, soft, and cooling breeze blows around in an agreeable way; all these auspicious signs are the same as those of former Buddhas; wherefore I know that this Bodhisattva will certainly arrive at perfect wisdom.

"And now, behold! from yonder man, a grass cutter, he obtains some pure and pliant grass, which spreading out beneath the tree, with upright body; there he takes his seat; his feet placed under him, not carelessly arranged, moving to and fro, but like the firmly fixed and compact body of a Naga; nor shall he rise again from off his seat till he has completed his undertaking."

And so Naga uttered these words by way of confirmation. The heavenly Nagas, filled with joy, caused a cool refereshing breeze to rise; the trees and grass were yet unmoved by it, and all the beasts, quiet and silent, looked on in wonderment.

These are the signs that Bodhisattva will certainly attain enlightenment.

Bodhisattva, his firmly fixed mind at rest, thoroughly exhausting the first principle of truth, he entered into deep and subtle contemplation. Every kind of Samadhi in order passed before his eyes. During the first watch he entered on "right perception" and in recollection all former births passed before his eyes. Born in such a place, of such a name, and downwards to his present birth, so through hundreds, thousands, myriads, all his births and deaths he knew. Countless in number were they, of every kind and sort; then knowing, too, his family relationships, great pity rose within his heart.

Rightly considering, inwardly he reflected from what source birth and death proceed. He was assured that age and death must come from birth as from a source. For since a man has born with him a body, that body must inherit pain. Then looking further whence comes birth, he saw it came from life-deeds done elsewhere; then with his Deva-eyes scanning these deeds, he saw they were not framed by Isvara. They were not self-caused, they were not personal existences, nor were they either uncaused; then, as one who breaks the first bamboo joint finds all the rest easy to separate, having discerned the cause of birth and death, he gradually came to see the truth; deeds come from Upadana, like as fire which catches hold of grass; Upadana comes from Trishna, just as a little fire inflames the mountains; Trishna comes from Vedana, the perception of pain and pleasure, the desire for rest; as the starving or the thirsty man seeks food and drink, so "sensation" brings "desire" for life; then contact is the cause of all sensation, producing the three kinds of pain or pleasure, even as by art of man the rubbing wood produces fire for any use or purpose; contact is born from the six entrances (senses).

The six entrances are caused by name and thing, just

as the germ grows to the stem and leaf; name and thing are born from knowledge, as the seed which germinates and brings forth leaves. Knowledge, in turn, proceeds from name and thing, the two are intervolved leaving no remnant; by some concurrent cause knowledge engenders name and thing, whilst by some other cause concurrent, name and thing engender knowledge. Just as a man and ship advance together, the water and the land mutually involved; thus knowledge brings forth name and thing; name and thing produce the roots. The roots engender contact; contact again brings forth sensation; sensation brings forth longing desire; longing desire produces Upadana. Upadana is the cause of deeds; and these again engender birth; birth again produces age and death; so does this one incessant round cause the existence of all living things.

Rightly illumined, thoroughly perceiving this, firmly established, thus was he enlightened; destroy birth, old age and death will cease; destroy Bhava then will birth cease; destroy "cleaving" then will Bhava end; destroy desire then will cleaving end; destroy sensation then will Trishna end. Destroy contact then will end sensation; destroy the six entrances, then will contact cease; the six entrances all destroyed, from this, moreover, names and things will cease. Knowledge destroyed, names and things will cease; names and things destroyed, then knowledge perishes; ignorance destroyed, then the constituents of individual life will die; the great Rishi was thus perfected in wisdom.

Thus perfected, Buddha then devised for the world's benefit the eightfold path, right sight, and so on, the only true path for the world to tread. Thus did he complete the end of "self," as fire goes out for want of grass; thus he had done what he would have men do; he first had found the way of perfect knowledge.

Buddha for those seven days, in contemplation lost, his heart at peace, beheld and pondered on the Bodhi tree, with gaze unmoved and never wearying:—"Now resting here, in this condition, I have obtained," he said, "my ever-shifting heart's desire, and now at rest I stand, escaped from self." The eyes of Buddha then considered "all that lives," and forthwith rose there in him deep compassion; much he desired to bring about their welfare, but how to gain for them that most excellent deliverance, from covetous desire, hatred, ignorance, and false teaching, this was the question; how to suppress this sinful heart by right direction; not by anxious use of outward means, but by resting quietly in thoughtful silence. Now looking back and thinking of his mighty vow, there rose one more within his mind a wish to preach the law; and looking carefully throughout the world, he saw how pain and sorrow ripened and increased everywhere.

Then Brahma-deva knowing his thoughts, and considering it right to request him to advance religion for the wider spread of the Brahma-glory, in the deliverance of all flesh from sorrow, coming, beheld upon the person of the reverend monk all the distinguishing marks of a great preacher, visible in an excellent degree; fixed and unmoved he sat in the possession of truth and wisdom, free from all evil impediments, with a heart cleansed from all insincerity or falsehood.

Then with reverent and a joyful heart, great Brahma stood and with hands joined, thus made known his request:— "What happiness in all the world so great as when a loving master meets the unwise; the world with all its occupants, filled with impurity and dire confusion, with heavy grief oppressed, or, in some cases, lighter sorrows, waits deliverance; the lord of men, having escaped by crossing the wide and mournful sea of birth and death, we now entreat to rescue others—those struggling creatures all engulfed therein; as the just worldly man, when he gets profit, gives some rebate withal. So the lord of men enjoying such religious gain, should also give somewhat to living things. The world indeed is bent on large personal gain, and hard it is to share one's own with others. O! let your loving heart be moved with pity towards the world burdened with vexing cares."

Thus having spoken by way of exhortation, with reverent mien he turned back to the Brahma heaven. Buddha, regarding the invitation of Brahma-deva, rejoiced at heart, and his design was strengthened; greatly was his heart of pity nourished, and purposed was his mind to preach. Thinking he ought to beg some food, each of the four kings offered him a Patra; Tathagata, in fealty to religion, received the four and joined them all in one. And now some merchant men were passing by, to whom "a virtuous friend," a heavenly spirit, said: "The great Rishi, the venerable monk, is dwelling in this mountain-grove, affording in the world a noble field for merit; go then and offer him a sacrifice!"

Hearing the summons, joyfully they went, and offered the first meal religiously. Having partaken of it, then he deeply pondered, who first should hear the law; he thought at once of Arada Kalama and Udraka Ramaputra, as being fit to accept the righteous law; but now they both were dead. Then next he thought of the five men, that they were fit to hear the first sermon. Bent then on this design to preach Nirvana, as the sun's glory bursts through the darkness, so went he on towards Benares, the place where dwelt the ancient Rishis. With eyes as gentle as the ox king's, his pace as firm and even as the lion's, because he would convert the world he went on towards the Kashi city. Step by step, like the king of beasts, did he advance watchfully through the grove of wisdom.

Turning the Wheel of Law

Tathagata piously composed and silent, radiant with glory, shedding light around, with unmatched dignity advanced alone, as if surrounded by a crowd of followers. Beside the way he encountered a young brahmin whose name was Upaka; struck with the deportment of the Bhikshu, he stood with reverent mien on the roadside. Joyously he gazed at such an unprecedented sight, and then, with closed hands, he spake as follows:

"The crowds who live around are stained with sin, without a pleasing feature, void of grace, and the great world's heart is everywhere disturbed; but you alone, your senses all composed, with visage shining as the moon when full, seem to have quaffed the water of the immortals' stream. The marks of beauty yours, as the great man's, the strength of wisdom, as an all sufficient, independent king's; what you have done must have been wisely done: what then your noble tribe and who your master?"

Answering he said, "I have no master; no honourable tribe; no point of excellence; self-taught in this profoundest doctrine, I have arrived at superhuman wisdom. That which behoves the world to learn, but through the world no learner found, I now myself and by myself have learned throughout; 'tis rightly called Sambodhi. That hateful family of griefs the sword of wisdom has destroyed; this then is what the world has named, and rightly named, the 'chiefest victory.' Through all Benares soon will sound the drum of life, no stay is possible—I have no name—nor do I seek profit or pleasure. But simply to declare the truth; to save men from pain, and to fulfil my ancient oath, to rescue all not yet delivered. The fruit of this my oath is ripened now, and I will follow out my ancient vow. Wealth, riches, self all given up, unnamed, I still am named 'Righteous Master.' And bringing profit to the world, I also have the name 'Great Teacher'; facing sorrows, not swallowed up by them, am I not rightly called 'Courageous Warrior?' If not a healer of diseases, what means the name of 'Good Physician?' Seeing the wanderer, not showing him the way, why then should I be called 'Good Master-guide?' Like as the lamp shines in the dark, without a purpose of its own, self-radiant, so burns the lamp of the Tathagata, without the shadow of a personal feeling. Bore wood in wood, there must be fire; the wind blows of its own free self in space; dig deep and you will come to water; this is the rule of self-causation. All the Munis who perfect wisdom, must do so at Gaya; and in the Kashi country they must first turn the Wheel of Righteousness."

The young brahmin Upaka, astonished, breathed the praise of such strange doctrine, and called to mind like thoughts he had before experienced; lost in thought at the wonderful occurrence, at every turning of the road he stopped to think; embarrassed in every step he took, Tathagata proceeding slowly onwards, came to the city of Kashi. The land so excellently adorned as the palace of Sakradevendra; the Ganges and Barana, two twin rivers flowed amidst; the woods and flowers and fruits so verdant, the peaceful cattle wandering together, the calm retreats free from vulgar noise, such was the place where the old Rishis dwelt.

Tathagata, glorious and radiant, redoubled the brightness of the place; the son of the Kaundinya tribe, and next Dasabala Kasyapa, and the third Vashpa, the fourth Asvajit, the fifth called Bhadra, practising austerities as hermits, seeing from far Tathagata approaching, sitting together all engaged in conversation said: "This Gautama, defiled by worldly indulgence, leaving the practice of austerities, now comes again to find us here, let us be careful not to rise in salutation, nor let us greet him when he comes, nor offer him the customary refreshments. Because he has broken his first vow, he has no claim to hospitality"—for men on seeing an approaching guest by rights prepare things for his present and his after wants. They arrange a proper resting couch, and take on themselves care for his comfort. Having spoken thus and so agreed, each kept his seat, resolved and fixed.

And now Tathagata slowly approached, when, lo! these men unconsciously, against their vow, rose and invited him to take a seat; offering to take his robe and Patra. They begged to wash and rub his feet, and asked him what he required more; thus in everything attentive, they honoured him and offered all to him as teacher. They did not cease however to address him still as Gautama, after his family.

Then spake the Lord to them and said: "Call me not after my private name, for it is a rude and careless way of speaking to one who had obtained Arhatship; but whether men respect or disrespect me, my mind is undisturbed and wholly quiet. But you—your way is not so courteous: let go, I pray, and cast away your fault. Buddha can save the world; they call him, therefore, Buddha. Towards all living things, with equal heart he looks as children, to call him then by his familiar name is to despise a father; this is sin."

Thus Buddha, by exercise of mighty love, in deep compassion spoke to them; but they, from ignorance and pride, despised the only wise and true one's words. They said that first he practised self-denial, but having reached thereby no profit, now giving rein to body, word, and thought, how by these means, they asked, has be become a Buddha? Thus equally entangled by doubts, they would not credit that he had attained the way. Thoroughly versed in highest truth, full of all-embracing wisdom, Tathagata on their account briefly declared to them the one true way; the foolish masters practising austerities, and those who love to gratify their senses, he pointed out to them these two distinctive classes, and how both greatly erred.

"Neither of these," he said, "has found the way of highest wisdom, nor are their ways of life productive of true rescue. The emaciated devotee by suffering produces in himself confused and sickly thoughts, not conducive even to worldly knowledge, how much less to triumph over sense! For he who tries to light a lamp with water, will not succeed in scattering the darkness, and so the man who tries with worn-out body to trim the lamp of wisdom shall not succeed, nor yet destroy his ignorance or folly. Who seeks with rotten wood to evoke the fire will waste his labour and get nothing for it; but boring hard wood into hard, the man of skill forthwith gets fire for his use.

"In seeking wisdom then it is not by these austerities a man may reach the law of life. But to indulge in pleasure is opposed to right: this is the fool's barrier against wisdom's light. The sensualist cannot comprehend the Sutras or the Sastras, how much less the way of overcoming all desire! As some man grievously afflicted eats food not fit to eat, and so in ignorance

aggravates his sickness, so can he get rid of lust who pampers lust? Scatter the fire amid the desert grass, dried by the sun, fanned by the wind—the raging flames who shall extinguish? Such is the fire of covetousness and lust, I, then, reject both these extremes: my heart keeps in the middle way.

"All sorrow at an end and finished, I rest at peace, all error put away; my true sight greater than the glory of the sun, my equal and unvarying wisdom, vehicle of insight—right words as it were a dwelling-place—wandering through the pleasant groves of right conduct, making a right life my recreation, walking along the right road of proper means, my city of refuge in right recollection, and my sleeping couch right meditation; these are the eight even and level roads by which to avoid the sorrows of birth and death. Those who come forth by these means from the slough, doing thus, have attained the end; such shall fall neither on this side or the other, amidst the sorrow-crowd of the two periods.

"The tangled sorrow-web of the three worlds by this road alone can be destroyed; this is my own way, unheard of before; by the pure eyes of the true law, impartially seeing the way of escape, I only I, now first make known this way; thus I destroy the hateful company of Trishna's host, the sorrows of birth and death, old age, disease, and all the unfruitful aims of men, and other springs of suffering. There are those who warring against desire are still influenced by desire; who whilst possessed of body, act as though they had none; who put away from themselves all sources of true merit—briefly will I recount their sorrowful lot. Like smothering a raging fire, though carefully put out, yet a spark left, so in their abstraction, still the germ of 'I', the source of great sorrow still surviving, perpetuates the suffering caused by lust, and the evil consequences of every kind of deed survive.

"These are the sources of further pain, but let these go and sorrow dies, even as the seed of corn taken from the earth and deprived of water dies; the concurrent causes not uniting, then the bud and leaf cannot be born; the intricate bonds of every

kind of existence, from the Deva down to the evil ways of birth, ever revolve and never cease; all this is produced from covetous desire; falling from a high estate to lower ones, all is the fault of previous deeds. But destroy the seed of covetousness and the rest, then there will be no intricate binding, but all effect of deeds destroyed, the various degrees of sorrow then will end for god. Having this, then, we must inherit that; destroying this, then that is ended too; no birth, old age, disease, or death; no earth, or water, fire, or wind. No beginning, end, or middle; and no deceptive systems of philosophy; this is the standpoint of wise men and sages; the certain and exhausted termination, complete Nirvana.

"Such do the eight right ways declare; this one expedient has no remains; that which the world sees not, engrossed by error I declare, I know the way to sever all these sorrow-sources; the way to end them is by right reason, meditating on these four highest truths, following and perfecting this highest wisdom. This is what means the 'knowing' sorrow; this is to cut off the cause of all remains of being; these destroyed, then all striving, too, has ended, the eight right ways have been assayed.

"Thus, too, the four great truths have been acquired, the eyes of the pure law completed. In these four truths, the equal, true or right, eyes not yet born, there is not mention made of gaining true deliverance; it is not said what must be done is done, nor that all is finished, nor that the perfect truth has been acquired. But now because the truth is known, then by myself is known 'deliverance gained,' by myself is known that 'all is done,' by myself is known 'the highest wisdom.'"

And having spoken thus respecting truth, the member of the Kaundinya family, and eighty thousand of the Deva host, were thoroughly imbued with saving knowledge. They put away defilement from themselves, they got the eyes of the pure law; Devas and earthly masters thus were sure, that what was to be done was done.

And now with lion-voice he joyfully inquired, and asked Kaundinya, "Knowest thou yet?"

Kaundinya forthwith answered Buddha, "I know the mighty master's law."

And for this reason, knowing it, his name was Ajnata Kaundinya. Amongst all the disciples of Buddha, he was the very first in understanding.

Then as he understood the sounds of the true law, hearing the words of the disciple—all the earth spirits together raised a shout triumphant, "Well done! deeply seeing the principles of the law, Tathagata, on this auspicious day, has set revolving that which never yet revolved, and far and wide, for gods and men, has opened the gates of immortality.

"Of this wheel the spokes are the rules of pure conduct; equal contemplation, their uniformity of length; firm wisdom is the tire; modesty and thoughtfulness, the rubbers (sockets in the nave in which the axle is fixed); right reflection is the nave; the wheel itself the law of perfect truth; the right truth now has gone forth in the world, not to retire before another teacher."

Thus the earth spirits shouted, the spirits of the air took up the strain, the Devas all joined in the hymn of praise, up to the highest Brahma heaven. The Devas of the triple world, now hearing what the great Rishi taught, in intercourse together spoke, "The widely honoured Buddha moves the world! Widespread, for the sake of all that lives, he turns the Wheel of the Law of complete purity!" The stormy winds, the clouds, the mists, all disappeared; down from space the heavenly flowers descended. The Devas revelled in their joys celestial, filled with unutterable gladness.

Spreading the New Way

And now those five men, Asvajit, Vashpa, and the others, having heard that Kaundinya "knew" the law, with humble mien and self-subdued, their hands joined, offered their homage, and looked with reverence in the teacher's face. Tathagata, by wise expedient, caused them one by one to embrace the law. And so from first to last the five Bhikshus obtained reason and subdued their senses, like the five stars which shine in heaven, waiting upon the brightening moon.

At this time in the town of Ku-i there was a noble's son called Yasas; lost in night-sleep suddenly he woke and when he saw his attendants all, men and women, with ill-clad bodies, sleeping, his heart was filled with loathing; reflecting on the root of sorrow, he thought how madly foolish men were immersed in it. Clothing himself, and putting on his jewels, he left his home and wandered forth; then on the way he stood and cried aloud, "Alas! alas! what endless chain of sorrows."

Tathagata, by night, was walking forth, and hearing sound like these, "Alas! what sorrow," forthwith repaid, "You are welcome! here, on the other hand, there is a place of rest—the most excellent, refreshing, Nirvana, quiet and unmoved, free from sorrow."

Yasas hearing Buddha's exhortation, there rose much joy within his heart. And in the place of the disgust he felt, the cooling streams of holy wisdom found their way, as when one enters first a cold pellucid lake. Advancing then, he came where Buddha was—his person decked with common ornaments, his mind already freed from all defects; by power of the good root obtained in other births, he quickly reahced the fruit of an Arhat. The secret light of pure wisdom's virtue enabled him to understand, on listening to the law; just as a pure silken fabric with ease is dyed a different colour. Thus having attained to self-illumination, and done that which was to be done, he was converted; then looking at his person richly ornamented, his heart was filled with shame.

Tathagata knowing his inward thoughts, in gathas spoke the following words: "Though ornamented with jewels, the heart may yet have conquered sense; looking with equal mind on all that lives, in such a case the outward form does not affect religion; the body, too, may wear the ascetic's garb, the heart, meanwhile be immersed in worldly thoughts; dwelling in lonely woods, yet covetous of worldly show, such men are after all mere worldlings; the body may have a wordly guise, the heart mount high to things celestial. The layman and the hermit are the same, when only both have banished thought of 'self,' but if the heart be twined with carnal bonds, what use the marks of bodily attention? He who wears martial decorations, does so because by valour he has triumphed over an enemy—so he who wears the hermit's coloured robe, does so for having vanquished sorrow as his foe."

Then he bade him come, and be a member of his order; and at the bidding, lo! his garments changed! and he stood wholly attired in hermit's dress, complete; in heart and outward look, a Sramana.

Now Yasas had in former days some light companions, in number fifty and four; when these beheld their friend a hermit, they, too, one by one, attained true wisdom. By virtue of deeds done in former births, these deeds now bore their perfect fruit. Just as when burning ashes are sprinkled by water, the water being dried, the flame bursts forth. So now, with those above, the disciples were altogether sixty, all Arhats; entirely obedient and instructed in the law of perfect discipleship.

So perfected he taught them further:

"Now ye have passed the stream and reached 'the other shore,' across the sea of birth and death; what should be done, ye now have done! and ye may now receive the charity of others. Go then through every country, convert those not yet converted; throughout the world that lies burnt up with sorrow, teach everywhere; instruct those lacking right instruction. Go, therefore! each one travelling by himself; filled with compassion, go! rescue and receive. I too will go alone, back to yonder Kia-ke mountain; where there are great Rishis, royal Rishis, Brahman-Rishis too, these all dwell there, influencing men according to their schools. The Rishi Kasyapa, enduring pain, reverenced by all the country, making converts too of many, him will I visit and convert."

Then the sixty Bhikshus respectfully receiving orders to preach, each according to his fore-determined purpose, following his inclination, went through every land.

The honoured of the world went on alone, till he arrived at the Kai-ke mountain, then entering a retired religious dell, he came to where the Rishi Kasyapa was. Now this one had a "fire grot" where he offered sacrifice, where an evil Naga dwelt, who wandered here and there in search of rest, through mountains and wild places of the earth. The honoured of the world, wishing to instruct this hermit and convert him, asked him, on coming, for a place to lodge that night.

Kasyapa, replying, spake to Buddha thus:

"I have no resting-place to offer for the night, only this fire grot where I sacrifice; this is a cool and fit place for the purpose, but an evil dragon dwells there, who is accustomed, as he can, to poison men."

Buddha replied, "Permit me only, and for the night I'll take my dwelling there."

Kasyapa made many difficulties, but the world-honoured one still asked the favour. Then Kasyapa addressed Buddha, "My mind desires no controversy, only I have my fears and apprehensions, but follow you your own good pleasures."

Buddha forthwith stepped within the fiery grot, and took his seat with dignity and deep reflection; and now the evil Naga seeing Buddha, belched forth in rage his fiery poison, and filled the place with burning vapour. But this could not affect the form of Buddha. Throughout the abode the fire consumed itself, the honoured of the world still sat composed: Even as Brahma, in the midst of the kalpafire that burns and reaches to the Brahma heavens, still sits unmoved, without a thought of fear or apprehension, so Buddha sat; the evil Naga seeing him, his face glowing with peace, and still unchanged, ceased his poisonous blast, his heart appeased; he bent his head and worshipped.

Kasyapa in the night seeing the fire-glow, sighed:—"Ah! alas! what misery! this most distinguished man is also burnt up by the fiery Naga."

Then Kasyapa and his followers at morning light came one and all to look. Now Buddha having subdued the evil

Naga, had straightaway placed him in his *patra*, beholding which, and seeing the power of Buddha, Kasyapa conceived within him deep and secret thoughts:—"This Gotama," he thought, "is deeply versed in religion, but still he said, 'I am a master of religion.' "

Then Buddha, as occasion offered, displayed all kinds of spiritual changes, influencing Kasyapa's heart-thoughts, changing and subduing them, making his mind pliant and yielding, until at length prepared to be a vessel of the true law, he confessed that his poor wisdom could not compare with the complete wisdom of the world-honoured one. And so, convinced at last, humbly submitting, he accepted right instruction. Thus Kasyapa, and five hundred of his followers following their master, virtuously submissive, in turn received the teaching of the law.

Kasyapa and all his followers were thus entirely converted. The Rishi then, taking his goods and all his sacrificial vessels, threw them together in the river, which floated down upon the surface of the current.

Then Buddha for the Kasyapas' sake, and for the benefit of the thousand Bhikshus, having preached, and done all that should be done, himself with purity and wisdom and all the concourse of his qualities excellently adorned, he gave them, as in charity, rules for cleansing sense.

At this time Bimbisara Raja, bowing his head, requested the honoured of the world to change his place of abode for the bamboo grove; graciously accepting it, Buddha remained silent. Then the king, having perceived the truth, offered his adoration and returned to his palace. The world-honoured, with the great congregation, proceeded on foot, to rest for awhile in the bamboo garden. There he dwelt to convert all that breathed, to kindle once for all the lamp of wisdom, to establish Brahma and the Devas, and to confirm the lives of saints and sages.

At this time Asvajit and Vashpa, with heart composed and every sense subdued, the time having come for begging food, entered into the town of Rajagriha. Unrivalled in the world were they for grace of person, and in dignity of carriage excelling all. The lords and ladies of the city seeing them, were filled with joy; those who were walking stood still, those before waited, those behind hastened on. Now the Rishi Kapila amongst all his numerous disciples had one of wide-spread fame, whose name was Sariputra; he, beholding the wonderful grace of the Bhikshus, their composed mien and subdued senses, their dignified walk and carriage, raising his hands, inquiring, said: "Young in years, but pure and graceful in appearance, such as I before have never seen. What law most excellent have you obeyed? and who your master that has taught you? and what the doctrine you have learned? Tell me, I pray you, and relieve my doubts."

Then of the Bhikshus, one, rejoicing at his question, with pleasing air and gracious words, replied: "The omniscient, born of the Ikshvaku family, the very first 'midst gods and men, this one is my great master. I am indeed but young, the sun of wisdom has but just arisen, how can I then explain the master's doctrine? Its meaning is deep and very hard to understand, but now, according to my poor wisdom, I will recount in brief the master's doctrine:—"Whatever things exist all spring from cause, the principles of birth and death may be destroyed, the way is by the means he has declared."

Then the twice-born Upaka, embracing heartily what he had heard, put from him all sense-pollution, and obtained the pure eyes of the law.

The Bhikshus after having begged their food, likewise went back to the bamboo grove. Sariputra on his arrival home rested with joyful face and full of peace. His friend, the honoured Mugalin, equally renowned for learning, seeing Sariputra in the distance, his pleasing air and lightsome step, spoke thus:—"As I now see thee, there is an unusual look I notice; your former nature seems quite changed, the signs of happiness I now observe, all indicate the possession of eternal truth: these marks are not uncaused."

Answering he said: "The words of the Tathagata are such as never yet were spoken," and then, requested, he declared what he had heard. Hearing the words and understanding them, he too put off the world's defilement, and gained the eyes of true religion, and now they both set out for Buddha's presence, with a large crowd of followers.

Buddha seeing the two worthies coming, thus spoke to his disciples:—"These two men who come shall be my two most eminent followers, one unsurpassed for wisdom, the other for powers miraculous." And then with Brahma's voice, profound and sweet, he forthwith bade them "Welcome!" Here is the pure and peaceful law, he said; here the end of all discipleship! Their hands grasping the triple-staff, their twisted hair holding the water-vessel, hearing the words of Buddha's welcome, they forthwith changed into complete Sramanas.

At this time there was a great householder whose name was "Friend of the Orphaned and Destitue"; he was very rich and widely charitable in helping the poor and needy. Now this man, coming far away from the north, even from the country of Kosala, stopped at the house of a friend whose name was Sheu-lo. Hearing that Buddha was in the world and dwelling in the bamboo grove near at hand, understanding moreover his renown and illustrious qualities, he set out that very night for the grove. Tathagata, well aware of his character, and that he was prepared to bring forth purity and faith, according to the case, called him by his true name, and for his sake addressed him in words of religion.

The nobleman, hearing the spoken law, forthwith attained the first degree of holiness: he emptied as it were, the sea of birth and death, one drop alone remaining. By practising, apart from men, the banishment of all desire, he soon attained the one impersonal condition, not as common folk do now-a-days who speculate upon the mode of true deliverance; for he who does not banish sorrow-causing samskaras does but involve himself in every kind of question; and though he reaches to the highest form of being, yet grasps not the one and only truth.

The nobleman, his heart receiving light, perceived throughout the most excellent system of truth. Simple, and of wisdom born; thus firmly settled in the true doctrine he lowly bent in worship at the feet of Buddha and with closed hands made his request:

"I dwell indeed at Sravasti, a land rich in produce, and enjoying peace; Prasenajit is the great king thereof, the offspring of the 'lion' family; his high renown and fame spread everywhere, reverenced by all both far and near. Now am I wishful there to found a Vihara, I pray you of your tenderness accept it from me. I know the heart of Buddha has no preferences, nor does he seek a resting-place from labour, but on behalf of all that lives refuse not my request."

Buddha, knowing the householder's heart, that his great charity was now the moving cause—untainted and unselfish charity, nobly considerate of the heart of all that lives—he said:

"Now you have seen the true doctrine, your guileless heart loves to exercise its charity: for wealth and money are inconstant treasures, 'twere better quickly to bestow such things on others.

"Yours, O friend! is the highest and the best degree of charity, without self-interest or thought of getting more. What your heart inclines you now to do, let it be quickly done and well completed! The uncertain and the lustful heart goes wandering here and there, but the pure eyes of virtue opening, the heart comes back and rests!" The nobleman accepting Buddha's teaching, his kindly heart receiving yet more light.

He invited Upatishya, his excellent friend, to accompany him on his return to Kosala; and then going round to select a pleasant site, he saw the garden of the heir-apparent, Jeta, the groves and limpid streams most pure. Proceeding where the prince was dwelling, he asked for leave to buy the ground; the prince, because he valued it so much, at first was not inclined to sell, but said at last:—"If you can cover it with gold then, but not else, you may possess it."

The nobleman, his heart rejoicing, forthwith began to spread his gold. The Jeta said: "I will not give, why then spread you your gold?" The nobleman replied, "Not give;

why then said you, 'Fill it with yellow gold'?" And thus they differed and contended both, till they resorted to the magistrate.

Meanwhile the people whispered much about his unwonted charity, and Jeta too, knowing the man's sincerity, asked more about the matter: what his reasons were. On his reply, "I wish to found a Vihara, and offer it to the Tathagata and all his Bhikshu followers," the prince, hearing the name of Buddha, received at once illumination, and only took one-half the gold, desiring to share in the foundation: "Yours is the land," he said, "but mine the trees; these will I give to Buddha as my share in the offering."

Then the noble took the land, Jeta the trees, and settled both in trust on Sariputra. Then they began to build the hall, labouring night and day to finish it. Lofty it rose and choicely decorated, as one of the four kings' palaces, in just proportions, following the directions, which Buddha had declared the right ones. Never yet so great a miracle as this! the priest shone in the streets of Sravasti! Tathagata, seeing the divine shelter, with all his holy ones resorted to the place to rest. No followers there to bow in prostrate service, his followers rich in wisdom only.

The nobleman reaping his reward, at the end of life ascended up to heaven, leaving to sons and grandsons a good foundation, through successive generations, to plough the field of merit.

In the past and present, there has been deliverance for all. Tathagata, when in the world; and now his relics—after his Nirvana; those who worship and revere these, gain equal merit; so also those who raise themselves by wisdom, and reverence the virtues of the Tathagata, cherishing religion, fostering a spirit of almsgiving, they gain great merit also. The noble and superlative law of Buddha ought to receive the adoration of the world.

2

Dhammachakka–Pavattana Sutta

The Wheel of Law

Reverence to the Blessed One, the Holy One, the Fully-Enlightened One.

Thus have I heard. The Blessed One was once staying at Benares, at the hermitage called Migadaya. And there the Blessed One addressed the company of the five Bhikshus, and said:

'There are two extremes, O Bhikkhus, which the man who has given up the world ought not to follow—the habitual practice, on the one hand, of those things whose attraction depends upon the passions, and especially of sensuality—a low and pagan way (of seeking satisfaction) unworthy, unprofitable, and fit only for the worldly-minded—and the habitual practice, on the other hand, of asceticism (or self-mortification), which is painful, unworthy, and unprofitable.

'There is a middle path, O Bhikkhus, avoiding these two extremes, discovered by the Tathagata—a path which opens the eyes, and bestows understanding, which leads to peace of mind, to the higher wisdom, to full enlightenment, to Nirva*n*a!

'What is that middle path, O Bhikkhus, avoiding these two extremes, discovered by the Tathagata—that path which opens the eyes, and bestows understanding, which leads to peace of mind, to the higher wisdom, to full enlightenment, to Nirvana? Verily! it is this noble eightfold path; that is to say:

'Right views;
Right aspirations;
Right speech;
Right conduct;
Right livelihood;
Right effort;
Right mindfulness; and
Right contemplation.

'This, O Bhikkhus, is that middle path, avoiding these two extremes, discovered by the Tathagata—that path which opens the eyes, and bestows understanding, which leads to peace of mind, to the higher wisdom, to full enlightenment, to Nirvana!

Now this, O Bhikkhus, is the noble truth concerning suffering:

'Birth is attended with pain, decay is painful, disease is painful, death is painful. Union with the unpleasant is painful, painful is separation from the pleasant; and any craving that is unsatisfied, that too is painful. In brief, the five aggregates which spring from attachment (the conditions of individuality and their cause) are painful.

'This then, O Bhikkhus, is the noble truth concerning suffering.

'Now this, O Bhikkhus, is the noble truth concerning the origin of suffering:

'Verily, it is that thirst (or craving), causing the renewal of existence, accompanied by sensual delight, seeking satisfaction now here, now there—that is to say, the craving for the gratification of the passions or the craving for a future life, or the craving for success in this present life.

'This then, O Bhikkhus, is the noble truth concerning the origin of suffering.

'Now this, O Bhikkhus, is the noble truth concerning

the destruction of suffering:

'Verily, it is the destruction, in which no passion remains, of this very thirst; the laying aside of, the getting rid of, the being free from, the harbouring no longer of this thirst.

'This then, O Bhikkhus, is the noble truth concerning the destruction of suffering.

'Now this, O Bhikkhus, is the noble truth concerning the way which leads to the destruction of sorrow. Verily! it is this noble eightfold path; that is to say:

'Right views;
Right aspirations;
Right speech;
Right conduct;
Right livelihood;
Right effort;
Right mindfulness; and
Right contemplation.

'This then, O Bhikkhus, is the noble truth concerning the destruction of sorrow.

'That this was the noble truth concerning sorrow, was not, O Bhikkhus, among the doctrines handed down, but there arose within me the eye to perceive it, there arose the knowledge of its nature, there arose the understanding of its cause, there arose the wisdom to guide in the path of tranquillity, there arose the light to dispel darkness from it.

'And again, O Bhikkhus, that I should comprehend that this was the noble truth concerning sorrow, though it was not amount the doctrines handed down, there arose within me the eye, there arose the knowledge, there arose the understanding, there arose the wisdom, there arose the light.

'And again, O Bhikkhus, that I had comprehended that this was the noble truth concerning sorrow, thought it was not among the doctrines handed down, there arose within me the eye, there arose the knowledge, there arose the understanding, there arose the wisdom, there arose the light.

'That this was the noble truth concerning the origin of sorrow, though it was not among the doctrines handed down, there arose within me the eye, there arose within me the knowledge, there arose the understanding, there arose the wisdom, there arose the light.

'And again, O Bhikkhus that I should put away the origin of sorrow, though the noble truth concerning it was not among the doctrines handed down, there arose within me the eye, there arose the knowledge, there arose the understanding, there arose the wisdom, there arose the light.

And again, O Bhikkhus, that I had fully put away the origin of sorrow, though the noble truth concerning it was not among the doctrines handed down, there arose within me the eye, there arose the knowledge, there arose the understanding, there arose the wisdom, there arose the light.

'That this, O Bhikkhus, was the noble truth concerning the destruction of sorrow, though it was not among the doctrines handed down, there arose within me the eye, there arose the knowledge, there arose the understanding, there arose the wisdom, there arose the light.

'And again, O Bhikkhus, that I should fully realise the destruction of sorrow, though the noble truth concerning it was not among the doctrines handed down, there arose within me the eye, there arose the knowledge, there arose the understanding, there arose the wisdom, there arose the light.

'And again, O Bhikkhus, that I had fully realised the destruction of sorrow, though the noble truth concerning it was not among the doctrines handed down, there arose within me the eye, there arose the knowledge, there arose the understanding, there arose the wisdom, there arose the light.

'That this was the noble truth concerning the way which leads to the destruction of sorrow, was not, O Bhikkshus, among the doctrines handed down, there arose within me the eye, there arose the knowledge, there arose the understanding, there arose the wisdom, there arose the light.

'And again, O Bhikkhus, that I should become versed in the way which leads to the destruction of sorrow, though the noble truth concerning it was not among the doctrines handed down, there arose within me the eye, there arose the knowledge, there arose the understanding, there arose the wisdom, there arose the light.

'And again, O Bhikkhus, that I had become versed in the way which leads to the destruction of sorrow, though the noble truth concerning it was not among the doctrines handed down, there arose within me the eye, there arose the knowledge, there arose the understanding, there arose the wisdom, there arose the light.

'So long, O Bhikkhus, as my knowledge and insight were not quite clear, regarding each of these four noble truths in this triple order, in this twelvefold manner—so long was I uncertain whether I had attained to the full insight of that wisdom which is unsurpassed in the heavens or on earth, among the whole race of Samanas and Brahmins, or of gods or men.

'But as soon, O Bhikkhus, as my knowledge and insight were quite clear regarding each of these four noble truths, in this triple order, in this twelvefold manner—then did I become certain that I had attained to the full insight of that wisdom which is unsurpassed in the heavens or on earth, among the whole race of Samanas and Brahmins, or of gods or men.

'And now this knowledge and this insight has arisen within me. Immovable is the emancipation of my heart. This is my last existence. There will now be no rebirth for me!'

Thus spake the Blessed One. The company of the five Bhikshus, glad at heart, exalted the words of the Blessed One. And when the discourse had been uttered, there arose within the venerable Kondanna the eye of truth, spotless, and without a stain, and he saw that whatsoever has an origin, in that is also inherent the necessity of coming to an end.

And when the royal chariot wheel of the truth had thus been set rolling onwards by the Blessed One, the gods of the earth gave forth a shout, saying:

'In Benares, at the hermitage of the Migadaya, the supreme wheel of the empire of Truth has been set rolling by the Blessed One—that wheel which not by any Samana or Brahmin, not by any god, not by any Brahma or Mara, not by any one in the universe, can ever be turned back!'

And when they heard the shout of the gods of the earth, the attendant gods of the four great kings, the guardian angels of the four quarters of the globe, gave forth a shout, saying :

'In Benares, at the hermitage of the Migadaya, the supreme wheel of the empire of Truth has been set rolling by the Blessed One—that wheel which not by any Samana or Brahmin, not by any god, not by any Brahma or Mara, not by any one in the universe, can ever be turned back!'

And thus as the gods in each of the heavens heard the shout of the inhabitants of the heaven beneath, they took up the cry until the gods in the highest heaven of heavens gave forth the shout, saying:

'In Benares, at the hermitage of the Migadaya, the supreme wheel of the empire of Truth has been set rolling by the Blessed One—that wheel which not by any Samana or Brahmin, not by any god, not by any Brahma or Mara, not by any one in the universe, can ever be turned back!'

And thus, in an instant, a second, a moment, the sound went up even to the world of Brahma: and this great ten-thousand-world-system quaked and trembled and was shaken violently, and an immeasurable bright light appeared in the universe, beyond even the power of the gods!

Then did the Blessed One give utterance to this exclamation of joy: 'Kondanna hath realised it. Kondanna hath realised it!' And so the venerable Kondanna acquired the name of Ajjata-Kondanna ('the Kondanna who realised').

3

Tevijja Sutta

The Three Shilas

The Problem of Brahma

This have I heard. At one time when the Blessed One was journeying through Kosala with a great company of the brethren, with about five hundred brethren, he came to the Brahmin village in Kosala which is called Manasakata. And there at Manasakata the Blessed One stayed in the mango grove, on the bank of the river Achiravati, to the south of Manasakata.

Now at that time many very distinguished and wealthy Brahmins were staying at Manasakata—Chanki the Brahmin, Tarukkha the Brahmin, Pokkharasati the Brahmin, Janussoni the Brahmin, Todeyya the Brahmin, and other very distinguished and wealthy Brahmins.

Now a conversation sprung up between Vasettha and Bharadvaja, when they were taking exercise after their bath and walking up and down in thoughtful mood, as to which was the true path, and which the false.

The young Brahmin Vasettha spake thus:

'This is the straight path, this the direct way which leads him who acts according to it, into a state of union with Brahma—I mean that which has been announced by the Brahmin Pokkarasati.

The young Brahmin Bharadvaja spake thus:

'This is the straight path, this the direct way which leads him who acts according to it, into a state of union with

Brahma—I mean that which has been announced by the Brahmin Tarukkha.'

But neither was the young Brahmin Vasettha able to convince the young Brahmin Bharadvaga, nor was the young Brahmin Bharadvaja able to convince the young Brahmin Vasettha.

Then the young Brahmin Vasettha said to the young Brahmin Bharadavaja:

'That Samana Gotama, Bharadvaja, of the Sakya clan, who left the Sakya tribe to adopt the religious life, is now staying at Manasakata, in the mango grove, on the bank of the river Achiravati, to the south of Manasakata. Now regarding that venerable Gotama, such is the high reputation that has been noised abroad, that he is said to be "a fully enlightened one, blessed and worthy, abounding in wisdom and goodness, happy, with knowledge of the world, unsurpassed as a guide to erring mortals, a teacher of gods and, men, a blessed Buddha." Come, then, Bharadvaja, let us go to the place where the Samana Gotama is; and when we have come there, let us ask the Samana Gotama touching this matter. What the Samana Gotama shall declare unto us, that let us bear in mind.'

'Very well, my friend!' said the young Brahmin Bharadvaja, in assent, to the young Brahmin Vasettha.

Then the young Brahmin Vasettha and the young Brahmin Bharadvaja went on to the place where the Blessed One was.

And when they had come there, they exchanged with the Blessed One the greetings and compliments of friendship and civility, and sat down beside him.

And while they were thus seated the young Brahmin Vasettha said to the Blessed One:

'As we, Gotama, were taking exercise and walking up and down, there sprung up a conversation between us on which was the true path and which the false. I said thus:

' "This is the straight path, this the direct way which

leads him, who acts according to it, into a state of union with Brahma—I mean that which has been announced by the Brahmin Pokkarasati."

'Bharadvaja said thus:

' "This is the straight path, this the direct way which leads him who acts according to it, into a state of union with Brahma—I mean that which has been announced by the Brahmin Tarukkha."

'Regarding this matter, Gotama, there is a strife, a dispute, a difference of opinion between us.'

'So you say, Vasettha, that you said thus:

' "This is the straight path, this the direct way which leads him who acts according to it, into a state of union with Brahma—I mean that which has been announced by the Brahmin Pokkarasati."

'While Bharadvaja said thus:

' "This is the straight path, this the direct way which leads him who acts according to it, into a state of union with Brahma—I mean that which has been announced by the Brahmin Tarukkha."

' Wherein, then, O Vasettha, is there a strife, a dispute, a difference of opinion between you?'

'Concerning the true path and the false, Gotama. Various Brahmins, Gotama, teach various paths—the Addhariya Brahmins, the Tittiriya Brahmins, the Chhandoka Brahmins, the Chhandava Brahmins, the Brahmachariya Brahmins. Are all those saving paths? Are they all paths which will lead him, who acts according to them, into a state of union with Brahma?

'Just, Gotama, as near a village or a town there are many and various paths, yet they all meet together in the village—just in that way are all the various paths taught by various Brahmins—the Addhariya Brahmins, the Tittiriya Brahmins, the Chhandoka Brahmins, the Chhandava Brahmins, the Brahmachariya Brahmins. Are all these saving paths? Are they all paths which will lead him, who acts according to them, into a state of union with Brahma?'

'Do you say that they all lead aright, Vasettha?'

'I say so, Gotama.'

'Do you really say that they all lead aright, Vasettha?'

'So I say, Gotama.'

'But then, Vasettha, is there a single one of the Brahmins versed in the Three Vedas who has ever seen Brahma face to face?'

'No, indeed, Gotama!'

'But is there then, Vasettha, a single one of the teachers of the Brahmins versed in the Three Vedas who has seen Brahma face to face?'

'No, indeed, Gotama!'

'But is there then, Vasettha, a single one of the pupils of the teachers of the Brahmins versed in the Three Vedas who has seen Brahma face to face?'

'No, indeed, Gotama!'

'But is there then, Vasettha, a single one of the Brahmins up to the seventh generation who has seen Brahma face to face?'

'No, indeed, Gotama!'

'Well then, Vasettha, those ancient Rishis of the Brahmins versed in the Three Vedas, the authors of the verses, the utterers of the verses, whose ancient form of words so chanted, uttered, or composed, the Brahmins of today chant over again or repeat; intoning or reciting exactly as has been intoned or recited—to wit, Atthaka, Vamaka, Vamadeva, Vessamitta, Yamataggi, Angirasa, Bharadvaja, Vasettha, Kassapa, and Bhagu—did even they speak thus, saying: "We know it, we have seen it, where Brahma is, whence Brahma is, whither Brahma is?" '

'Not so, Gotama!'

'Then you say, Vasettha that not one of the Brahmins, or of their teachers, or of their pupils, even up to the seventh generation, has ever seen Brahma face to face. And that even the Rishis of old, the authors and utterers of the verses, of the ancient form of words which the Brahmins of today so carefully intone and recite precisely as they have been handed down—even they did not pretend to know or to have seen where or whence or whither Brahma is. So that the Brahmins versed in the Three Vedas have forsooth said thus: "What we know not, what we have not seen, to a state of union with that we can show the way, and can say: 'This is the straight path, this is the direct way which leads him who acts according to it, into a state of union with Brahma!' "

'Now what think you, Vasettha? Does it not follow, this being so, that the talk of the Brahmins, versed though they be in the Three Vedas, is foolish talk?'

'In sooth, Gotama, that being so, it follows that the talk of the Brahmins versed in the Three Vedas is foolish talk!'

'Verily, Vasettha, that Brahmins versed in the Three Vedas should be able to show the way to a state of union with that which they do not know, neither have seen—such a condition of things has no existence!

'Just, Vasettha, as when a string of blind men are clinging one to the other, neither can the foremost see, nor can the middle one see, nor can the hindmost see—just even so, methinks, Vasettha, is the talk of the Brahmins versed in the Three Vedas but blind talk: the first sees not, the middle one sees not, nor can the latest see. The talk then of these Brahmins versed in the Three Vedas turns out to be ridiculous, mere words, a vain and empty thing!'

•

'Now what think you, Vasettha? Can the Brahmins versed in the Three Vedas—like other, ordinary, folk—see the sun and the moon as they pray to, and praise, and worship them, turning round with clasped hands towards the place whence they rise and where they set?'

'Certainly, Gotama, they can.'

'Now what think you, Vasettha? The Brahmins versed in the Three Vedas, who can very well—like other, ordinary, folk—see the sun and the moon as they pray to, and praise, and worship them, turning round with clasped hands to the place whence they rise and where they set—are those Brahmins, versed in the Three Vedas, able to point out the way to a state of union with the sun or the moon, saying: "This is the straight path, this the direct way which leads him who acts according to it, to a state of union with the sun or the moon?" '

'Certainly not, Gotama!'

'So you say, Vasettha, that the Brahmins are not able to point out the way to union with that which they have seen, and you further say that neither any one of them, nor of their pupils, nor of their predecessors even to the seventh generation has ever seen Brahma. And you further say that even the Rishis of old, whose words they hold in such deep respect, did not pretend to know, or to have seen where, or whence, or whither Brahma is. Yet these Brahmins versed in the Three Vedas say, forsooth, that they can point out the way to union with that which they know not, neither have seen! Now what think you, Vasettha? Does it not follow that, this being so, the talk of the Brahmins, versed though they be in the Three Vedas, is foolish talk?'

'In sooth, Gotama, that being so, it follows that the talk of the Brahmins versed in the Three Vedas is foolish talk!'

'Very good, Vasettha. Verily then, Vasettha, that Brahmins versed in the Three Vedas should be able to show the way to a state of union with that which they do not know neither have seen—such a condition of things has no existence.

•

'Just, Vasettha, as if a man should say, "How I long for, how I love the most beautiful woman in this land!"

'And people should ask him, "Well! good friend! this most beautiful woman in the land whom you thus love and long for, do you know whether that beautiful woman is a noble lady or a Brahmin woman, or of the trader class, or a Shudra?"

'But when so asked he should answer "No."

'And when people should ask him, "Well! good friend! this most beautiful woman in all the land, whom you so love and long for, do you know what the name of that most beautiful woman is, or what is her family name, whether she be tall or short, dark or of medium complexion, black or fair, in what village or town or city she dwells?"

'But when so asked he should answer "No."

'And then people should say to him, "So then, good friend, whom you know not, neither have seen, her do you love and long for?"

'And then when so asked he should answer "Yes." '

'Now what think you, Vasettha? Would it not turn out, that being so, that the talk of that man was foolish talk?'

'In sooth, Gotama, it would turn out, that being so, that the talk of that man was foolish talk!'

'And just even so, Vasettha, though you say that the Brahmins are not able to point out the way to union with that which they have seen, and you further say that neither any one of them, nor of their pupils, nor of their predecessors even to the seventh generation has ever seen Brahma. And you further say that even the Rishis of old, whose words they hold in such deep respect, did not pretend to know, or to have seen where, or whence, or whither Brahma is. Yet these Brahmins versed in the Three Vedas say, forsooth, that they can point out the way to union with that which they know not, neither have seen! Now what think you, Vasettha? Does it not follow that, this being so, the talk of the Brahmans, versed though they be in the Three Vedas, is foolish talk?'

'In sooth, Gotama, that being so, it follows that the talk of the Brahmins versed in the Three Vedas is foolish talk!'

'Very good, Vasettha. Verily then, Vasettha, that Brahmins versed in the Three Vedas should be able to show the way to a state of union with that which they do not know, neither have seen—such a condition of things has no existence.'

•

'Just, Vasettha, as if a man should make a staircase in the place where four roads cross, to mount up into a mansion. And people should say to him, "Well, good friend, this mansion, to mount up into which you are making this staircase, do you know whether it is in the east, or in the south, or in the west, or in the north? Whether it is high or low or of medium size?'

'And when so asked he should answer "No."'

'And people should say to him, "But then, good friend, you are making a staircase to mount up into something—taking it for a mansion—which, all the while, you know not, neither have seen!"

'And when so asked he should answer "Yes."'

'Now what think you, Vasettha? Would it not turn out, that being so, that the talk of that man was foolish talk?'

'In sooth, Gotama, it would turn out, that being so, that the talk of that man was foolish talk!'

'And just even so, Vasettha, though you say that the Brahmins are not able to point out the way to union with that which they have seen, and you further say that neither any one of them, nor of their pupils, nor of their predecessors even to the seventh generation has ever seen Brahma. And you further say that even the Rishis of old, whose words they hold in such deep respect, did not pretend to know, or to have seen where, or whence or whither Brahma is. Yet these Brahmins versed in the Three Vedas say, forsooth, that they can point out the way to union with that which they know not, neither have seen! Now what think you, Vasettha? Does it not follow that, this being so, the talk of the Brahmins versed in the Three Vedas is foolish talk?'

'In sooth, Gotama, that being so, it follows that the talk of the Brahmins versed in the Three Vedas is foolish talk!'

'Very good, Vasettha. Verily then, Vasettha, that Brahmins versed in the Three Vedas should be able to show the way to a state of union with that which they do not know, neither have seen—such condition of things has no existence.'

•

'Again, Vasettha, if this river Achiravati were full of water even to the brim, and overflowing. And a man with business on the other side, bound for the other side, should come up, and want to cross over. And he, standing on this bank, should invoke the further bank, and say, "Come hither, O further bank! come over to this side!"

'Now what think you, Vasettha? Would the further bank of the river Achiravati, by reason of that man's invoking and praying and hoping and praising, come over to this side?'

'Certainly not, Gotama!'

'In just the same way, Vasettha, do the Brahmins versed in the Three Vedas—omitting the practice of those qualities which really make a man a Brahmin, and adopting the practice of those qualities which really make men not Brahmins—say thus: "Indra we call upon, Soma we call upon, Varuna we call upon, Isana we call upon, Prajapati we call upon, Brahma we call upon, Mahiddhi we call upon, Yama we call upon!" Verily, Vasettha, that those Brahmins versed in the Three Vedas, but omitting the practice of those qualities which really make a man a Brahmin, and adopting the practice of those qualities which really make men not Brahmins—that they, by reason of their invoking and praying and hoping and praising, should, after death and when the body is dissolved, become united with Brahma—verily such a condition of things has no existence!'

•

'Just, Vasettha, as if this river Achiravati were full, even to the brim, and overflowing. And a man with business on the other side, bound for the other side, should come up, and want to cross over. And he, on this bank, were to be bound tightly, with his arms behind his back, by a strong chain. Now what think you, Vasettha, would that man be able to get over from this bank of the river Achiravati to the further bank?'

'Certainly not, Gotama!'

'In the same way, Vasettha, there are five things leading to lust, which are called in the Discipline of the Noble One a "chain" and a "bond."'

'What are the five?'

'Forms perceptible to the eye; desirable, agreeable, pleasant, attractive forms, that are accompanied by lust and cause delight. Sounds of the same kind perceptible to the ear. Odours of the same kind perceptible to the nose. Tastes of the same kind perceptible to the tongue. Substances of the same kind perceptible to the body by touch. These five things predisposing to passion are called in the discipline of the Noble One a "chain" and a "bond." And these five things predisposing to lust, Vasettha, do the Brahmins versed in the Three Vedas cling to, they are infatuated by them, guilty of them, see not the danger of them, know not how unreliable they are, and so enjoy them.

'And verily, Vasettha, that Brahmins versed in the Three Vedas, but omitting the practice of those qualities which really make a man a Brahmin, and adopting the practice of those qualities which really make men non-Brahmins—clinging to these five things predisposing to passion, infatuated by them, guilty of them, seeing not their danger, knowing not their unreliability, and so enjoying them—that these Brahmins should after death, on the dissolution of the body, become united to Brahma—such a condition of things has no existence.'

•

'Again, Vasettha, if this river Achiravati were full of water even to the brim, and overflowing. And a man with business on the other side, bound for the other side, should come up, and want to cross over. And if he covering himself up, even to his head, were to lie down, on this bank, to sleep.

'Now what think you, Vasettha? Would that man be able to get over from this bank of the river Achiravati to the further bank?'

'Certainly not, Gotama!'

'And in the same way, Vasettha, there are these five hindrances, in the Discipline of the Noble One, which are called "veils," and are called "hindrances," and are called "obstacles," and are called "entanglements."

'Which are the five?'

'The hindrance of lustful desire,
The hindrance of malice,
The hindrance of sloth and idleness,
The hindrance of pride and self-righteousness,
The hindrance of doubt.

'These are the five hindrances, Vasettha, which, in the Discipline of the Noble One, are called veils, and are called hindrances, and are called obstacles, and are called entanglements.

'Now with these five hindrances, Vasettha, the Brahmins versed in the Three Vedas are veiled, hindered, obstructed, and entangled.

'And verily, Vasettha, that Brahmins versed in the Three Vedas, but omitting the practice of those qualities which really make a man a Brahmin, and adopting the practice of those qualities which really make men non-Brahmins—veiled, hindered, obstructed, and entangled by these Five Hindrances—that these Brahmins should after death, on the dissolution of the body, become united to Brahma—such a condition of things has no existence.'

•

'Now what think you, Vasettha, and what have you

heard from the Brahmins aged and well-stricken in years, when the learners and teachers are talking together? Is Brahma in possession of wives and wealth, or is he not?'

'He is not, Gotama.'

'Is his mind full of anger, or free from anger?'

'Free from anger, Gotama.'

'Is his mind full of malice, or free from malice?'

'Free from malice, Gotama.'

'Is his mind depraved, or pure?'

'It is pure, Gotama.'

'Has he self-mastery, or has he not?'

'He has, Gotama.'

'Now what think you, Vasettha, are the Brahmins versed in the Three Vedas in the possession of wives and wealth, or are they not?'

'They are, Gotama.'

'Have they anger in their hearts, or have they not?'

'They have, Gotama.'

'Do they bear malice, or do they not?'

'They do, Gotama.'

'Are they pure in heart, or are they not?'

'They are not, Gotama.'

'Have they self-mastery, or have they not?'

'They have not, Gotama.'

'Then you say, Vasettha, that the Brahmins are in possession of wives and wealth, and that Brahma is not. Can there, then, be agreement and likeness between the Brahmins with their wives and property, and Brahma, who has none of these things?'

'Certainly not, Gotama!'

'Very good, Vasettha. But, verily, that these Brahmins versed in the Three Vedas, who live married and wealthy should after death, when the body is dissolved, become united with Brahma, who has none of these things—such a condition of thins has no existence.'

'Then you say, too, Vasettha, that the Brahmins bear anger and malice in their hearts, and are sinful and uncontrolled, whilst Brahma is free from anger and malice, and sinless, and has self-mastery. Now can there, then, be concord and likeness between the Brahmins and Brahma?'

'Certainly not, Gotama!'

'Very good, Vasettha. That these Brahmins versed in the Three Vedas and yet bearing anger and malice in their hearts, sinful, and uncontrolled, should after death, when the body is dissolved, become united to Brahma, who is free from anger and malice, sinless, and has self-mastery—such a condition of things has no existence.'

'So that thus then, Vasettha, the Brahmins, versed though they be in the Three Vedas, while they sit down in confidence, are sinking down in the mire; and so sinking they are arriving only at despair, thinking the while that they are crossing over into some happier land.

'Therefore is it that the threefold wisdom of the Brahmins, wise in their Three Vedas, is called a waterless desert, their threefold wisdom is called a pathless jungle, their threefold wisdom is called destruction!'

•

When he had thus spoken, the young Brahmin Vasettha said to the Blessed one:

'It has been told me, Gotama, that the Samana Gotama knows the way to the state of union with Brahma.'

'What do you think, Vasettha, is not Manasakata near to this spot, not distant from this spot?'

'Just so, Gotama. Manasakata is near to, is not far from here.'

'Now what think you, Vasettha, suppose there were a man born in Manasakata, and people should ask him, who never till that time had left Manasakata, which was the way to Manasakata. Would that man, born and brought up in Manasakata, be in any doubt or difficulty?'

'Certainly not, Gotama! And why? If the man had been born and brought up in Manasakata, every road that leads to Manasakata would be perfectly familiar to him.'

'That man, Vasettha, born and brought up at Manasakata might, if he were asked the way to Manasakata, fall into doubt and difficulty, but to the Tathagata, when asked touching the path which leads to the world of Brahma, there can be neither doubt nor difficulty. For Brahma, I know, Vasettha, and the world of Brahma, and the path which leadeth unto it. Yea, I know it even as one who has entered the Brahma world, and has been born within it!'

•

When he had thus spoken, Vasettha the young Brahmin said to the Blessed One:

'So has it been told me, Gotama, even that the Samana Gotama knows the way to a state of union with Brahma. It is well! Let the Venerable Gotama be pleased to show us the way to a state of union with Brahma, let the Venerable Gotama save the Brahmin race!'

'Listen then, Vasettha, and give ear attentively, and I will speak!'

'So be it, Lord!' said the young Brahmin Vasettha, in assent, to the Blessed One.

Then the Blessed One spake, and said: 'Know, Vasettha, that from time to time a Tathagata is born into the world, a fully Enlightened One, blessed and worthy, abounding in wisdom and goodness, happy, with knowledge of the world, unsurpassed as a guide to erring mortals, a teacher of gods and men, a Blessed Buddha. He, by himself, thoroughly understands, and sees, as it were, face to face this universe—the world below with all its spirits, and the worlds above, of Mara and of Brahma—and all creatures, Samanas and Brahmins, gods and men, and he then makes his knowledge known to others. The truth doth he proclaim both in its letter and in its spirit, lovely in its origin, lovely in its progress, lovely in its consummation: the higher life doth he make known, in all its purity and in all its perfectness.

'A householder, or one of his children, or a man of inferior birth in any class, listens to that truth. On hearing the truth he has faith in the Tathagata, and when he has acquired that faith he thus considers with himself:

' "Full of hindrances is household life, a path defiled by passion: free as the air is the life of him who has renounced all worldly things. How difficult is it for the man who dwells at home to live the higher life in all its fulness, in all its purity, in all its bright perfection! Let me then cut off my hair and beard, let me clothe myself in the orange-coloured robes, and let me go forth from a household life into the homeless state!"

'Then before long, forsaking his portion of wealth, be it great or be it small; forsaking his circle of relatives, be they many or be they few, he cuts off his hair and beard, he clothes himself in the orange-coloured robes, and he goes forth from the household life into the homeless state.

'When he has thus become a recluse he passes a life self-restrained according to the rules of the Patimokkha; uprightness is his delight, and he sees danger in the least of those things he should avoid; he adopts and trains himself in the precepts; he encompasses himself with holiness in word and deed; he sustains his life by means that are quite pure; good is his conduct, guarded the door of his senses; mindful and self-possessed, he is altogether happy.!'

The Short Conducts *(The Chula Silam)*

'Now wherein, Vasettha, is his conduct good?

'Herein, O Vasettha, that putting away the murder of that which lives, he abstains from destroying life. The cudgel and the sword he lays aside; and, full of modesty and pity, he is compassionate and kind to all creatures that have life!

'This is the kind of goodness that he has.

'Putting away the theft of that which is not his, he abstains from taking anything not given. He takes only what is given, therewith is he content, and he passes his life in honesty and in purity of heart!

'This, too, is the kind of goodness that he has.

'Putting away inchastity, he lives a life of chastity and purity, averse to the low habit of sexual intercourse.

'This, too, is the kind of goodness that he has.

'Putting away lying, he abstains from speaking falsehood. He speaks truth, from the truth he never swerves; faithful and trustworthy, he injures not his fellow man by deceit.

'This, too, is the kind of goodness that he has.

'Putting away slander, he abstains from calumny. What he hears here he repeats not elsewhere to raise a quarrel against the people here: what he hears elsewhere he repeats not here to raise a quarrel against the people there. Thus he lives as a binder together of those who are divided, an encourager of those who are friends, a peacemaker, a lover of peace, impassioned for peace, a speaker of words that make for peace.

'This, too, is the kind of goodness that he has.

'Putting away bitterness of speech, he abstains from harsh language. Whatever word is humane, pleasant to the ear, lovely, reaching to the heart, urbane, pleasing to the people, beloved of the people—such are the words he speaks.

'This, too, is the kind of goodness that he has.

'Putting away foolish talk, he abstains from vain conversation. In season he speaks; he speaks that which is; he speaks fact; he utters good doctrine; he utters good discipline; he speaks, and at the right time, that which redounds to profit, is well-grounded, is well-defined, and is full of wisdom.

'This, too, is the kind of goodness that he has.

'He refrains from injuring any herb or any creature. He takes but one meal a day; abstaining from food at night time, or at the wrong time. He abstains from dancing, singing, music, and theatrical shows. He abstains from wearing, using, or adorning himself with garlands, and scents, and unguents, and he abstains from lofty couches and large beds.

'This, too, is the kind of goodness that he has.

'He abstains from the getting of silver or gold. He abstains from the getting of grain uncooked. He abstains from the getting of flesh that is raw. He abstains from the getting of any woman or girl. He abstains from the getting of bondmen or bondwomen. He abstains from the getting of sheep or goats. He abstains from the getting of fowls or swine. He abstains from the getting of elephants, cattle, horses, and mares. He abstains from the getting of fields or lands.

'This, too, is the kind of goodness that he has.

'He refrains from carrying out those commissions on which messengers can be sent. He refrains from buying and selling. He abstains from tricks with false weights, alloyed metals, or false measures. He abstains from bribery, cheating, fraud, and crooked ways.

'This, too, is the kind of goodness that he has.

'He refrains from maiming, killing, imprisoning, highway robbery, plundering villagers, or obtaining money by threats of violence.

'This, too, is the kind of goodness that he has.

The Middle Conducts *(The Majjhima Silam)*

'Or whereas some Samana-Brahmins, who live on the food provided by the faithful, continue addicted to injuring plants or vegetables: that is to say, the germs arising from roots, the germs arising from trunks of trees, the germs arising from joints, the germs arising from buds, or the germs arising from seeds. He, on the other hand, refrains from injuring such plants or animals.

'This, too, is the kind of goodness that he has.

'Or whereas some Samana-Brahmins, who live on the food provided by the faithful, continue addicted to storing up property: that is to say, meat, drink, clothes, equipages, beds, perfumes, and grain. He, on the other hand, refrains from storing up such property.

'This, too, is the kind of goodness that he has.

'Or whereas some Samana-Brahmins, who live on the

food provided by the faithful, continue addicted to witnessing public spectacles: that is to say, dancing, singing, concerts, theatrical representations, recitations, instrumental music, funeral ceremonies, drummings, balls, gymnastics, tumblings, feasts in honour of the dead, combats between elephants, horses, buffaloes, bulls, goats, rams, cocks, and quails, cudgel-playing, boxing, wrestling, fencing, musters, marching, and reviews of troops. He, on there other hand, refrains from such public spectacles.

'This, too, is the kind of goodness that he has.

'Or whereas some Samana-Brahmins, who live on the food provided by the faithful, continue addicted to occupying their time with games detrimental to their progress in virtue: that is to say, with a board of sixty-four squares, or of one hundred squares; tossing up; hopping over diagrams formed on the ground; removing substances from a heap without shaking the remainder; dicing; trapball; sketching rude figures; tossing balls; blowing trumpets; ploughing matches; tumbling; forming mimic windmills; guessing at measures; chariot races; archery; shooting marbles from the fingers; guessing other people's thoughts; and mimicking other people's acts. He, on the other hand, refrains from such games detrimental to virtue.

'This, too, is the kind of goodness that he has.

'Or whereas some Samana-Brahmins, who live on the food provided by the faithful, continue addicted to the use of elevated and ornamented couches or things to recline upon: that is to say, of large couches; ornamented beds; coverlets with long fleece; embroidered counterpanes; woollen coverlets, plain or worked with thick flowers; cotton coverlets, worked with knots, or dyed with figures of animals; fleecy carpets; carpets inwrought with gold or with silk; far-spreading carpets; rich elephant housings, trappings, or harness; rugs for chariots; skins of the tiger or antelope; and pillows or cushions ornamented with gold lace or embroidery. He, on the other hand, refrains from the use of such elevated or ornamented couches or things to recline upon.

'This, too, is the kind of goodness that he has.

'Or whereas some Samana-Brahmins, who live on the food provided by the faithful, continue addicted to the use of articles for the adornment of their persons: that is to say, unguents; fragrant oils; perfumed baths; shampooings; mirrors; antimony for the eyebrows and eyelashes; flowers; cosmetics; dentifrices; bracelets; diadems; handsome walking-sticks; tiaras; swords; umbrellas; embroidered slippers; fillets; jewelry; fans of the buffalo tail; and long white garments. He, on the other hand, refrains from the use of such articles for the adornment of the person.

'This, too, is the kind of goodness that he has.

'Or whereas some Samana-Brahmins, who live on the food provided by the faithful, continue addicted to mean talk: that is to say, tales of kings, of robbers, or of ministers of state; tales of arms, of war, of terror; conversation respecting meats, drinks, clothes, couches, garlands, perfumes, relationships, equipages, streets, villages, towns, cities, provinces, women, warriors, demigods; fortune-telling; hidden treasures in jars; ghost stories; empty tales; disasters by sea; accidents on shore; things which are, and things which are not. He, on the other hand, refrains from such mean conversation.

'This, too, is the kind of goodness that he has.

'Or whereas some Samana-Brahmins, who live on the food provided by the faithful, continue addicted to wrangling: that is to say, to saying, "You are ignorant of this doctrine and discipline, but I understand them!" "What do you know of doctrine or discipline?" "You are heterodox, but I am orthodox!" "My discourse is profitable, but yours is worthless!" "That which you should speak first you speak last, and that which you should speak last you speak first!" "What you have long studied I have completely overturned!" "Your errors are made quite plain!" "You are disgraced!" "Go away and escape from this disputation; or if not, extricate yourself from your difficulties!" He, on the other hand, refrains from such wrangling.

'This, too, is the kind of goodness that he has.

'Or whereas some Samana-Brahmins, who live on the food provided by the faithful, continue addicted to performing the servile duties of a go-between: that is to say, between kings, ministers of state, soldiers, Brahmins, people of property, or young men, who say, "Come here!" "Go there!" "Take this to such a place!" "Bring that here!" But he refrains from such servile duties of a messenger.

'This, too, is the kind of goodness that he has.

'Or whereas some Samana-Brahmins, who live on the food provided by the faithful, continue addicted to hypocrisy: that is to say, they speak much; they make high professions; they disparage others; and they are continually thirsting after gain. But he refrains from such hypocritical craft.

'This, too, is the kind of goodness that he has.

The Long Conducts *(The Maha Silam)*

'Or whereas some Samana-Brahmins, who live on the food provided by the faithful, continue to gain a livelihood by such low arts, by such lying practices as these: that is to say, by divination from marks on the body; by auguries; by the interpretation of prognostics, of dreams, and of omens, good or bad by divinations from the manner in which cloth and other such things have been bitten by rats; by sacrifices to the god of fire, offerings of Dabbha grass, offerings with a ladle, offerings of husks, of bran, of rice, of clarified butter, of oil, and of liquids ejected from the mouth; and by bloody sacrifices; by teaching spells for preserving the body, for determining lucky sites, for protecting fields, for luck in war, against ghosts and goblins, to secure good harvests, to cure snake bites, to serve as antidotes for poison, and to cure bites of scorpions or rats; by divination, by the flight of hawks, or by the croaking of ravens; by guessing at length of life; by teaching spells to ward off wounds; and by pretended knowledge of the language of beasts.—

'He, on the other hand, refrains from seeking a livelihood by such low arts, by such lying practices.

'This, too, is the kind of goodness that he has.

'Or whereas some Samana-Brahmins, who live on the food provided by the faithful, continue to gain a livelihood by such low arts, by such lying practices as these: that is to say, by explaining the good and bad points in jewels, sticks, garments, swords, arrows, bows, weapons of war, women, men, youths, maidens, male and female slaves, elephants, horses, bulls, oxen, goats, sheep, fowl, snipe, iguanas, long-eared creatures, turtle, and deer.—

'He, on the other hand, refrains from seeking a livelihood by such low arts, by such lying practices.

'This, too, is the kind of goodness that he has.

'Or whereas some Samana-Brahmins, who live on the food provided by the faithful, continue to gain a livelihood by such low arts, by such lying practices as these: that is to say, by foretelling future events, as these:

' "There will be a sortie by the king." "There will not be a sortie by the king." "The king within the city will attack." "The king outside the city will retreat." "The king within the city will gain the victory." "The king outside the city will be the conqueror." "The king inside the city will be vanquished." Thus prophesying to this one victory and to that one defeat.—

'He, on the other hand, refrains from seeking a livelihood by such low arts, by such lying practices.

'This, too, is the kind of goodness that he has.

'Or whereas some Samana-Brahmins, who live on the food provided by the faithful, continue to gain a livelihood by such low arts, by such lying practices as these: that is to say, by predicting—

' "There will be an eclipse of the moon." "There will be an eclipse of the sun." "There will be an eclipse of a planet." "The sun and the moon will be in conjunction." "The sun and the moon will be in opposition." "The planets will be in conjunction." "The planets will be in opposition." "There will be falling meteors, and fiery coruscations in the atmosphere." "There will be earthquakes, thunderbolts, and forked lightnings." "The rising and setting of the sun, moon, or planets will be cloudy or clear." And then: "The eclipse of the moon will have such and such a result." "The eclipse of the sun will have such and such a result." "The sun and the moon being in conjunction will have such and such a result." "The sun and the moon being in opposition will have such and such a result." "The planets being in conjunction will have such and such a result." "The planets being in opposition will have such and such a result." "The falling meteors and fiery coruscations in the atmosphere will have such and such a result." "The earthquakes, thunderbolts, and forked lightnings will have such and such a result." "The rising and setting of the sun, moon, or planets, cloudy or clear, will have such and such a result."

'He, on the other hand, refrains from seeking a livelihood by such low arts, by such lying practices.

'This, too, is the kind of goodness that he has.

'Or whereas some Samana-Brahmins, who live on the food provided by the faithful, continue to gain a livelihood by such low arts, by such lying practices as these: that is to say, by predicting—

' "There will be an abundant rainfall." "There will be a deficient rainfall." "There will be an abundant harvest." "There will be famine." "There will be tranquillity." "There will be disturbances." "The season will be sickly." "The season will be healthy." Or by drawing deeds, making up accounts, giving pills, making verses, or arguing points of casuistry.—

'He, on the other hand, refrains from seeking a livelihood by such low arts, by such lying practices.

'This, too, is the kind of goodness that he has.

'Or whereas some Samana-Brahmins, who live on the food provided by the faithful, continue to gain a livelihood by such low arts, by such lying practices as these: that is to say, by giving advice touching the taking in marriage, or the giving in marriage; the forming of alliances, or the dissolution of connections; the calling in property, or the laying of it out. By teaching spells to procure prosperity, or to cause adversity to others; to remove sterility; to produce dumbness, locked-jaw, deformity, or deafness. By obtaining oracular responses by the aid of a mirror, or from a young girl, or from a god. By worshipping the sun, or by worshipping Brahma; by spitting fire out of their mouths, or by laying hands on people's heads.—

'He, on the other hand, refrains from seeking a livelihood by such low arts, by such lying practices.

'This, too, is the kind of goodness that he has.

'Or whereas some Samana-Brahmans, who live on the food provided by the faithful, continue to gain a livelihood by such low arts, by such lying practices as these: that is to say, by teaching the ritual for making vows and performing them; for blessing fields; for imparting virility and rendering impotent; for choosing the site of a house; for performing a house-warming. By teaching forms of words to be used when cleansing the mouth, when bathing, and when making offerings to the god of fire. By prescribing medicines to produce vomiting or purging, or to remove obstructions in the higher or lower intestines, or to relieve headache. By preparing oils for the ear, collyriums, catholicons, antimony, and cooling drinks. By practising cautery, midwifery, or the use of root decoctions or salves.—

'He, on the other hand, refrains from seeking a livelihood by such low arts, by such lying practices.

'This, too, is the kind of goodness that he has.

The Way

'And he lets his mind pervade one quarter of the world with thoughts of Love, and so the second, and so the third, and so the fourth. And thus the whole wide world, above, below, around, and everywhere, does he continue to pervade with heart of Love, far-reaching, grown great, and beyond measure.

'Just, Vasettha, as a mighty trumpeter makes himself heard—and that without difficulty—in all the four directions; even so of all things that have shape or life, there is not one that he passes by or leaves aside, but regards them all with mind set free, and deep-felt love.

'Verily this, Vasettha, is the way to a state of union with Brahma.

'And he lets his mind pervade one quarter of the world with thoughts of pity, sympathy, and equanimity, and so the second, and so the third, and so the fourth. And thus the whole wide world, above, below, around, and everywhere, does he continue to pervade with heart of pity, sympathy, and equanimity, far-reaching, grown great, and beyond measure.

'Just, Vasettha, as a mighty trumpeter makes himself heard—and that without difficulty—in all the four directions; even so of all things that have shape or life, there is not one that he passes by or leaves aside, but regards them all with mind set free, and deep-felt pity, sympathy, and equanimity.

'Verily this, Vasettha, is the way to a state of union with Brahma.'

'Now what think you, Vasettha, will the Bhikkhu who lives thus be in possession of women and of wealth, or will he not?'

'He will not, Gotama!'

'Will he be full of anger, or free from anger?'

'He will be free from anger, Gotama!'

'Will his mind be full of malice, or free from malice?'

'Free from malice, Gotama!'

'Will his mind be sinful, or pure?'

'It will be pure, Gotama!'

'Will he have self-mastery, or will he not?'

'Surely he will, Gotama!'

'Then you say, Vasettha, that the Bhikkhu is free from household cares, and that Brahma is free from household cares. Is there then agreement and likeness between the Bhikkhu and Brahma?'

'There is, Gotama!'

'Very good, Vasettha. Then in sooth, Vasettha, that the Bhikkhu who is free from household cares should after death, when the body is dissolved, become united with Brahma, who is the same—such a condition of things is every way possible!

'And so you say, Vasettha, that the Bhikkhu is free from anger, and free from malice, pure in mind, and master of himself; and that Brahma is free from anger, and free from malice, pure in mind, and master of himself. Then in sooth, Vasettha, that the Bhikkhu who is free from anger, free from malice, pure in mind, and master of himself should after death, when the body is dissolved, become united with Brahma, who is the same—such a condition of things is every way possible!'

When he had thus spoken, the young Brahmins Vasettha and Bharadvaja addressed the Blessed One, and said:

'Most excellent, Lord, are the words of thy mouth, most excellent! Just as if a man were to set up that which is thrown down, or were to reveal that which is hidden away, or were to point out the right road to him who has gone astray, or were to bring a lamp into the darkness, so that those who have eyes can see external forms;—just even so, Lord, has the truth been made known to us, in many a figure, by the Blessed One. And we, even we, betake ourselves, Lord, to the Blessed One as our refuge, to the Truth, and to the Brotherhood. May the Blessed One accept us as disciples, as true believers, from this day forth, as long as life endures!'

4

Dhammapada

The Good Path

The *Dhammapada* is one of the most practical ethical handbooks of Buddhism. It is included in the canon of Buddhistic scriptures, and is one of the books which can be read with delight to-day by those who are classed as general readers. It is divided into 26 chapters, and the keynote of it is struck by the sentence: "The virtuous man is happy in this world, and he is happy in the next; he is happy in both. He is happy when he thinks of the good he has done; he is still more happy when going on the good path."

The first step in the "good path" is earnestness, for as the writer says, "Earnestness is the path of immortality, Nirvana, thoughtlessness the path of death; those who are in earnest do not die, those who are thoughtless are as if dead already." Earnestness, in this connection, evidently means the power of reflection, and of abstracting the mind from mundane things.

There is something very inspiring in the sentence, "When the learned man drives away vanity by earnestness, he, the wise, climbing the terraced heights of wisdom, looks down upon the fools: free from sorrow he looks upon the sorrowing crowd, as one that stands on a mountain looks down upon them that stand upon the plain."

The Twin Verses

All that we are is the result of what we have thought: it is founded on our thoughts, it is made up of our thoughts. If a man speaks or acts with an evil thought, pain follows him, as the wheel follows the foot of the ox that draws the carriage.

All that we are is the result of what we have thought: it is founded on our thoughts, it is made up of our thoughts. If a man speaks or acts with a pure thought, happiness follows him, like a shadow that never leaves him.

"He abused me, he beat me, he defeated me, he robbed me"—in those who harbour such thoughts hatred will never cease.

"He abused me, he beat me, he defeated me, he robbed me"—in those who do not harbour such thoughts hatred will cease.

For hatred does not cease by hatred at any time: hatred ceases by love—this is an old rule.

The world does not know that we must all come to an end here; but those who know it, their quarrels cease at once.

He who lives looking for pleasures only, his senses uncontrolled, immoderate in his food, idle, and weak, Mara (the temper) will certainly overthrow him, as the wind throws down a weak tree.

He who lives without looking for pleasures, his senses well controlled, moderate in his food, faithful and strong, him Mara will certainly not overthrow, any more than the wind throws down a rocky mountain.

He who wishes to put on the yellow dress without having cleansed himself from sin, who disregards also temperance and truth, is unworthy of the yellow dress.

But he who has cleansed himself from sin, is well grounded in all virtues, and endowed also with temperance and truth, he is indeed worthy of the yellow dress.

They who imagine truth in untruth, and see untruth

in truth, never arrive at truth, but follow vain desires.

They who know truth in truth, and untruth in untruth, arrive at truth, and follow true desires.

As rain break through an ill-thatched house, passion will break through an unreflecting mind.

As rain does not breaks through a well-thatched house, passion will not break through a well-reflecting mind.

The evil-doer mourns in this world, and he mourns in the next; he mourns in both. He mourns and suffers when he sees the evil result of his own work.

The virtuous man delights in this world, and he delights in the next; he delights in both. He delights and rejoices, when he sees the purity of his own work.

The evil-doer suffers in this world, and he suffers in the next; he suffers in both. He suffers when he thinks of the evil he has done; he suffers more when going on the evil path.

The virtuous man is happy in this world, and he is happy in the next; he is happy in both He is happy when he thinks of the good he has done; he is still more happy when going on the good path.

The thoughtless man, even if he can recite a large portion of the law, but is not a doer of it, has no share in the priesthood, but is like a cowherd counting the cows of others.

The followers of the law, even if he can recite only a small portion of the law, but, having forsaken passion and hatred and foolishness, possesses true knowledge and serenity of mind, he, caring for nothing in this world or that to come, has indeed a share in the priesthood.

Earnestness

Earnestness is the path of immortality, Nirvana, thoughtlessness the path of death. Those who are in earnest do not die, those who are thoughtless are as if dead already.

Having understood this clearly, those who are advanced in earnestness delight in earnestness, and rejoice in the knowledge of the elect.

These wise people, meditative, steady, always possessed of strong powers, attain to Nirvana, the highest happiness.

If an earnest person has roused himself, if he is not forgetful, if his deeds are pure, if he acts with consideration, if he restrains himself, and lives according to law—then his glory will increase.

By rousing himself, by earnestness, by restraint and control, the wise man may make for himself an island which no flood can overwhelm.

Fools follow after vanity. The wise man keeps earnestness as his best jewel.

Follow not after vanity, nor after the enjoyment of love and lust! He who is earnest and meditative, obtains ample joy.

When the learned man drives away vanity by earnestness, he, the wise, climbing the terraced heights of wisdom, looks down upon the fools: free from sorrow he looks upon the sorrowing crowd, as one that stands on a mountain looks down upon them that stand upon the plain.

Earnest among the thoughtless, awake among the sleepers, the wise man advances like a racer, leaving behind the hack.

By earnestness did Maghavan (Indra) rise to the lordship of the gods. People praise earnestness; thoughtlessness is always blamed.

A Bhikshu who delights in earnestness, who looks with fear on thoughtlessness, moves about like fire, burning all his fetters, small or large.

A Bhikshu who delights in reflection, who looks with fear on thoughtlessness, cannot fall away from his perfect state—he is close upon Nirvana.

Thought

As a fletcher makes straight his arrow, a wise man makes straight his trembling and unsteady thought, which is difficult to guard, difficult to hold back.

As a fish taken from his watery home and thrown on the dry ground, our thought trembles all over in order to escape the dominion of Mara, the tempter.

It is good to tame the mind, which is difficult to hold in and flighty, rushing wherever it listeth; a tamed mind brings happiness.

Let the wise man guard his thoughts, for they are difficult to perceive, very artful, and they rush wherever they list; thoughts well guarded bring happiness.

Those who bridle their mind which travels far, moves about alone, is without a body, and hides in the chamber of the heart, will be free from the bonds of Mara, the tempter.

If a man's faith is unsteady, if he does not know the true law, if his peace of mind is troubled, his knowledge will never be perfect.

If a man's thoughs are not dissipated, if his mind is not perplexed, if he has ceased to think of good or evil, then there is no fear for him while he is watchful.

Knowing that this body is fragile like a jar, and making his thought firm like a fortress, one should attack Mara, the tempter, with the weapon of knowledge, one should watch him when conquered, and should never rest.

Before long, alas! this body will lie on the earth, despised, without understanding, like a useless log.

Whatever a hater may do to a hater, or an enemy to an enemy, a wrongly-directed mind will do him greater mischief.

Not a mother, not a father, will do so much, nor any other relatives; a well-directed mind will do us greater service.

Flowers

Who shall overcome this earth, and the world of Yama, the lord of the departed, and the world of the gods? Who shall find out the plainly shown path of virtue, as a clever man finds the right flower?

The disciple will overcome the earth, and the world of

Yama, and the world of the gods. The disciple will find out the plainly shown path of virtue, as a clever man finds the right flower.

He who knows that this body is like froth, and has learnt that it is as unsubstantial as a mirage, will break the flower-pointed arrow of Mara, and never see the king of death.

Death carries off a man who is gathering flowers, and whose mind is distracted, as a flood carries off a sleeping village.

Death subdues a man who is gathering flowers, and whose mind is distracted, before he is satiated in his pleasures.

As the bee collects nectar and departs without injuring the flower, or its colour or scent, so let a sage dwell in his village.

Not the perversities of others, not their sins of commission or omission, but his own misdeeds and negligences should a sage take notice of.

Like a beautiful flower, full of colour, but without scent, are the fine but fruitless words of him who does not act accordingly.

But, like beautiful flower, full of colour and full of scent, are the fine and fruitful words of him who acts accordingly.

As many kinds of wreaths can be made from a heap of flowers, so many good things may be achieved by a mortal when once he is born.

The scent of flowers does not travel against the wind, nor that of sandalwood, or the Tagara and Mallika flowers; but the odour of good people travels even against the wind: a good man pervades every place.

Sandalwood or Tagara, a lotus-flower, or a Vassiki, among these sorts of perfumes, the perfume of virute is unsurpassed.

Mean is the scent that comes from Tagara and sandalwood; the perfume of those who possess virtue rises up to the gods as the highest.

Of the people who possess these vitures, who live without thoughtlessness, and who are emancipated through true knowledge, Mara, the tempter, never finds the way.

As on a heap of rubbish cast upon the highway the lily will grow full of sweet perfume and delight, thus among those who are mere rubbish, the disciple of the truly enlightened Buddha shines forth by his knowledge above the blinded worldling.

The Fool

Long is the night to him who is awake; long is a mile to him who is tired; long is life to the foolish who do not know the true law.

If a traveller does not meet with one who is his better, or his equal, let him firmly keep to his solitary journey; there is no companionship with a fool.

"These sons belong to me, and this wealth belongs to me," with such thoughts a fool is tormented. He himself does not belong to himself; how much less sons and wealth?

The fool who knows his foolishness, is wise at least so far. But a fool who thinks himself wise, he is called a fool indeed.

If a fool be associated with a wise man even all his life, he will perceive the truth as little as a spoon perceives the taste of soup.

If an intelligent man be associated for one minute only with a wise man, he will soon perceive the truth, as the tongue perceives the taste of soup.

Fools of poor understanding have themselves for their greatest enemies, for they do evil deeds which bear bitter fruits.

That deed is not well done of which a man must repent, and the reward of which he receives crying and with a tearful face.

No, that deed is well done of which a man does not repent, and the reward of which he receives gladly and cheerfully.

As long as the evil deed does not bear fruit, the fool thinks, it is like honey; but when it ripens, then the fool suffers grief.

Let a fool month after month eat his food like an ascetic with the tip of a blade of Kusa-grass, yet is he not worth the sixteenth particle of those who have well weighed the law.

An evil deed, like newly-drawn milk, does not turn suddenly; smouldering, like fire covered by ashes, it follows the fool.

And when the evil deed, after it has become known, turns to sorrow for the fool, then it destroys his bright lot, nay, it cleaves his head.

Let the fool wish for a false reputation, for precedence among the Bhikshus, for lordship in the convents, for worship among other people!

"May both the layman and he who has left the world think that this is done by me; may they be subject to me in everything which is to be done or is not to be done," thus is the mind of the fool, and his desire and pride increase.

"One is the road that leads to wealth, another the road that leads to Nirvana"—if the Bhikshu, the disciple of Buddha, has learnt this, he will not yearn for honour, he will strive after separation from the world.

The Wise Man

If you see a man who shows you what is to be avoided, who administers reproofs, and is intelligent, follow that wise man as you would one who tells of hidden treasures; it will be better, not worse, for him who follows him.

Let him admonish, let him teach, let him forbid what is improper!—he will be beloved of the good, by the bad he will be hated.

Do not have evil-doers for friends, do not have low people for friends: have virtuous people for friends, have for friends the best of men.

He who drinks in the law lives happily with a serene

mind: the sage rejoices always in the law, as preached by the elect.

Well-makers lead the water wherever they like; fletchers bend the arrow; carpenters bend a log of wood; wise people fashion themselves.

As a solid rock is not shaken by the wind, wise people falter not amidst blame and praise.

Wise people, after they have listened to the laws, become serene, like a deep, smooth, and still lake.

Good men indeed walk warily under all circumstances; good men speak not out of a desire for sensual gratification; whether touched by happiness or sorrow wise people never appear elated or depressed.

If, whether for his own sake, or for the sake of others, a man wishes neither for a son, nor for wealth, nor for lordship, and if he does not wish for his own success by unfair means, then he is good, wise, and virtuous.

Few are there among men who arrive at the other shore, become Arhats; the other people here run up and down the shore.

But those who, when the law has been well preached to them, follow the law, will pass over the dominion of death, however difficult to cross.

A wise man should leave the dark state of ordinary life, and follow the bright state of the Bhikshu. After going from his home to a homeless state, he should in his retirement look for enjoyment where enjoyment seemed difficult. Leaving all pleasures behind, and calling nothing his own, the wise man should purge himself from all the troubles of the mind.

Those whose mind is well grounded in the seven elements of knowledge, who without clinging to anything, rejoice in freedom from attachment, whose appetites have been conquered, and who are full of light, they are free even in this world.

The Venerable

There is no suffering for him who has finished his journey, and abandoned grief, who has freed himself of all sides, and thrown off all fetters.

They exert themselves with their thoughts well-collected, they do not tarry in their abode; like swans who have left their lake, they leave their house and home.

Men who have no riches, who live on recognized food, who have perceived void and unconditioned freedom, Nirvana, their path is difficult to understand, like that of birds in the air. He whose appetites are stilled, who is not absorbed in enjoyment, who has perceived void and unconditioned freedom, Nirvana, his path is difficult to understand, like that of birds in the air.

The gods even envy him whose senses, like horses well broken in by the driver, have been subdued, who is free from pride, and free from appetites; such a one who does his duty is tolerant like the earth, or like a threshold; he is like a lake without mud; no new births are in store for him.

His thought is quiet, quiet are his word and deed, when he has obtained freedom by true knowledge, when he has thus become a quiet man.

The man who is free from credulity, but knows the uncreated, who has cut all ties, removed all temptations, renounced all desires, he is the greatest of men.

In a hamlet or in a forest, on sea or on dry land, wherever venerable persons (Arahanta) dwell, that place is delightful.

Forests are delightful; where the world finds no delight, there the passionless will find delight, for they look not for pleasures.

The Thousands

Even though a speech be of a thousand words, but made up of senseless words, one word of sense is better, which if a man hears, he becomes quiet.

Even though a Gatha (poem) be of a thousand words, but made up of senseless words, one word of a Gatha is better, which if a man hears, be becomes quiet.

Though a man recite a hundred Gathas made up of senseless words, one word of the law is better, which if a man hears, he becomes quiet.

If one man conquer in battle a thousand times a thousand men and if another conquer himself, he is the greatest of conquerors.

One's own self conquered is better than all other people; not even a god, a Gandharva, not Mara could change into defeat the victory of a man who has vanquished himself, and always lives under restraint.

If a man for a hundred years sacrifice month by month with a thousand, and if he but for one moment pay homage to a man whose soul is grounded in true knowledge, better is that homage than a sacrifice for a hundred years.

If a man for a hundred years worship Agni in the forest, and if he but for one moment pay homage to a man whose soul is grounded in true knowledge, better is that homage than sacrifice for a hundred years.

Whatever a man sacrifice in this world as an offering or as an oblation for a whole year in order to gain merit, the whole of it is not worth a quarter a pence; reverence shown to the righteous is better.

He who always greets and constantly reveres the aged, four things will increase to him: life, beauty, happiness, power.

But he who lives a hundred years, vicious and unrestrained, a life of one day is better if a man is virtuous and reflecting.

And he who lives a hundred years, ignorant and unrestrained, a life of one day is better if a man is wise and reflecting.

And he who lives a hundred years, idle and weak, a life of one day is better if a man has attained firm strength.

And he who lives hundred years, not seeing beginning and end, a life of one day is better if a man sees beginning and end.

And he who lives a hundred years, not seeing the immortal place, a life of one day is better if a man sees the immortal place.

And he who lives a hundred years, not seeing the highest law, a life of one day is better if a man sees the highest law.

Evil

A man should hasten towards the good, and should keep his thought away from evil; if a man does what is good slothfully, his mind delights in evil.

If a man commits a sin, let him not do it again; let him not delight in sin: the accumulation of evil is painful.

If a man does what is good, let him do it again; let him delight in it: the accumulation of good is delightful.

Even an evil-doer sees happiness so long as his evil deed does not ripen; but when his evil deed ripens, then does the evil-doer see evil.

Even a good man sees evil days so long as his good deed does not ripen; but when his good deed ripens, then does the good man see good things.

Let not man think lightly of evil, saying in his heart, it will not come nigh unto me. Even by the falling of water-drops a water-pot is filled; the fool becomes full of evil, even if he gather it little by little.

Let no man think lightly of good, saying in his heart. it will not come nigh unto me. Even by the falling of water-drops a water-pot is filled; the wise man becomes full of good, even if he gather it little by little.

Let a man avoid evil deeds, as a merchant, if he has few companions and carries much wealth, avoids a dangerous road; a man who loves life avoids poison.

He who has no wound on his hand, may touch poison with his hand; poison does not affect one who has no wound; nor is there evil for one who does not commit evil.

If a man offend a harmless, pure, and innocent person, the evil falls back upon that fool, like light dust thrown up against the wind.

Some people are born again; evil-doers go to hell; righteous people go to heaven; those who are free from all worldly desires attain Nirvana.

Not in the sky, not in the midst of the sea, not if we enter into the clefts of the mountains, is there known a spot in the whole world where a man might by freed from an evil deed.

Not in the sky, not in the midst of the sea, not if we enter into the clefts of the mountains, is there known a spot in the whole world where death could not overcome the mortal.

Punishment

All men tremble at punishment, all men fear death; remember that you are like unto them, and do not kill, nor cause slaughter.

All men tremble at punishment, all men love life; remember that thou art like unto them, and do not kill, nor cause slaughter.

He who, seeking his own happiness, punishes or kills beings who also long for happiness, will not find happiness after death.

He who, seeking his own happiness, does not punish or kill beings who also long for happiness, will find happiness after death.

Do not speak harshly to anyone; those who are spoken to will answer thee in the same way. Angry speech is painful: blows for blows will touch thee.

If, like a shattered gong, thou utter nothing, then thou hast reached Nirvana; anger is not known to thee.

As a cowherd with his staff drives his cows into the stable, so do Age and Death drive the life of men.

A fool does not know when he commits his evil deeds:

but the wicked man burns by his own deeds, as if burnt by fire.

He who inflicts pain on innocent and harmless persons, will soon come to one of these ten states:

He will have cruel suffering, loss, injury of the body, heavy affliction, or loss of mind.

A misfortune coming from the king, or a fearful accusation, or loss of relations, or destruction of treasures.

Lightning-fire will burn his houses; and when his body is destroyed, the fool will go to hell.

Not nakedness, not platted hair, not dirt, not fasting, or lying on the earth, not rubbing with dust, not sitting motionless, can purify a mortal who has not overcome desires.

He who, though dressed in fine apparel, exercises tranquillity, is quiet, subdued, restrained, chaste, and has ceased to find fault with all other beings, he indeed is a Brahmin, a Sramana, a Bhikshu.

Is there in this world any man so restrained by shame that he does not provoke reproof, as a noble horse the whip?

Like a noble horse when touched by the whip, be ye strenuous and eager, and by faith, by virtue, by energy, by meditation, by discernment of the law, you will overcome this great pain, perfect in knowledge and in behaviour, and never forgetful.

Well-makers lead the water wherever they like; fletchers bend the arrow; carpenters bend a log of wood; good people fashion themselves.

Old Age

How is there laughter, how is there joy, as this world is always burning? Do you not seek a light, ye who are surrounded by darkness?

Look at this dressed-up lump, covered with wounds, joined together, sickly, full of many schemes, but which has not strength, no hold!

This body is wasted, full of sickness, and frail; this heap of corruption breaks to pieces, life indeed ends in death.

After one has looked at those gray bones, thrown away like gourds in the autumn, what pleasure is there left in life!

After a stronghold has been made of the bones, it is covered with flesh and blood, and there dwell in it old age and death, pride and deceit.

The brilliant chariots of kings are destroyed, the body also approaches destruction, but the virute of good people never approaches destruction—thus do the good say to the good.

A man who has learnt little, grows old like an ox; his flesh grows, but his knowledge does not grow.

Looking for the maker of this tabernacle, I have run through a course of many births, not finding him; and painful is birth again and again. But now, maker of the tabernacle, thou hast been seen; thou shalt not make up this tabernacle again. All thy rafters are broken, thy ridge-pole is sundered; the mind, approaching the Eternal, Nirvana, has attained to the extinction of all desires.

Men who have not observed proper discipline, and have not gained wealth in their youth, perish like old herons in a lake without fish.

Men who have not observed proper discipline, and have not gained wealth in their youth, lie, like broken bows, sighing after the past.

Self

If a man hold himself dear, let him watch himself carefully; during one at least out of the three watches a wise man should be watchful.

Let each man direct himself first to what is proper, then let him teach others; thus a wise man will not suffer.

If a man make himself as he teaches others to be, then, being himself well subdued, he may subdue others; for one's own self is difficult to subdue.

Self is the lord of self, who else could be the lord? With self well subdued, a man finds a lord such as few can find.

The evil done by one's self, self-forgotten, self-bred, crushes the foolish, as a diamond breaks even a precious stone.

He whose wickedness is very great brings himself down to that state where his enemy wishes him to be, as a creeper does with the tree which it surrounds.

Bad deeds, and deeds hurtful to ourselves, are easy to do; what is beneficial and good, that is very difficult to do.

The foolish man who scorns the rule of the Arhat, of the Arya, of the virtuous, and follows a false doctrine, he bears fruit to his own destruction, like the fruits of the Katthaka reed.

By one's self the evil is done, by one's self one suffers; by one's self evil is left undone, by one's self one is purified. The pure and the impure stand and fall by themselves, no one can purify another.

Let no one forget his own duty for the sake of another's however great; let a man, after he has discerned his own duty, be always attentive to his duty.

The World

Do not follow the evil law! Do not live on in thoughtlessness! Do not follow false doctrine! Be not a friend of the world.

Rouse thyself! do not be idle! Follow the law of virtue! The virtuous rest in bliss in this world and in the next.

Follow the law of virtue; do not follow that of sin. The virtuous rest in bliss in this world and in the next.

Look upon the world as you would on a bubble, look upon it as you would on a mirage: the king of death does not see him who thus looks down upon the world.

Come, look at this world, glittering like a royal chariot; the foolish are immersed in it, but the wise do not touch it.

He who formerly was reckless and afterwards became sober, brightens up this world, like the moon when freed from clouds.

He whose evil deeds are covered by good deeds, brightens up this world, like the moon when freed from clouds.

This world is dark, few only can see here; a few only go to heaven, like birds escaped from the net.

The swans go on the path of the sun, they go miraculously through the ether; the wise are led out of this world, when they have conquered Mara and his train.

If a man has transgressed the one law, and speaks lies, and scoffs at another world, there is no evil he will not do.

The uncharitable do not go to the world of the gods; fools only do not praise liberality; a wise man rejoices in liberality, and through it becomes blessed in the other world.

Better than sovereignty over the earth, better than going to heaven, better than lordship over all worlds, is the reward of Sotapatti, the first step in holiness.

Buddha–The Awakened

He whose conquest cannot be conquered again, into whose conquest no one in this world enters, by what track can you lead him, the Awakened, the Omniscient, the trackless?

He whom no desire with its snares and poisons can lead astray, by what track can you lead him, the Awakened, the Omniscient, the trackless?

Even the gods envy those who are awakened and not forgetful, who are given to meditation, who are wise, and who delight in the repose of retirement from the world.

Difficult to obtain is the conception of men, difficult is the life of mortals, difficult is the hearing of the True Law, difficult is the birth of the Awakened the attainment of Buddhahood.

Not to commit any sin, to do good, and to purify one's mind, that is the teaching of all the awakened.

The Awakened call patience the highest penance, long-suffering the highest Nirvana; for he is not an anchorite who strikes others, he is not an ascetic who insults others.

Not to blame, not to strike, to live restrained under the

law, to be moderate in eating, to sleep and sit alone, and to dwell on the highest thoughts—this is the teaching of the Awakened.

There is no satisfying lusts, even by a shower of gold pieces; he who knows that lusts have a short taste and cause pain, he is wise; even in heavenly pleasures he finds no satisfaction, the disciple who is fully awakened delights only in the destruction of all desires.

Men, driven by fear, go to many a refuge, to mountains and forests, to groves and sacred trees. But that is not a safe refuge, that is not the best refuge; a man is not delivered from all pains after having gone to that refuge.

He who takes refuge with Buddha, the Law, and the Church; he who, with clear understanding, sees the four holy truths: pain, the origin of pain, the destruction of pain, and the eightfold holy way that leads to the quieting of pain;—that is the safe refuge, that is the best refuge; having gone to that refuge, a man is delivered from all pain.

A supernatural person, a Buddha, is not easily found: he is not born everywhere. Wherever such a sage is born, that race prospers.

Happy is the arising of the Awakened, happy is the teaching of the True Law, happy is peace in the church, happy is the devotion of those who are at peace.

He who pays homage to those who deserve homage, whether the awakened, Buddha, or their disciples, those who have overcome the host of evils, and crossed the flood of sorrow, he who pays homage to such as have found deliverance and know no fear, his merit can never be measured by anyone.

Happiness

We live happily indeed, not hating those who hate us! among men who hate us we dwell free from hatred! We live happily indeed, free from ailments among the ailing! among men who are ailing let us dwell free from ailments!

We live happily indeed, free from greed among the

greedy! among men who are greedy let us dwell free from greed!

We live happily indeed, though we call nothing our own! We shall be like the bright gods, feeding on happiness!

Victory breeds hatred, for the conquered is unhappy. He who has given up both victory and defeat, he, the contented, is happy.

There is no fire like passion, there is no losing throw like hatred; there is no pain like this body; there is no happiness higher than rest.

Hunger is the worst of diseases, the elements of the body the greatest evil; if one knows this truly, that is Nirvana, the highest happiness.

Health is the greatest of gifts, contentedness the best riches; trust is the best of relationships, Nirvana the highest happiness.

He who has tasted the sweetness of solitude and tranquillity, is free from fear and free from sin, while he tastes the sweetness of drinking in the law.

The sight of the Arya is good, to live with them is always happiness; if a man does not see fools, he will be truly happy.

He who walks in the company of fools suffers a long way; company with fools, as with an enemy, is always painful; company with the wise is pleasure, like meeting with kinsfolk.

Therefore, one ought to follow the wise, the intelligent, the learned, the much enduring, the dutiful, the elect; one ought to follow such a good and wise man, as the moon follows the path of the stars.

Pleasure

He who gives himself to vanity, and does not give himself to meditation, forgetting the real aim of life and grasping at pleasure, will in time envy him who has exerted himself in meditation.

Let no man ever cling to what is pleasant, or to what is unpleasant. Not to see what is pleasant is pain, and it is pain to see what is unpleasant.

Let, therefore, no man love anything; loss of the beloved is evil. Those who love nothing, and hate nothing, have no fetters.

From pleasure comes grief, from pleasure comes fear; he who is free from pleasure knows neither grief nor fear.

From affection comes grief, from affection comes fear; he who is free from affection knows neither grief nor fear.

From lust comes grief, from lust comes fear; he who is free from lust knows neither grief nor fear.

From love comes grief, from love comes fear; he who is free from love knows neither grief nor fear.

From greed comes grief, from greed comes fear; he who is free from greed knows neither grief nor fear.

He who possesses virtue and intelligence, who is just, speaks the truth, and does what is his own business, him the world will hold dear.

He in whom a desire for the Ineffable (Nirvana) has sprung up, who in his mind is satisfied, and whose thoughts are not bewildered by love, he is called Urdhvamsrotas, carried upwards by the stream.

Kinsmen, friends, and lovers salute a man who has been long away, and returns safe from afar.

In like manner his good works receive him who has done good, and has gone from this world to the other;—as kinsmen receive a friend on his return.

Anger

Let a man leave anger, let him forsake pride, let him overcome bondage! No sufferings befall the man who is not attached to name and form, and who calls nothing his own.

He who holds back rising anger like a rolling chariot, him I call a real driver; other people are but holding the reins.

Let a man overcome anger by love, let him overcome evil by good; let him overcome the greedy by liberality, the liar by truth!

Speak the truth, do not yield to anger; give, if thou art asked for little; by these three steps thou wilt go near the gods.

The sages who injure nobody, and who always control their body, they will go to the unchangeable place, Nirvana, where, if they have gone, they will suffer no more.

Those who are ever watchful, who study day and night, and who strive after Nirvana, their passions will come to an end.

This is an old saying, O Atula, this is not as if of today: "They blame him who sits silent, they blame him who speaks much, they also blame him who says little; there is no one on earth who is not blamed."

There never was, there never will be, nor is there now, a man who is always blamed, or a man who is always praised.

But he whom those who discriminated praise continually day after day, as without blemish, wise, rich in knowledge and virtue, who would dare to blame him, like a coin made of gold from the Jambu river? Even the gods praise him, he is praised even by Brahman.

Beware of bodily anger, and control thy body! Leave the sins of the body, and with thy body practise virtue!

Beware of the anger of the tongue, and control thy tongue! Leave the sins of the tongue, and practise virtue with thy tongue!

Beware of the anger of the mind, and control thy mind! Leave the sins of the mind, and practise virtue with thy mind!

The wise who control their body, who control their tongue, the wise who control their mind, are indeed well controlled.

Impurity

Thou art now like a sear leaf, the messengers of Yama have come near to thee; thou standest at the door of thy departure, and thou hast no provision for thy journey.

Make thyself an island, work hard, be wise! When thy impurities are blown away, and thou art free from guilt, thou wilt enter into the heavenly world of the Arya.

Thy life has come to an end, thou art come near to death Yama, there is no resting-place for thee on the road, and thou hast no provision for thy journey.

Make thyself an island, work hard, be wise! When thy impurities are blown away, and thou art free from guilt, thou wilt not enter again into birth and decay.

Let a wise man blow off the impurities of himself, as a smith blows off the impurities of silver, one by one, little by little, and from time to time.

As the impurity which springs from the iron, when it springs from it, destroys it; thus do a transgressor's own works lead him to the evil path.

The taint of prayers is non-repetition; the taint of houses, non-repair; the taint of complexion is sloth; the taint of a watchman, alertlessness.

Bad conduct is the taint of woman, niggardliness the taint of a benefactor; tainted are all evil ways, in this world and in the next.

But there is a taint worse than all taints—ignorance is the greatest taint. O mendicants! throw off that taint, and become taintless!

Life is easy to live for a man who is without shame: a crow hero, a mischief-maker, an insulting, bold, and wretched fellow.

But life is hard to live for a modest man, who always looks for what is pure, who is disinterested, quiet, spotless, and intelligent.

He who destroys life, who speaks untruth, who in the world takes what is not given him, who goes to another man's wife; and the man who gives himself to drinking intoxicating liquors, he, even in this world, digs up his own root.

O man, know this, that the unrestrained are in a bad state; take care that greediness and vice do not bring thee to grief for a long time!

The world gives according to their faith or according to their pleasure: if a man frets about the food and the drink given to others, he will find no rest either by day or by night.

He in whom that feeling is destroyed, and taken out with the very root, finds rest by day and by night.

There is no fire like passion, there is no shark like hatred, there is no snare like folly, there is no torrent like greed.

The fault of others is easily perceived, but that of one's self is difficult to perceive; a man winnows his neighbour's faults like chaff, but his own fault he hides, as a cheat hides the bad die from the player.

If a man looks after the faults of others, and is always inclined to be offended, his own passions will grow, and he is far from the destruction of passions.

There is no path through the air, a man is not a Samana outwardly. The world delights in vanity, the Tathagatas are free from vanity.

There is no path through the air, a man is not a Samana outwardly. No creatures are eternal; but the awakened Buddha are never shaken.

The Just

A man is not just if he carries a matter by violence; no, he who distinguishes both right and wrong, who is learned and guides others, not by violence, but by the same law, being a guardian of the law and intelligent, he is called just.

A man is not learned because he talks much; he who is patient, free from hatred and fear, he is called learned.

A man is not a supporter of the law because he talks much; even if a man has learnt little, but sees the law bodily, he is a supporter of the law, a man who never neglects the law.

A man is not an elder because his head is gray; his age may be ripe, but he is called "Old-in-vain."

He in whom there is truth, virtue, pity, restraint, moderation, he who is free from impurity and is wise, he is called an elder.

An envious, stingy, dishonest man does not become respectable by means of much talking only, or by the beauty of his complexion.

He in whom all this is destroyed, and taken out with the very root, he, when freed from hatred, is called respectable.

Not by tonsure does an undisciplined man who speaks falsehood become a Samana; can a man be a Samana who is still held captive by desire and greediness?

He who always quiets the evil, whether small or large, he is called a Samana, a quiet man, because he has quieted all evil.

A man is not a Bhikshu simply because he asks others for alms; he who adopts the whole law is a Bhikshu not he who only begs.

He who is above good and evil, who is chaste, who with care passes through the world, he indeed is called a Bhikshu.

A man is not a Muni because he observes silence if he is foolish and ignorant; but the wise who, as with the balance, chooses the good and avoids evil, he is a Muni, and is a Muni thereby; he who in this world weighs both sides is called a Muni.

A man is not an Arya because he injures living creatures; because he has pity on all living creatures, therefore is a man called Arya.

Not only by discipline and vows, not only by much learning, not by entering into a trance, not by sleeping alone, do I earn the happiness of release which no worldling can know. O Bhikshu, he who has obtained the extinction of desires has obtained confidence.

The Way

The best of ways is the eightfold; the best of truths the four words; the best of virtues passionlessness; the best of men he who has eyes to see.

This is the way, there is no other that leads to the purifying of intelligence. Go on this path! This is the confusion of Mara, the tempter.

If you go on this way, you will make an end of pain! The way preached by me, when I had understood the removal of the thorns in the flesh.

You yourself must make an effort. The Tathagatas are only preachers. The thoughtful who enter the way are freed from the bondage of Mara.

"All created things perish," he who knows and sees this becomes passive in pain; this is the way to purity.

"All created things are grief and pain," he who knows and sees this becomes passive in pain; this is the way that leads to purity.

"All forms are unreal," he who knows and sees this becomes passive in pain; this is the way that leads to purity.

He who does not rouse himself when it is time to rise, who, though young and strong, is full of sloth, whose will and thought are weak, that lazy and idle man never finds the way to knowledge.

Watching his speech, well restrained in mind, let a man never commit any wrong with his body! Let a man but keep these three roads of action clear, and he will achieve the way which is taught by the wise.

Through zeal knowledge is gained, through lack of zeal knowledge is lost; let a man who knows this double path of gain and loss thus place himself that knowledge may grow.

Cut down the whole forest of desires, not a tree only! Danger comes out of the forest of desires. When you have cut down both the forest of desires and its undergrowth, then, Bhikshus, you will be rid of the forest and of desires!

So long as the desire of man towards women, even the smallest, is not destroyed, so long is his mind in bondage, as the calf that drinks milk is to its mother.

Cut out the love of self, like an autumn lotus, with thy hand! Cherish the road of peace. Nirvana has been shown by Sugata (Buddha).

"Here I shall dwell in the rain, here in winter and summer," thus the fool meditates, and does not think of death.

Death comes and carries off that man, honoured for his children and flocks, his mind distracted, as a flood carries off a sleeping village.

Sons are no help, nor a father, nor relations; there is no help from kinsfolk for one whom death has seized.

A wise and well-behaved man who knows the meaning of this should quickly clear the way that leads to Nirvana.

Miscellaneous

If by leaving a small pleasure one sees a great pleasure, let a wise man leave the small pleasure, and look to the great.

He who, by causing pain to others, wishes to obtain pleasure for himself, he, entangled in the bonds of hatred, will never be free from hatred.

What ought to be done is neglected, what ought not to be done is done; the desires of unruly, thoughtless people are always increasing.

But they whose whole watchfulness is always directed to their body, who do not follow what ought not to be done, and who steadfastly do what ought to be done, the desires of such watchful and wise people will come to an end.

A true Brahmin goes scathless, though he have killed father and mother, and two valiant kings, though he has destroyed a kingdom with all its subjects.

A true Brahmin goes scathless, though he have killed father and mother, and two holy kings, and an eminent man besides.

The disciples of Gotama are always well awake, and their thoughts day and night are always set on Buddha.

The disciples of Gotama are always well awake, and their thoughts day and night are always set on the law.

The disciples of Gotama are always well awake, and their thoughts day and night are always set on the church.

The disciples of Gotama are always well awake, and

their thoughts day and night are always set on their body.

The disciples of Gotama are always well awake, and their thoughts day and night always delights in compassion.

The disciples of Gotama are always well awake, and their thoughts day and night always delights in meditation.

It is hard to leave the world to become a friar, it is hard to enjoy the world; hard is the monastery, painful are the houses; painful it is to dwell with equals to share everything in common, and the itinerant mendicant is beset with pain. Therefore let no man be an itinerant mendicant, and he will not be beset with pain.

A man full of faith, if endowed with virtue and glory, is respected, whatever place he may choose.

Good people shine from afar, like the snowy mountains; bad people are not seen, like arrows shot by night.

Sitting alone, lying down alone, walking alone without ceasing, and alone subduing himself, let a man be happy near the edge of a forest.

The Downward Course

He who says what is not goes to hell; he also who, having done a thing, says I have not done it. After death both are equal: they are men with evil deeds in the next world.

Many men those shoulders are covered with the yellow gown are ill-conditioned and unrestrained; such evil-doers by their evil deeds go to hell.

Better it would be to swallow a heated iron ball, like flaring fire, than that a bad unrestrained fellow should live on the charity of the land.

Four things does a reckless man gain who covets his neighbour's wife—demerit, an uncomfortable bed, thirdly, punishment, and lastly, hell.

There is demerit, and the evil way to hell: there is the short pleasure of the frightened in the arms of the frightened, and the king imposes heavy punishment; therefore let no man think of his neighbour's wife.

As a grass-blade, if badly grasped, cuts the arm, badly practised asceticism leads to hell.

An act carelessly performed, a broken vow, and hesitating obedience to discipline (Brahmachariyam), all these bring no great reward.

If anything is to be done, let a man do it, let him attack it vigorously! A careless pilgrim only scatters the dust of his passions more widely.

An evil deed is better left undone, for a man repents of it afterwards; a good deed is better done, for having done it, one does not repent.

Like a well-guarded frontier fort, with defences within and without, so let a man guard himself. Not a moment should escape, for they who allow the right moment to pass, suffer pain when they are in hell.

They who are ashamed of what they ought not to be ashamed of, and are not ashamed of what they ought to be ashamed of, such men, embracing false doctrines, enter the evil path.

They who fear when they ought not to fear, and fear not when they ought to fear, such men, embracing false doctrines, enter the evil path.

They who see sin where there is no sin, and see no sin where there is sin, such men, embracing false doctrines, enter the evil path.

They who see sin where there is sin, and no sin where there is no sin, such men, embracing the true doctrine, enter the good path.

The Elephant

Silently I endured abuse as the elephant in battle endures the arrow sent from the bow: for the world is ill-natured.

They lead a tamed elephant to battle, the king mounts a tamed elephant; the tamed is the best among men, he who silently endures abuse.

Mules are good, if tamed, and noble Sindhu horses, and

elephants with large tusks; but he who tames himself is better still.

For with these animals does no man reach the untrodden country, Nirvana, where a tamed man goes on a tamed animal—on his own well-tamed self.

The elephant called Dhanapalaka, his temples running with pungent sap, and who is difficult to hold, does not eat a morsel when bound; the elephant longs for the elephant grove.

If a man becomes fat and a great eater, if he is sleepy and rolls himself about, that fool, like a hog fed on grains, is born again and again.

This mind of mine went formerly wandering about as it liked, as it listed, as it pleased; but I shall now hold it in thoroughly, as the rider who holds the hook holds in the furious elephant.

Be not thoughtless, watch your thoughts! Draw yourself out of the evil way, like an elephant sunk in mud.

If a man find a prudent companion who walks with him, is wise, and lives soberly, he may walk with him, overcoming all dangers, happy, but considerate.

If a man find no prudent companion who walks with him, is wise, and lives soberly, let him walk alone, like a king who has left his conquered country behind—like an elephant in the forest.

It is better to live alone: there is no companionship with a fool; let a man walk alone, let him commit no sin, with few wishes, like an elephant in the forest.

If the occasion arises, friends are pleasant; enjoyment is pleasant, whatever be the cause; a good work is pleasant in the hour of death; the giving up of all grief is pleasant.

Pleasant in the world is the state of a mother, pleasant the state of a father, pleasant the state of a Samana, pleasant the state of a Brahmin.

Pleasant is virtue lasting to old age, pleasant is a faith firmly rooted; pleasant is attainment of intelligence, pleasant is avoiding of sins.

Thirst

The thirst of a thoughtless man grows like a creeper; he runs from life to life, like a monkey seeking fruit in the forest.

Whomsoever this fierce poisonous thirst overcomes, in this world, his sufferings increase like the abounding Birana grass.

But from him who overcomes this fierce thirst, difficult to be conquered in this world, sufferings fall off, like water-drops from a lotus leaf.

This salutary word I tell you, "Do ye, as many as are here assembled, dig up the root of thirst, as he who wants the sweet-scented Usira root must dig up the Birana grass, that Mara, the tempter, may not crush you again and again, as the stream crushes the reeds.

As a tree, even though it has been cut down, is firm so long as its root is safe, and grows again, thus, unless the feeders of thirst are destroyed, this pain of life will return again and again.

He whose thirty-six streams are strongly flowing in the channels of pleasure, the waves—his desires which are set on passion—will carry away that misguided man.

The channels run everywhere, the creeper of passion stands sprouting; if you see the creeper springing up, cut its root by means of knowledge.

A creature's pleasures are extravagant and luxurious; given up to pleasure and deriving happiness, men undergo again and again birth and decay.

Beset with lust, men run about like a snared hare; held in fetters and bonds, they undergo pain for a long time, again and again.

Beset with lust, men run about like a snared hare; let therefore the mendicant drive out thirst, by striving after passionlessness for himself.

He who, having got rid of the forest of lust after having reached Nirvana, gives himself over to lust, and who, when free from lust, runs to lust, look at that man! though free, he runs into bondage.

Wise people do not call that a strong fetter which is made of iron, wood, or hemp; passionately strong is the care for precious stones and rings, for sons and a wife.

The fetter wise people call strong which drags down, yields, but is difficult to undo; after having cut this at last, people leave the world, free from cares, and leaving the pleasures of love behind.

Those who are slaves to passions, run down the stream of desires, as a spider runs down the web which he has made himself; when they have cut this, at last, wise people go onwards, free from cares, leaving all pain behind.

Give up what is before, give up what is behind, give up what is between, when thou goest to the other shore of existence; if thy mind is altogether free, thou wilt not again enter into birth and decay.

If a man is tossed about by doubts, full of strong passions, and yearning only for what is delightful, his thirst will grow more and more, and he will indeed make his fetters strong.

If a man delights in quieting doubts, and, always reflecting, dwells on what is not delightful, he certainly will remove, nay, he will cut the fetter of Mara.

He who has reached the consummation, who does not tremble, who is without thirst and without sin, he has broken all the thorns of life: this will be his last body.

He who is without thirst and without affection, who understands the words and their interpretation, who knows the order of letters, those which are before and which are after, he has received his last body, he is called the great sage, the great man.

"I have conquered all, I know all, in all conditions of life I am free from taint; I have left all, and through the destruction of thirst I am free; having learnt myself, whom should I indicate as my teacher?"

The gift of the law exceeds all gifts; the sweetness of the law exceeds all sweetness; the delight in the law exceeds all delights; the extinction of thirst overcomes all pain.

Riches destroy the foolish, if they look not for the other shore; the foolish by his thirst for riches destroys himself, as if he were destroying others.

The fields are damaged by weeds, mankind is damaged by passion: therefore a gift bestowed on the passionless brings great reward.

The fields are damaged by weeds, mankind is damaged by hatred: therefore a gift bestowed on the passionless brings great reward.

The fields are damaged by weeds, mankind is damaged by vanity: therefore a gift bestowed on the passionless brings great reward.

The fields are damaged by weeds, mankind is damaged by lust: therefore a gift bestowed on the passionless brings great reward.

The Bhikshu

Restraint in the eye is good, good is restraint in the ear, in the nose restraint is good, good is restraint in the tongue.

In the body restraint is good, good is restraint in speech, in thought restraint is good, good is restraint in all things. A Bhikshu, restrained in all things, is freed from all pain.

He who controls his hand, he who controls his feet, he who controls his speech, he who is well controlled, he who delights inwardly, who is collected, who is solitary and content, him they call Bhikshu.

The Bhikshu who controls his mouth, who speaks wisely and calmly, who teaches the meaning and the law, his word is sweet.

He who dwells in the law, delights in the law, meditates on the law, recollects the law: that Bhikshu will never fall away from the true law.

Let him not despise what he has received, nor ever envy others: a mendicant who envies others does not obtain peace of mind.

A Bhikshu who, though he receives little, does not despise

what he has received, even the gods will praise him, if his life is pure, and if he is not slothful.

He who never identifies himself with name and form, and does not grieve over what is no more, he indeed is called a Bhikshu.

The Bhikshu who behaves with kindness, who is happy in the doctrine of Buddha, will reach the quiet place, Nirvana, happiness arising from the cessation of natural inclinations.

O Bhikshu, empty this boat! if emptied, it will go quickly; having cut off passion and hatred, thou wilt go to Nirvana.

Cut off the five fetters, leave the five, rise above the five. A Bhikshu, who has escaped from the five fetters, he is called Oghatinna—"saved from the flood."

Meditate, O Bhikshu, and be not heedless! Do not direct thy thought to what gives pleasure, that thou mayest not for thy heedlessness have to swallow the iron ball in hell, and that thou mayest not cry out when burning, "This is pain."

Without knowledge there is no meditation, without meditation there is no knowledge: he who has knowledge and meditation is near unto Nirvana.

A Bhikshu who has entered his empty house, and whose mind is tranquil, feels a more than human delight when he sees the law clearly.

As soon as he has considered the origin and destruction of the elements of the body, he finds happiness and joy which belong to those who know the immortal Nirvana.

And this is the beginning here for a wise Bhikshu: watchfulness over the senses, contentedness, restraint under the law; keep noble friends whose life is pure, and who are not slothful.

Let him live in charity, let him be perfect in his duties; then in the fulness of delight he will make an end of suffering.

As the Vassika plant sheds its withered flowers, men should shed passion and hatred, O ye Bhikshus!

The Bhikshu whose body and tongue and mind are quieted, who is collected, and has rejected the baits of the world, he is called quiet.

Rouse thyself by thyself, examine thyself by thyself, thus self-protected and attentive wilt thou live happily, O Bhikshu!

For self is the lord of self, self is the refuge of self; therefore curb thyself as the merchant curbs a noble horse.

The Bhikshu, full of delight, who is happy in the doctrine of Buddha will reach the quiet place, Nirvana, happiness consisting in the cessation of natural inclinations.

He who, even as a young Bhikshu, applies himself to the doctrine of Buddha, brightens up this world, like the moon when free from clouds.

The Brahmin

Stop the stream valiantly, drive away the desires, O Brahmin! When you have understood the destruction of all that was made, you will understand that which was not made.

If the Brahmin has reached the other shore in both laws, in restraint and contemplation, all bonds vanish from him who has obtained knowledge.

He for whom there is neither the hither nor the further shore, nor both, him, the fearless and unshackled, I call indeed a Brahmin.

He who is thoughtful, blameless, settled, dutiful, without passions, and who has attained the highest end, him I call indeed a Brahmin.

The sun is bright by day, the moon shines by night, the warrior is bright in his armour, the Brahmin is bright in his meditation; but Buddha, the Awakened, is bright with splendour day and night.

Because a man is rid of evil, therefore he is called Brahmin; because he walks quietly, therefore he is called Samana; because he has sent away his own impurities, therefore he is called a pilgrim.

No one should attack a Brahmin, but no Brahmin, if attacked, should let himself fly at his aggressor! Woe to him who strikes a Brahmin, more woe to him who flies at his aggressor!

It advantages a Brahmin not a little if he holds his mind back from the pleasures of life; the more all wish to injure has vanished, the more all pain will cease.

Him I call indeed a Brahmin who does not offend by body, word, or thought, and is controlled on these three points.

He from whom he may learn the law, as taught by the Well-awakened Buddha, him let him worship assiduously, as the Brahmin worships the sacrificial fire.

A man does not become a Brahmin by his plaited hair, by his family, or by birth; in whom there is truth and righteousness, he is blessed, he is a Brahmin.

What is the use of plaited hair, O fool! what of the raiment of goat-skins? Within thee there is ravening, but the outside thou makest clean.

The man who wears dirty raiments, who is emaciated and covered with veins, who meditates alone in the forest, him I call indeed a Brahmin.

I do not call a man a Brahmin because of his origin or of his mother. He is indeed arrogant, and he is wealthy: but the poor, who is free from all attachments, him I call indeed a Brahmin.

Him I call indeed a Brahmin who, after cutting all fetters, never trembles, is free from bonds and unshackled.

Him I call indeed a Brahmin who, after cutting the strap and the thong, the rope with all that pertains to it, has destroyed all obstacles, and is awakened.

Him I call indeed a Brahmin who, though he has committed no offence, endures reproach, stripes, and bonds: who has endurance for his force, and strength for his army.

Him I call indeed a Brahmin who is free from anger, dutiful, virtuous, without appetites, who is subdued, and has received his last body.

Him I call indeed a Brahmin who does not cling to sensual pleasures, like water on a lotus leaf, like a mustard seed on the point of a needle.

Him I call indeed a Brahmin who, even here, knows

the end of his own suffering, has put down his burden, and is unshackled.

Him I call indeed a Brahmin whose knowledge is deep, who possesses wisdom, who knows the right way and the wrong, and has attained the highest end.

Him I call indeed a Brahmin who keeps aloof both from laymen and from mendicants, who frequents no houses, and has but few desires.

Him I call indeed a Brahmin who without hurting any creatures, whether feeble or strong, does not kill nor cause slaughter.

Him I call indeed a Brahmin who is tolerant with the intolerant, mild with the violent, and free from greed among the greedy.

Him I call indeed a Brahmin from whom anger and hatred, pride and hypocrisy have dropped like a mustard seed from the point of a needle.

Him I call indeed a Brahmin who utters true speech, instructive and free from harshness, so that he offend no one.

Him I call indeed a Brahmin who takes nothing in the world that is not given him, be it long or short, small or large, good or bad.

Him I call indeed a Brahmin who fosters no desires for this world or for the next, has no inclinations, and is unshackled.

Him I call indeed a Brahmin who has no interests, and when he has understood the truth, does not say How, how? and who has reached the depth of the Immortal.

Him I call indeed a Brahmin who in this world has risen above both ties, good and evil, who is free from grief, from sin, and from impurity.

Him I call indeed a Brahmin who is bright like the moon, pure, serene, undisturbed, and in whom all gayety is extinct.

Him I call indeed a Brahmin who has traversed this miry road, the impassable world, difficult to pass, and its vanity, who has gone through, and reached the other shore, is thoughtful, steadfast, free from doubts, free from attachment, and content.

Him I call indeed a Brahmin who in this world, having abandoned all desires, travels about without a home, and in whom all concupiscence is extinct.

Him I call indeed a Brahmin who, having abandoned all longings, travels about without a home, and in whom all covetousness is extinct.

Him I call indeed a Brahmin who, after leaving all bondage to men, has risen above all bondage to the gods, and is free from all and every bondage.

Him I call indeed a Brahmin who has left what gives pleasure and what gives pain, who is cold, and free from all germs of renewed life: the hero who has conquered all the worlds.

Him I call indeed a Brahmin who knows the destruction and the return of beings everywhere, who is free from bondage, welfaring, Sugata, and awakened, Buddha.

Him I call indeed a Brahmin whose path the gods do not know, nor Gandharvas, nor men, whose passions are extinct, and who is an Arhat.

Him I call indeed a Brahmin who calls nothing his own, whether it be before, behind, or between; who is poor, and free from the love of the world.

Him I call indeed a Brahmin, the manly, the noble, the hero, the great sage, the conqueror, the indifferent, the accomplished, the awakened.

Him I call indeed a Brahmin who knows his former abodes, who sees heaven and hell, has reached the end of births, is perfect in knowledge, a sage, and whose perfections are all perfect.

5

The Prajna-Paramita Vajrachchhedika

The Perfect Wisdom Doctrine of the Diamond-Cutter

Adoration to the blessed Arya-Prajna-Paramita!

Thus it was heard by me: At one time Bhagavat (the blessed Buddha) dwelt in Shravasti, in the grove of Jeta, in the garden of Anathapindada, together with a large company of Bhikshus, *viz.* with 1250 Bhikshus, with many noble-minded Bodhisattvas.

Then Bhagavat having in the forenoon put on his undergarment, and having taken his bowl and cloak, entered the great city of Shravasti to collect alms. Then Bhagavat, after he had gone to the great city of Shravasti to collect alms, performed the act of eating, and having returned from his round in the afternoon, he put away his bowl and cloak, washed his feet, and sat down on the seat intended for him, crossing his legs, holding his body upright, and turning his reflection upon himself. Then many Bhikshus approached to where Bhagavat was, saluted his feet with their heads, turned three times round him to the right, and sat down on one side.

At that time again the venerable Subhuti came to that assembly and sat down. Then rising from his seat and putting his robe over one shoulder, kneeling on the earth with his right knee, he stretched out his folded hands towards

Bhagavat and said to him: 'It is wonderful, O Bhagavat, it is exceedingly wonderful, O Sugata, how much the noble-minded Bodhisattvas have been favoured with the highest favour by the Tathagata, the holy and fully enlightened! It is wonderful how much the noble-minded Bodhisattvas have been instructed with the highest instruction by the Tathagata, the holy and fully enlightened! How then, O Bhagavat, should the son or the daughter of a good family, after having entered on the path of the Bodhisattvas, behave, how should he advance, and how should he restrain his thoughts?'

After the venerable Subhuti had thus spoken, Bhagavat said to him: 'Well said, well said, Subhuti! So it is, Subhuti, so it is, as you say. The noble-minded Bodhisattvas have been favoured with the highest favour by the Tathagata, the noble-minded Bodhisattvas have been instructed with the highest instruction by the Tathagata. Therefore, O Subhuti, listen and take it to heart, well and rightly. I shall tell you, how any one who has entered on the path of Bodhisattvas should behave, how he should advance, and how he should restrain his thoughts.' Then the venerable Subhuti answered the Bhagavat and said: 'So be it, O Bhagavat.'

•

Then the Bhagavat thus spoke to him: 'Any one, O Subhuti, who has entered here on the path of the Bodhisattvas must thus frame his thought: As many beings as there are in this world of beings, comprehended under term of beings (either born of eggs, or from the womb, or from moisture, or miraculously), with form or without form, with name or without name, or neither with nor without name, as far as any known world of beings is known, all these must be delivered by me in the perfect world of Nirvana. And yet, after I have thus delivered immeasurable beings, not one single being has been delivered. And why? If, O Subhuti, a Bodhisattva had any idea of a being, he could not be called a Bodhisattva, one who is fit to become a Buddha. Any why?

Because, O Subhuti, no one is to be called a Bodhisattva, for whom there should exist the idea of a being, the idea of a living being, or the idea of a person.'

'And again, O Subhuti, a gift should not be given by a Bodhisattva, while he believes in objects; a gift should not be given by him, while he believes in anything; a gift should not be given by him, while he believes in form; a gift should not be given by him, while he believes in the special qualities of sound, smell, taste, and touch. For thus, O Subhuti, should a gift be given by a noble-minded Bodhisattva, that he should not believe even in the idea of cause. And why? Because that Bodhisattva, O Subhuti, who gives a gift, without believing in anything, the measure of his stock of merit is not easy to learn.'—'What do you think, O Subhuti, is it easy to learn the measure of space in the eastern quarter?' Subhuti said: 'Not indeed, O Bhagavat.'—Bhagavat said: 'In like manner, is it easy to learn the measure of space in the southern, western, northern quarters, below and above (nadir and zenith), in quarters and subquarters, in the ten quarters all round?' Subhuti said: 'Not indeed, O Bhagavat.' Bhagavat said: 'In the same manner, O Subhuti, the measure of the stock of merit of a Bodhisattva, who gives a gift without believing in anything, is not easy to learn. And thus indeed, O Subhuti, should one who has entered on the path of Bodhisattvas give a gift, that he should not believe even in the idea of cause.'

'Now what do you think, O Subhuti, should a Tathagata be known by the possession of signs?' Subhuti said: 'Not indeed, O Bhagavat, a Tathagata is not to be known by the possession of signs. And why? Because what has been preached by the Tathagata as the possession of signs, that is indeed the possession of no-signs.'

After this, Bhagavat spoke thus to the venerable Subhuti: 'Wherever there is, O Subhuti, the possession of signs, there is falsehood; wherever there is no possession of signs, there is no falsehood. Hence the Tathagata is to be seen, known, from no-signs as signs.'

After this, the venerable Subhuti spoke thus to the Bhagavat: 'Forsooth, O Bhagavat, will there be any beings in the future, in the last time, in the last moment, in the last 500 years, during the time of the decay of the good Law, who, when these very words of the Sutras are being preached, will frame a true idea?' The Bhagavat said: 'Do not speak thus, Subhuti. Yes, there will be some beings in the future, in the last time, in the last moment, in the last 500 years, during the decay of the good Law, who will frame a true idea when these very words are being preached.

'And again, O Subhuti, there will be noble-minded Bodhisattvas, in the future, in the last time, in the last moment, in the last 500 years, during the decay of the good Law, there will be strong and good and wise beings, who, when these very words of the Sutras are being preached, will frame a true idea. But those noble-minded Bodhisattvas, O Subhuti, will not have served one Buddha only, and the stock of their merit will not have been accumulated under one Buddha only; on the contrary, O Subhuti, those noble-minded Bodhisattvas will have served many hundred thousands of Buddhas, and the stock of their merit will have been accumulated under many hundred thousands of Buddhas; and they, when these very words of the Sutras are being preached, will obtain one and the same faith. They are known, O Subhuti, by the Tathagata through his Buddha-knowledge; they are seen, O Subhuti, by the Tathagata through his Buddha-eye; they are understood, O Subhuti, by the Tathagata. All these, O Subhuti, will produce and will hold fast an immeasurable and innumerable stock of merit. And why? Because, O Subhuti, there does not exist in those noble-minded Bodhisattvas the idea of self, there does not exist the idea of a being, the idea of a living being, the idea of a person. Nor does there exist, O Subhuti, for these noble-minded Bodhisattvas the idea of quality (dharma), nor of no-quality. Neither does there exist, O Subhuti, any idea or no-idea. And why? Because, O Subhuti, if there existed for these noble-minded Bodhisattvas the idea of quality, then they would believe in a self, they would believe in a being, they would believe in a living being, they would believe in a person. And if there existed for them the idea of no-quality, even then they would believe in a self, they would believe in a being, they would believe in a living being, they would believe in a person. And why? Because, O Subhuti, neither quality nor no-quality is to be accepted by a noble-minded Bodhisattva. Therefore this hidden saying has been preached by the Tathagata: "By those who know the teaching of the law, as like unto a raft, all qualities indeed must be abandoned; much more no-qualities." '

•

And again Bhagavat spoke thus to the venerable Subhuti: 'What do you think, O Subhuti, is there anything (dharma) that was known by the Tathagata under the name of the highest perfect knowledge, or anything that was taught by the Tathagata?'

After these words, the venerable Subhuti spoke thus to Bhagavat: 'As I, O Bhagavat, understand the meaning of the preaching of the Bhagavat, there is nothing that was known by the Tathagata under the name of the highest perfect knowledge, nor is there anything that is taught by the Tathagata. And why? Because that thing which was known or taught by the Tathagata is incomprehensible and inexpressible. It is neither a thing nor no-thing. And why? Because the holy persons are of imperfect power.'

Bhagavat said: 'What do you think, O Subhuti, if a son or daughter of a good family filled this sphere of a million millions of worlds with the seven gems or treasures, and gave it as a gift to the holy and enlightened Tathagatas, would that son or daughter of a good family on the strength of this produce a large stock of merit?' Subhuti said: 'Yes, O Bhagavat, yes, O Sugata, that son or daughter of a good family would on the strength of this produce a large stock of merit. And why? Because, O Bhagavat, what was preached by the Tathagata as the stock of merit, that was preached by the Tathagata as no-stock of merit. Therefore the Tathagata preaches: "A stock of merit, a stock of merit indeed!" ' Bhagavat said: 'And if, O Subhuti, the son or daughter of a good family should fill this sphere of a million millions of worlds with the seven treasures and should give it as a gift to the holy and enlightened Tathagatas, and if another after taking from this treatise of the Law one Gatha of four lines only should fully teach others and explain it, he indeed would on the strength of this produce a larger stock of merit immeasurable and innumerable. And why? Because, O Subhuti, the highest perfect knowledge of the holy and enlightened Tathagatas is produced from it; the blessed Buddhas are produced from it. And why? Because, O Subhuti, when the Tathagata preached: "The qualities of Buddha, the qualities of Buddha indeed!" they were preached by him as no-qualities of Buddha. Therefore they are called the qualities of Buddha.'

Bhagavat said: 'Now, what do you think, O Subhuti, does a Srota-apanna, the first grader who has entered the stream, think in this wise: The fruit of Srota-apatti has been obtained by me?' Subhuti said: 'Not indeed, O Bhagavat, a Srota-apanna does not think in this wise: The fruit of Srota-apatti has been obtained by me. And why? Because, O Bhagavat, he has not obtained any particular state (dharma). Therefore he is called a Srota-apanna. He has not obtained any form, nor sounds, nor smells, nor tastes, nor things that can be touched. Therefore he is called a Srota-apanna. If, O Bhagavat, a Srota-apanna were to think in this wise: The fruit of Srota-apatti has been obtained by me, he would believe in a self, he would believe in a being, he would believe in a living being, he would believe in a person.'

Bhagavat said: 'What do you think, O Subhuti, does a Sakridagamin, the second grader who returns once, think in this wise: The fruit of a Sakridagamin has been obtained by me?' Subhuti said: 'Not indeed, O Bhagavat, a Sak*ri*dagamin does not think in this wise: The fruit of a Sakridagamin has been obtained by me. And why? Because he is not an individual being (dharma), who has obtained the state of a Sakridagamin. Therefore he is called a Sakridagamin.'

Bhagavat said: 'What do you think, O Subhuti, does an Anagamin, who never returns and becomes Arhat, think in this wise: the fruit of an Anagamin has been obtained by me?' Subhuti said: 'Not indeed, O Bhagavat, an Anagamin does not think in this wise: The fruit of an Anagamin has been obtained by me. And why? Because he is not an individual being, who has obtained the state of an Anagamin. Therefore he is called an Anagamin.'

Bhagavat said: 'What do you think, O Subhuti, does an Arhat think in this wise: The fruit of an Arhat has been obtained by me?' Subhuti said: 'Not indeed, O Bhagavat, an Arhat does not think in this wise: The fruit of an Arhat has been obtained by me. And why? Because he is not an individual being, who is called an Arhat. Therefore he is called an Arhat. And if, O Bhagavat, an Arhat were to think in this wise: The state of an Arhat has been obtained by me, he would believe in a self, he would believe in a being, he would believe in a living being, he would believe in a person.

'And why? I have been pointed out, O Bhagavat, by the holy and fully enlightened Tathagata, as the foremost of those who dwell in virtue. I, O Bhagavat, am an Arhat, freed from passion. And yet, O Bhagavat, I do not think in this wise: I am an Arhat, I am freed from passion. If, O Bhagavat, I should think in this wise, that the state of an Arhat has been obtained by me, then the Tathagata would not have truly prophesied of me, saying: "Subhuti, the son of a good family, the foremost of those dwelling in virtue, does not dwell anywhere, and therefore he is called a dweller in virtue, a dweller in virtue indeed!" '

Bhagavat said: ' What do you think, O Subhuti, is there anything (dharma) which the Tathagata has adopted from the Tathagata Dipankara, the holy and fully enlightened?' Subhuti said: 'Not indeed, O Bhagavat; there is not anything which the Tathagata has adopted from the Tathagata Dipankara, the holy and fully enlightened.'

Bhagavat said: 'If, O Subhuti, a Bodhisattva should say: "I shall create numbers of worlds," he would say what is untrue. And why? Because, O Subhuti, when the Tathagata preached: "Numbers of worlds, numbers of worlds indeed!" they were preached by him as no-numbers. Therefore they are called numbers of worlds.

'Therefore, O Subhuti, a noble-minded Bodhisattva should in this wise frame an independent mind, which is to be framed as a mind not believing in anything, not believing in form, not believing in sound, smell, taste, and anything that can be touched. Now, for instance, O Subhuti, a man might have a body and a large body, so that his size should be as large as the king of mountains, Sumeru. Do you think then, O Subhuti, that his selfhood, he himself, would be large?' Subhuti said: 'Yes, O Bhagavat, yes, O Sugata, his selfhood would be large. And why? Because, O Bhagavat, when the Tathagata preached: "Selfhood, selfhood indeed!" it was preached by him as no-selfhood. Therefore it is called selfhood.'

•

Bhagavat said: 'What do you think, O Subhuti, if there were as many Ganga rivers as there are grains of sand in the large river Ganga, would the grains of sand be many?' Subhuti said: 'Those Ganga rivers would indeed be many, much more the grains of sand in those Ganga rivers.' Bhagavat said: 'I tell you, O Subhuti, I announce to you, If a woman or man were to fill with the seven treasures as many worlds as there would be grains of sand in those Ganga rivers and present them as a gift to the holy and fully enlightened Tathagatas—What do you think, O Subhuti, would that woman or man on the strength of this produce a large stock of merit?' Subhuti said: 'Yes, O Bhagavat, yes, O Sugata, that woman or man would on the strength of this produce a large stock of merit, immeasurable and innumerable.' Bhagavat said: 'And if, O Subhuti, a woman or man having filled so many worlds with the seven treasures should give them as a gift to the holy and enlightened Tathagatas, and if another son or daughter of a good family, after taking from this treatise of the Law one Gatha of four lines only, should fully teach others and explain it, he, indeed, would on the strength of this produce a larger stock of merit, immeasurable and innumerable.'

'Then again, O Subhuti, that part of the world in which, after taking from this treatise of the Law one Gatha of four lines only, it should be preached or explained, would be like a Chaitya, holy shrine, for the whole world of gods, men, and spirits; what should we say then of those who learn the whole of this treatise of the Law to the end, who repeat it, understand it, and fully explain it to others? They, O Subhuti, will be endowed with the highest wonder. And in that place, O Subhuti, there dwells the teacher, or one after another holding the place of the wise preceptor.'

After these words, the venerable Subhuti spoke thus to Bhagavat: 'O Bhagavat, how is this treatise of the Law called, and how can I learn it?' After this, Bhagavat spoke thus to the venerable Subhuti: 'This treatise of the Law, O Subhuti, is called the Prajna-paramita, Transcendent wisdom, and you should learn it by that name. And why? Because, O Subhuti, what was preached by the Tathagata as the Prajna-paramita, that was preached by the Tathagata as no-Paramita. Therefore it is called the Prajna-paramita.

'Then, what do you think, O Subhuti, is there anything

(dharma) that was preached by the Tathagata?' Subhuti said: 'Not indeed, O Bhagavat, there is not anything that was preached by the Tathagata.'

Bhagavat said: 'What do you think, O Subhuti,—the dust of the earth which is found in this sphere of a million millions of worlds, is that much?' Subhuti said: 'Yes, O Bhagavat, yes, O Sugata, that dust of the earth would be much. And why? Because, O Bhagavat, What was preached by the Tathagata as the dust of the earth, that was preached by the Tathagata as no-dust. Therefore it is called the dust of the earth. And what was preached by the Tathagata as the sphere of worlds, that was preached by the Tathagata as no-sphere. Therefore it is called the sphere of worlds.'

Bhagavat said: ' What do you think, O Subhuti, is a holy and fully enlightened Tathagata to be seen, known, by the thirty-two signs of a hero?' Subhuti said: 'No indeed, O Bhagavat; a holy and fully enlightened Tathagata is not to be seen, known, by the thirty-two signs of a hero. And why? Because what was preached by the Tathagata as the thirty-two signs of a hero, that was preached by the Tathagata as no-signs. Therefore they are called the thirty-two signs of a hero.'

Bhagavat said: 'If, O Subhuti, a woman or man should day by day sacrifice his life, selfhood, as many times as there are grains of sand in the river Ganga, and if he should thus sacrifice his life for as many kalpas as there are grains of sand in the river Ganga, and if another man, after taking from this treatise of the Law one Gatha of four lines only, should fully teach others and explain it, he indeed would on the strength of this produce a larger stock of merit, immeasurable and innumerable.'

•

At that time, the venerable Subhuti was moved by the power of the Law, shed tears, and having wiped his tears, he thus spoke to Bhagavat: 'It is wonderful, O Bhagavat, it is exceedingly wonderful, O Sugata, how fully this teaching of the Law has been preached by the Tathagata for the benefit of those beings who entered on the foremost path the path that leads to Nirvana, and who entered on the best path, from whence, O Bhagavat, knowledge has been produced in me. Never indeed, O Bhagavat, has such a teaching of the Law been heard by me before. Those Bodhisattvas, O Bhagavat, will be endowed with the highest wonder, who when this Sutra is being preached hear it and will frame to themselves a true idea. And why? Because what is a true idea is not a true idea. Therefore the Tathagata preaches: "A true idea, a true idea indeed!"

'It is no wonder to me, O Bhagavat, that I accept and believe this treatise of the Law, which has been preached. And those beings also, O Bhagavat, who will exist in the future, in the last time, in the last moment, in the last 500 years, during the time of the decay of the good Law, who will learn this treatise of the Law, O Bhagavat, remember it, recite it, understand it, and fully explain it to others, they will indeed be endowed with the highest wonder.

'But, O Bhagavat, there will not arise in them any idea of a self, any idea of a being, of a living being, or a person, nor does there exist for them any idea or no-idea. Any why? Because, O Bhagavat, the idea of a self is no-idea, and the idea of a being, or a living being, or a person is no-idea. And why? Because the blessed Buddhas are freed from all ideas.'

After these words, Bhagavat thus spoke to the venerable Subhuti: 'So it is, O Subhuti, so it is. Those beings, O Subhuti, who when this Sutra was being recited here will not be disturbed or frightened or become alarmed, will be endowed with the highest wonder. And why? Because, O Subhuti, this was preached by the Tathagata, as the Parama-paramita, which is no-Paramita. And, O Subhuti, what the Tathagata preaches as the Parama-paramita, that was preached also by immeasurable blessed Buddhas. Therefore it is called the Parama-paramita.

'And, O Subhuti, the Paramita or the highest perfection of endurance belonging to a Tathagata, that also is no-Paramita. And why? Because, O Subhuti, at the time when the king of Kalinga cut my flesh from every limb, I had no idea of a self, of a being, of a living being, or of a person; I had neither an idea nor no-idea. And why? Because, O Subhuti, if I at that time had had an idea of a self, I should also have had an idea of malevolence. If I had had an idea of a being, or of a living being, or of a person, I should also have had an idea of malevolence. And why? Because, O Subhuti, I remember the past 500 births, when I was the Rishi Kshantivadin, preacher of endurance. At that time also, I had no idea of a self, of a being, of a living being, of a person. Therefore then, O Subhuti, a noble-minded Bodhisattva, after putting aside all ideas, should raise his mind to the highest perfect knowledge. He should frame his mind so as not to believe, depend, in form, sound, smell, taste, or anything that can be touched, in something (dharma), in nothing or anything. And why? Because what is believed is not believed, not to be depended on. Therefore the Tathagata preaches: "A gift should not be given by a Bodhisattva who believes in anything, it should not be given by one who believes in form, sound, smell, taste, or anything that can be touched."

'And again, O Subhuti, a Bodhisattva should in such wise give his gift for the benefit of all beings. And why? Because, O Subhuti, the idea of a being is no-idea. And those who are thus spoken of by the Tathagata as all beings are indeed no-beings. And why? Because, O Subhuti, a Tathagata says what is real, says what is true, says the things as they are; a Tathagata does not speak untruth.

'But again, O Subhuti, whatever doctrine has been perceived, taught, and meditated on by a Tathagata, in it there is neither truth nor falsehood. And as a man who has entered the darkness would not see anything, thus a Bodhisattva is to be considered who is immersed in objects, and who being immersed in objects gives a gift. But as a man who has eyes would, when the night becomes light, and the sun has risen, see many things, thus a Bodhisattva is to be considered who is not immersed in objects, and who not being immersed in objects gives a gift.

'And again, O Subhuti, if any sons or daughters of good families will learn this treatise of the Law, will remember, recite, and understand it, and fully explain it to others, they, O Subhuti, are known by the Tathagata through his Buddha-knowledge, they are seen, O Subhuti, by the Tathagata through his Buddha-eye. All these beings, O Subhuti, will produce and hold fast an immeasurable and innumerable stock of merit.'

•

'And if, O Subhuti, a woman or man sacrificed in the morning as many lives as there are grains of sand in the river Ganga and did the same at noon and the same in the evening, and if in this way they sacrificed their lives for a hundred thousands of Niyutas of Kotis of ages, and if another, after hearing this treatise of the Law, should not oppose it, then the latter would on the strength of this produce a larger stock of merit, immeasurable and innumerable. What should we say then of him who after having written it, learns it, remembers it, understands it, and fully explains it to others?

'And again, O Subhuti, this treatise of the Law is incomprehensible and incomparable. And this treatise of the Law has been preached by the Tathagata for the benefit of those beings who entered on the foremost path, the path that leads to Nirvana, and who entered on the best path. And those who will learn this treatise of the Law, who will remember it, recite it, understand it, and fully explain it to others, they are known, O Subhuti, by the Tathagata through his Buddha-knowledge, they are seen, O Subhuti, by the Tathagata through his Buddha-eye. All these beings, O Subhuti, will be endowed with an immeasurable stock of merit, they will be endowed with an incomprehensible, incomparable, immeasurable and unmeasured stock of merit.

All these beings, O Subhuti, will equally remember the Bodhi, the highest Buddha-knowledge, will recite it, and understand it. And why? Because it is not possible, O Subhuti, that this treatise of the Law should be heard by beings of little faith, by those who believe in self, in beings, in living beings, and in persons. It is impossible that this treatise of the Law should be heard by beings who have not acquired the knowledge of Bodhisattvas, or that it should be learned, remembered, recited, and understood by them. The thing is impossible.

'And again, O Subhuti, that part of the world in which this Sutra will be propounded, will have to be honoured by the whole world of gods, men, and evil spirits, will have to be worshipped, and will become like a Chaitya.'

'And, O Subhuti, sons or daughters of a good family who will learn these very Sutras, who will remember them, recite them, understand them, thoroughly take them to heart, and fully explain them to others, they will be overcome, they will be greatly overcome. And why? Because, O Subhuti, whatever evil deeds these beings have done in a former birth, deeds that must lead to suffering, those deeds these beings, owing to their being overcome, after they have seen the Law, will destroy, and they will obtain the knowledge of Buddha.

'I remember, O Subhuti, in the past, before innumerable and more than innumerable kalpas, there were eighty-four hundred thousands of Niyutas of Kotis of Buddhas following after the venerable and fully enlightened Tathagata Dipankara, who were pleased by me, and after being pleased were not displeased. And if, O Subhuti, these blessed Buddhas were pleased by me, and after being pleased were not displeased, and if on the other hand people at the last time, at the last moment, in the last 500 years, during the time of the decay of the good Law, will learn these very Sutras, remember them, recite them, understand them, and fully explain them to others, then, O Subhuti, in comparison with their stock of merit that former stock of merit will not come to one hundredth part, nay, not to one thousandth part, not to a hundred thousandth part, not to a ten millionth part, not to a hundred millionth part, not to a hundred thousand ten millionth part, not to a hundred thousands of Niyutas ten millionth part. It will not bear number, nor fraction, nor counting, nor comparison, nor approach, nor analogy.

'And if, O Subhuti, I were to tell you the stock of merit of those sons or daughters of good families, and how large a stock of merit those sons or daughters of good families will produce, and hold fast at that time, people would become distracted and their thoughts would become bewildered. And again, O Subhuti, as this treatise of the Law preached by the Tathagata is incomprehensible and incomparable, its rewards also must be expected to be incomprehensible.'

•

At that time the venerable Subhuti thus spoke to the Bhagavat: 'How should a person, after having entered on the path of the Bodhisattvas, behave, how should he advance, and how should he restrain his thoughts?' Bhagavat said: 'He who has entered on the path of Bodhisattvas should thus frame his thought: All beings must be delivered by me in the perfect world of Nirvana; and yet after I have thus delivered these beings, no being has been delivered. And why? Because, O Subhuti, if a Bodhisattva had any idea of beings, he could not be called a Bodhisattva, and so on from the idea of a living being to the idea of a person; if he had any such idea, he could not be called a Bodhisattva. And why? Because, O Subhuti, there is no such thing (dharma) as one who has entered on the path of the Bodhisattvas.

'What do you think, O Subhuti, is there anything which the Tathagata has adopted from the Tathagata Dipankara with regard to the highest perfect knowledge?' After this, the venerable Subhuti spoke thus to the Bhagavat: 'As far as I, O Bhagavat, understand the meaning of the preaching of the Bhagavat, there is nothing which has been adopted by the Tathagata from the holy and fully enlightened

Tathagata Dipankara with regard to the highest perfect knowledge.' After this, Bhagavat thus spoke to the venerable Subhuti: 'So it is, Subhuti, so it is. There is not, O Subhuti, anything which has been adopted by the Tathagata from the holy and fully enlightened Tathagata Dipankara with regard to the highest perfect knowledge. And if, O Subhuti, anything had been adopted by the Tathagata, the Tathagata Dipankara would not have prophesied of me, saying : "Thou, O boy, wilt be in the future the holy and fully enlightened Tathagata called Sakyamuni." Because then, O Subhuti, there is nothing that has been adopted by the holy and fully enlightened Tathagata with regard to the highest perfect knowledge, therefore I was prophesied by the Tathagata Dipankara, saying: "Thou, boy, wilt be in the future the holy and fully enlightened Tathagata called Sakyamuni."

'And why, O Subhuti, the name of Tathagata? It expresses true suchness. And who Tathagata, O Subhuti? It expresses that he had no origin. And why Tathagata, O Subhuti? It expresses the destruction of all qualities. And why Tathagata, O Subhuti? It expresses one who had no origin whatever. And why this? Because, O Subhuti, no-origin is the highest goal.

'And whosoever, O Subhuti, should say that, by the holy and fully enlightened Tathagata, the highest perfect knowledge has been known, he would speak an untruth, and would slander me, O Subhuti, with some untruth that he has learned. And why? Because there is no such thing, O Subhuti, as has been known by the Tathagata with regard to the highest perfect knowledge. And in that, O Subhuti, which has been known and taught by the Tathagata, there is neither truth nor falsehood. Therefore the Tathagata preaches: "All things are Buddha-things." And why? Because what was preached by the Tathagata, O Subhuti, as all things, that was preached as no-things; and therefore all things are called Buddha-things.

'Now, O Subhuti, a man might have a body and a large body.' The venerable Subhuti said: 'That man who was spoken of by the Tathagata as a man with a body, with a large body, he, O Bhagavat, was spoken of by the Tathagata as without a body, and therefore he is called a man with a body and with a large body.'

Bhagavat said: 'So it is, O Subhuti; and if a Bodhisattva were to say: "I shall deliver all beings," he ought not to be called a Bodhisattva. And why? Is there anything, O Subhuti, that is called a Bodhisattva?' Subhuti said: 'Not indeed, Bhagavat, there is nothing which is called Bodhisattva.' Bhagavat said: 'Those who were spoken of as beings, beings indeed, O Subhuti, they were spoken of as no-beings by the Tathagata, and therefore they are called beings. Therefore the Tathagata says: "All beings are without self, all beings are without life, without manhood, without a personality."

'If, O Subhuti, a Bodhisattva were to say: "I shall create numbers of worlds," he would say what is untrue. And why? Because, what were spoken of as numbers of worlds, numbers of worlds indeed, O Subhuti, these were spoken of as no-numbers by the Tathagata, and therefore they are called numbers of worlds.

'A Bodhisattva, O Subhuti, who believes that all things are without self, that all things are without self, he has faith, he is called a noble-minded Bodhisattva by the holy and fully enlightened Tathagata.'

•

Bhagavat said: 'What do you think, O Subhuti, has the Tathagatta the bodily eye?' Subhuti said: 'So it is, O Bhagavat, the Tathagata has the bodily eye.'

Bhagavat said: 'What do you think, O Subhuti, has the Tathagata the heavenly eye?' Subhuti said: 'So it is, O Bhagavat, the Tathagata has the heavenly eye.'

Bhagavat said: 'What do you think, O Subhuti, has the Tathagata the eye of knowledge?' Subhuti said: 'So it is, O Bhagavat, the Tathagata has the eye of knowledge.'

Bhagavat said: 'What do you think, O Subhuti, has the Tathagata the eye of the Law?' Subhuti said: 'So it is, O Bhagavat, the Tathagata has the eye of the Law.'

Bhagavat said: 'What do you think, O Subhuti, has the Tathagata the eye of Buddha?' Subhuti said: 'So it is, O Bhagavat, the Tathagata has the eye of Buddha.'

Bhagavat said: 'What do you think, O Subhuti, as many grains of sand as there are in the great river Ganga—were they preached by the Tathagata as grains of sand?' Subhuti said: 'So it is, O Bhagavat, so it is, O Sugata, they were preached as grains of sand by the Tathagata.' Bhagavat said: 'What do you think, O Subhuti, if there were as many Ganga rivers as there are grains of sand in the great river Ganga; and, if there were as many worlds as there are grains of sand in these, would these worlds be many?' Subhuti said: 'So it is, O Bhagavat, so it is, O Sugata, these worlds would be many.' Bhagavat said: 'As many beings as there are in all those worlds, I know the manifold trains of thought of them all. Any why? Because what was preached as the train of thoughts, the train of thoughts indeed, O Subhuti, that was preached by the Tathagata as no-train of thoughts, and therefore it is called the train of thoughts. And why? Because, O Subhuti, a past thought is not perceived, a future thought is not perceived, and the present thought is not perceived.'

'What do you think, O Subhuti, if a son or a daughter of a good family should fill this sphere of a million millions of worlds with the seven treasures, and give it as a gift to holy and fully enlightened Buddhas, would that son or daughter of a good family produce on the strength of this a large stock of merit?' Subhuti said: 'Yes, a large one.' Bhagavat said: 'So it is, Subhuti, so it is; that son or daughter of a good family would produce on the strength of this a large stock of merit, immeasurable and innumerable. And why? Because what was preached as a stock of merit, a stock of merit indeed, O Subhuti, that was preached as no-stock of merit by the Tathagata, and therefore it is called a stock of merit. If, O Subhuti, there existed a stock of merit, the Tathagata would not have preached: "A stock of merit, a stock of merit indeed!" '

'What do you think then, O Subhuti, is a Tathagata to be seen, known, by the shape of his visible body?' Subhuti said: 'Not indeed, O Bhagavat, a Tathagata is not to be seen, known, by the shape of his visible body. And why? Because, what was preached, O Bhagavat, as the shape of the visible body, the shape of the visible body indeed, that was preached by the Tathagata as no-shape of the visible body, and therefore it is called the shape of the visible body.'

Bhagavat said: 'What do you think, O Subhuti, should a Tathagata be seen, known, by the possession of signs?' Subhuti said: 'Not indeed, O Bhagavat, a Tathagata is not to be seen, known, by the possession of signs. And why? Because what was preached by the Tathagata as the possession of signs, that was preached as non-possession of signs by the Tathagata, and therefore, it is called the possession of signs.'

Bhagavat said: 'What do you think, O Subhuti, does the Tathagata think in this wise: The Law has been taught by me?' Subhuti said: 'Not indeed, O Bhagavat, does the Tathagata think in this wise: The Law has been taught by me.' Bhagavat said: 'If a man should say that the Law has been taught by the Tathagata, he would say what is not true; he would slander me with untruth which he has learned. And why? Because, O Subhuti, it is said the teaching of the Law, the teaching of the Law indeed. O Subhuti, there is nothing that can be perceived by the name of the teaching of the Law.'

•

After this, the venerable Subhuti spoke thus to the Bhagavat: 'Forsooth, O Bhagavat, will there be any beings in the future, in the last time, in the last moment, in the last 500 years, during the time of the decay of the good

Law, who, when they have heard these very Laws, will believe?' Bhagavat said: 'These, O Subhuti, are neither beings nor no-beings. And why? Because, O Subhuti, those who were preached as beings, beings indeed, they were preached as no-beings by the Tathagata, and therefore, they are called beings.'

'What do you think then, O Subhuti, is there anything which has been known by the Tathagata in the form of the highest perfect knowledge?' The venerable Subhuti said: 'Not indeed, O Bhagavat, there is nothing, O Bhagavat, that has been known by the Tathagata in the form of the highest perfect knowledge.' Bhagavat said: 'So it is, Subhuti, so it is. Even the smallest thing is not known or perceived there, therefore it is called the highest perfect knowledge.'

'Also, Subhuti, all is the same there, there is no difference there, and therefore it is called the highest perfect knowledge. Free from self, free from being, free from life, free from personality, that highest perfect knowledge is always the same, and thus known with all good things. And why? Because, what were preached as good things, good things indeed, O Subhuti, they were preached as no-thing by the Tathagata, and therefore they are called good things.'

'And if, O Subhuti, a woman or man, putting together as many heaps of the seven treasures as there are Sumerus, kinds of mountains, in the sphere of a million millions of worlds, should give them as a gift to holy and fully enlightened Tathagatas; and if a son or a daughter of good family, after taking from this treatise of the Law, this Prajna-paramita, one Gatha of four lines only, should teach it to others, then, O Subhuti, compared with his stock of merit, the former stock of merit would not come to the one hundredth part,' etc., till 'it will not bear an approach.'

'What do you think then, O Subhuti, does a Tathagata

think in this wise: Beings have been delivered by me? You should not think so, O Subhuti. And why? Because there is no being, O Subhuti, that has been delivered by the Tathagata. And, if there were a being, O Subhuti, that has been delivered by the Tathagata, then the Tathagata would believe in self, believe in a being, believe in a livng being, and believe in a person. And what is called a belief in self, O Subhuti, that is preached as no-belief by the Tathagata. And this is learned by children and ignorant persons; and they who were preached as children and ignorant persons, O Subhuti, were preached as no-persons by the Tathagata, and therefore, they are called children and ignorant persons.'

'What do you think then, O Subhuti, is the Tathagata to be seen, known, by the possession of signs?' Subhuti said: 'Not indeed, O Bhagavat. So far as I know the meaning of the preaching of the Bhagavat, the Tathagata is not to be seen, known, by the possession of signs.' Bhagavat said: 'Good, good, Subhuti, so it is, Subhuti; so it is, as you say; a Tathagata is not to be seen, known, by the possession of signs. And why ? Because, O Subhuti, if the Tathagata were to be seen, known, by the possession of signs, a wheel-turning king also would be a Tathagata; therefore a Tathagata is not to be seen, known, by the possession of signs.' The venerable Subhuti spoke thus to the Bhagavat: 'As I understand the meaning of the preaching of the Bhagavat, a Tathagata is not to be seen, known, by the possession of signs.' Then the Bhagavat at that moment preached these two Gathas:

They who saw me by form, and they who heard me by sound,

They engaged in false endeavours, will not see me. A Buddha is to be seen, known, from the Law; for the Buddhas have the Law-body;

And the nature of the Law cannot be understood, nor can it be made to be understood.

'What do you think then, O Subhuti, has the highest

perfect knowledge been known by the Tathagata through the possession of signs? You should not think so, O Subhuti. And why? Because, O Subhuti, the highest perfect knowledge would not be known by the Tathagata through the possession of signs. Nor should anybody, O Subhuti, say to you that the destruction of annihilation of anything is proclaimed by those who have entered on the path of the Bodhisattvas.'

•

'And if, O Subhuti, a son or a daughter of a good family were to fill worlds equal to the number of grains of sand of the river Ganga with the seven treasures, and give them as a gift to holy and fully enlightened Tathagatas; and if a Bodhisattva acquired endurance in selfless and uncreated things, then the latter will on the strength of this produce a larger stock of merit, immeasurable and innumerable.'

'But, O Subhuti, a stock of merit should not be appropriated by a noble-minded Bodhisattva.' The venerable Subhuti said: 'Should a stock of merit, O Bhagavat, not be appropriated by a Bodhisattva?' Bhavagat said: 'It should be appropriated, O Subhuti; it should not be appropriated; and therefore it is said: It should be appropriated.'

'And again, O Subhuti, if anybody were to say that the Tathagata goes, or comes or stands or sits, or lies down, he, O Subhuti, does not understand the meaning of my preaching. And why? Because the word Tathagata means one who does not go to anywhere, and does not come from anywhere; and therefore he is called the Tathagata, truly come, holy and fully enlightened.'

'And again, O Subhuti, if a son or a daughter of a good family were to take as many worlds as there are grains of earth-dust in this sphere of a million millions of worlds, and reduce them to such fine dust as can be made with immeasurable strength, like what is called a mass of the smallest atoms, do you think, O Subhuti, would that be a mass of many atoms?' Subhuti said: 'Yes, Bhagavat, yes, Sugata, that would be a mass of many atoms. And why? Because, O Bhagavat, if it were a mass of many atoms, Bhagavat would not call it a mass of many atoms. And why? Because, what was preached as a mass of many atoms by the Tathagata, that was preached as no-mass of atoms by the Tathagata; And therefore it is called a mass of many atoms. And what was preached by the Tathagata as the sphere of a million millions of worlds, that was preached by the Tathagata as no-sphere of worlds; and therefore it is called the sphere of a million millions of worlds. And why? Because, O Bhagavat, if there were a sphere of worlds, there would exist a belief in matter; and what was preached as a belief in matter by the Tathagata, that was preached as no-belief by the Tathagata; and therefore it is called a belief in matter.' Bhagavat said: 'And a belief in matter itself, O Subhuti, is unmentionable and inexpressible; it is neither a thing nor no-thing, and this is known by children and ignorant persons.'

'And why? Because, O Subhuti, if a man were to say that belief in self, belief in a being, belief in life, belief in personality had been preached by the Tathagata would he be speaking truly?' Subhuti said: 'Not indeed, Bhagavat, not indeed, Sugata; he would not be speaking truly. And why? Because, O Bhagavat, what was preached by the Tathagata as a belief in self, that was preached by the Tathagata as no-belief; therefore it is called belief in self.'

Bhagavat said: 'Thus then, O Subhuti, are all things to be perceived, to be looked upon, and to be believed by one who has entered on the path of the Bodhisattvas. And in this wise are they to be perceived, to be looked upon, and to be believed, that a man should believe neither in the idea of a thing nor in the idea of a no-thing. And why? Because, by saying: The idea of a thing, the idea of a thing indeed, it has been preached by the Tathagata as no-idea of a thing.'

'And, O Subhuti, if a noble-minded Bodhisattva were to fill immeasurable and innumerable spheres of worlds with the seven treasures, and give them as a gift to holy and fully enlightened Tathagatas; and if a son or a daughter of a good family after taking from this treatise of the Law, this Prajna-paramita, one Gatha of four lines only, should learn it, repeat it, understand, it, and fully explain it to others, then the latter would on the strength of this produce a larger stock of merit, immeasurable and innumerable. And how should be explain it? As in the sky:

'Stars, darkness, a lamp, a phantom, dew, a bubble. A dream, a flash of lightining, and a cloud–thus we should—look upon the world all that was made.

'Thus he should explain; therefore it is said: He should explain.'

Thus spoke the Bhagavat enraptured. The elder Subhuti, and the friars, nuns, the faithful laymen and women, and the Bodhisattvas also, and the whole world of gods, men, evil spirits and fairies, praised the preaching of the Bhagavat.

Prajna-Paramita Hridaya Sutra (The Heart of Perfect Wisdom)

Adoration to the Omniscient!

This I heard: At one time the Bhagavat (Lord Buddha) dwelt as Rajagriha, on the hill Gridhrakuta, together with a large number of Bhikshus and a large number of Bodhisattvas.

At that time the Bhagavat was absorbed in a meditation, called Gambhiravasambodha. And at the same time the great Bodhisattva Aryavalokiteshvara, performing his study in the deep Prajna-paramita, thought thus: 'There are the five Skandhas, and those he considered as something by nature empty.

Then the venerable Sariputra, through Buddha's power, thus spoke to the Bodhisattva Aryavalokiteshvara: 'If the son or daughter of a family wishes to perform the study in the deep Prajna-paramita, how is he to be taught?'

On this the great Bodhisattva Aryavalokiteshvara thus spoke to the venerable Sariputra: 'If the son or daughter of a family wishes to perform the study in the deep Prajna-paramita, he must think thus:

'There are five Skandhas, and these he considered as by their nature empty. Form is emptiness, and emptiness indeed is form. Emptiness is not different from form, form is not different from emptiness. What is form that is emptiness, what is emptiness that is form. Thus perception, name, conception, and knowledge also are emptiness. Thus, O Sariputra, all things have the character of emptiness, they have no beginning, no end, they are faultless and not faultless, they are not imperfect and not perfect. Therefore, O Sariputra, here in this emptiness there is no form, no perception, no name, no concept, no knowledge. No eye, ear, nose, tongue, body, and mind. No form, sound, smell, taste, touch, and objects. There is no eye,' etc., till we come to 'there is no mind, no objects, no mind knowledge. There is no knowledge, no ignorance, no destruction of ignorance,' till we come to 'there is no decay and death, no destruction of decay and death; there are not the Four Truths, viz., that there is pain, origin of pain, stoppage of pain, and the path to it. There is no knowledge, no obtaining, no not-obtaining of Nirvana. Therefore, O Sariputra, as there is no obtaining of Nirvana, a man who has approached the Prajna-paramita of the Bodhisattvas, dwells for a time enveloped in consciousness. But when the envelopment of consciousness has been annihilated, then he becomes free of all fear, beyond the reach of change, enjoying final Nirvana.

'All Buddhas of the past, present, and future, after approaching the Prajna-paramita, have awoke to the highest perfect knowledge.

'Therefore we ought to know the great verse of the Prajna-paramita, the verse of the great wisdom, the unsurpassed verse, the verse which appeases all pain—it is truth, because it is not false—the verse proclaimed in the Prajna-paramita:

"O wisdom, gone, gone, gone to the other, shore, landed at the other shore, Svaha!"

'Thus, O Sariputra, should a Bodhisattva teach in the study of the deep Prajna-paramita.'

Then when the Bhagavat had risen from that meditation, he gave his approval to the venerbale Bodhisattva Avalokitesvara, saying: 'Well done, well done, noble son! So it is, noble son. So indeed must this study of the deep Prajna-paramita be peformed. As it has been described by thee, it is applauded by Arhat Tathagatas.'

Thus spoke Bhagavat with joyful mind. And the venerable Sariputra, and the honourable Bodhisattva Avalokitesvara, and the whole assembly, and the world of gods, men, demons, and fairies praised the speech of the Bhagavat.

6

Sukhavati Vyuha

The Land of Bliss

Adoration to the Omniscient!!

Thus it was heard by me: At one time the Blessed Bhagavat (Lord Buddha) dwelt at Shravasti, in the Jeta-grove, in the garden of Anathapindaka, together with a large company of Bhikshus *viz.* with twelve hundred and fifty Bhikshus, all of them acquainted with the five kinds of knowledge, elders, great disciples, and Arhats, such as Sariputra, the elder, Mahamaudgalyayana, Mahakasyapa, Mahakapphina, Mahakatyayana, Mahakaushthila, Revata, Shuddhipanthaka, Nanda, Ananda, Rahula, Gavampati, Bharadvaja, Kalodayin, Vakkula, and Aniruddha. He dwelt together with these and many other great disciples, and together with many noble-minded Boddhisattvas, such as Manjusri, the prince, the Bodhisattva Ajita, the Boddhisattva Gandhahastin, the Bodhisattva Nityodyukta, the Bodhisattva Anikshiptadhura. He dwelt together with them and many other noble-minded Bodhisattvas, and with Shakra, the Indra, or King of the Devas, and with Brahmin Sahampati. With these and many other hundred thousand sons of the gods, Bhagavat dwelt at Shravasti.

Then Bhagavat addressed the honoured Sariputra and said, 'O Sariputra, after you have passed from here over a hundred thousand kotis of Buddha countries there is in the Western part a Buddha country, a world called Sukhavati, the happy country. And there a Tathagata, called Amitayus, an Arhat, fully enlightened, dwells now, and remains, and supports himself, and teaches the Law.

'Now what do you think, Sariputra, for what reason is that world called Sukhavati? In that world Sukhavati, O Sariputra, there is neither bodily nor mental pain for living beings. The sources of happiness are innumerable there. For that reason is that world called Sukhavati the happy country.

'And again, O Sariputra, that world Sukhavati is adorned with seven terraces, with seven rows of palm-trees, and with strings of bells. It is enclosed on every side, beautiful, brilliant with the four gems, gold, silver, beryl and crystal. With such arrays of excellences peculiar to a Buddha country is that Buddha country adorned.

'And again, O Sariputra, in that world Sukhavati there are lotus lakes, adorned with the seven gems, gold, silver, beryl, crystal, red pearls, diamonds, and corals as the seventh. They are full of water which possesses the eight good qualities, their waters rise as high as the fords and bathing-places, so that even crows may drink there; they are strewn with golden sand. And in these lotus-lakes there are all around on the four sides four stairs, beautiful and brilliant with the four gems, gold, silver, beryl, crystal. And on every side of these lotus-lakes gem-trees are growing, beautiful and brilliant with the seven gems, gold, silver, beryl, crystal, red pearls, diamonds, and corals as the seventh. And in those lotus-lakes lotus-flowers are growing, blue, blue-coloured, of blue splendour, blue to behold; yellow, yellow-coloured, of yellow splendour, yellow to behold; red, red-coloured, of red splendour, red to behold; white, white-coloured, of white splendour, white to behold; beautiful, beautifully-coloured, of beautiful splendour, beautiful to behold, and in circumference as large as the wheel of a chariot.

'And again, O Sariputra, in that Buddha country there are heavenly musical instruments always played on, and the earth is lovely and of golden colour. And in that Buddha country a flower-rain of heavenly Mandarava blossoms pours down three times every day, and three times every night. And the beings who are born there worship before their morning meal a hundred thousand kotis of Buddhas by going to other worlds; and having showered a hundred thousand kotis of flowers upon each Tathagata, they return to their own world in time for the afternoon rest. With such array of excellences peculiar to a Buddha country is that Buddha country adorned.

'And again, O Sariputra, there are in that Buddha country swans, curlews, and peacocks. Three times every night, and three times every day, they come together and perform a concert each uttering his own note. And from them thus uttering proceeds a sound proclaiming the five virtues, the five powers, and the seven steps leading towards the highest knowledge. When the men there hear that sound, remembrance of Buddha, remembrance of the Law, remembrance of the Church, rises in their mind.

'Now, do you think, O Sariputra, that there are beings who have entered into the nature of animals birds, etc.? This is not to be thought of. The very name of hells is unknown in that Buddha country, and likewise that of descent into animal bodies and of the realm of Yama. No, these tribes of birds have been made on purpose by the Tathagata Amitayus, and they utter the sound of the Law.

'And again, O Sariputra, when those rows of palm-trees and strings of bells in that Buddha country are moved by the wind, a sweet and enrapturing sound proceeds from them. Yes, O Sariputra, as from a heavenly musical instrument consisting of a hundred thousand kotis of sounds, when played by Aryas, a sweet and enrapturing sound proceeds from those rows of palm-trees and strings of bells moved by the wind. And when the men hear that sound, reflection on Buddha arises in them, reflection on the Law, reflection on the Church.

'Now what do you think, O Sariputra, for what reason is that Tathagata called Amitayus? The length of life, ayus, O Sariputra, of that Tathagata and of those men there is immeasurable, amita. Therefore is that Tathagata called Amitayus. And ten kalpas have passed, O Sariputra, since that Tathagata awoke to perfect knowledge.

'And what do you think, O Sariputra, for what reason

is that Tathagata called Amitabha? The splendour, abha, O Sariputra, of that Tathagata is unimpeded over all Buddha countries. Therefore is that Tathagata called Amitabha.

'And there is, O Sariputra, an innumerable assembly of disciples with that Tathagata, purified and venerable persons, whose number it is not easy to count.

'And again, O Sariputra, of those beings also who are born in the Buddha country of the Tathagata Amitayus as purified Bodhisattvas, never to return again and bound by one birth only, of those Bodhisattvas also, O Sariputra, the number is not easy to count, except they are reckoned as infinite in number.

'Then again all beings, O Sariputra, ought to make fervent prayer for that Buddha country. And why? Because they come together there with such excellent men. Beings are not born in that Buddha country of the Tathagata Amitayus as a reward and result of good works performed in this present life. No, whatever son or daughter of a family shall hear the name of the blessed Amitayus the Tathagata, and having heard it, shall keep it in mind, and with thoughts undisturbed shall keep it in mind for one, two, three, four, five, six or seven nights,—when that son or daughter of a family comes to die, then that Amitayus, the Tathagata, surrounded by an assembly of disciples and followed by a host of Bodhisattvas, will stand before them at their hour of death, and they will depart this life with tranquil minds. After their death they will be born in the world Sukhavati, in the Buddha country of the same Amitayus, the Tathagata. Therefore, then, O Sariputra, having perceived this cause and effect, I with reverence say thus, Every son and every daughter of a family ought with their whole mind to make fervent prayer for that Buddha country.

'And now, O Sariputra, as I here at present glorify that world, thus in the East, O Sariputra, other blessed Buddhas, led by the Tathagata Akshobhya, the Tathagata Merudhvaja, the Tathagata Mahameru, the Tathagata Meruprabhasa, and the Tathagata Manjudhvaja, equal in number to the sand of the river Ganga, comprehend their own Buddha countries in their speech, and then reveal them. Accept this repetition of the law, called the "Favour of all Buddhas," which magnifies their inconceivable excellences.

'Thus also in the South do other blessed Buddhas, led by the Tathagata Chandrasuryapradipa, the Tathagata Yasahprabha, the Tathagata Maharchiskandha, the Tathagata Merupradipa, the Tathagata Anantavirya, equal in number to the sand of the river Ganga, comprehend their own Buddha countries in their speech, and then reveal them.

'Thus also in the West do other blessed Buddhas, led by the Tathagata Amitayus, the Tathagata Amitaskandha, the Tathagata Amitadhvaja, the Tathagata Mahaprabha, the Tathagata Maharatnaketu, the Tathagata Shuddharashmiprabha, equal in number to the sand of the river Ganga, comprehend, their own Buddha countries.'

'Thus also in the North do other blessed Buddhas, led by the Tathagata Maharchiskandha, the Tathagata Vaisvanaranirghosha, the Tathagata Dundubhisvaranirghosha, the Tathagata Dushpradharsha, the Tathagata Adityasambhava, the Tathagata Jaleniprabha, the Tathagata Prabhakara, equal in number to the sand of the river Ganga comprehend their own Buddha countries.

'Thus also in the Nadir do other blessed Buddhas, led by the Tathagata Simha, the Tathagata Yasas, the Tathagata Yashahprabhava, the Tathagata Dharma, the Tathagata Dharmadhara, the Tathagata Dharmadhvaja, equal in number to the sand of the river Ganga comprehend their own Buddha countries.

'Thus also in the Zenith do other blessed Buddhas, led by the Tathagata Brahmaghosha, the Tathagata Nakshatraraja, the Tathagata Indraketudhvajaraja, the Tathagata Gandhottama, the Tathagata Gandhaprabhasa, the Tathagata Maharchiskandha, the Tathagata Ratnakusumasampushpitagatra, the Tathagata Salendraraja, the Tathagata Ratnotpalasri, the Tathagata Sarvarthadarsa, the Tathagata Sumerukalpa, equal in number to the sand of the river Ganga comprehend their own Buddha countries.

'Now what do you think, O Sariputra, for what reason

is that repetition of the Law called the Favour of all Buddhas? Every son or daughter of a family who shall hear the name of that repetition of the Law and retain in their memory the names of those blessed Buddhas, will be favoured by the Buddhas, and will never return again, being once in possession of the transcendent true knowledge. Therefore, then, O Sariputra, believe, accept, and do not doubt of me and those blessed Buddhas!

'Whatever sons or daughters of a family shall make mental prayer for the Buddha country of that blessed Amitayus, the Tathagata, or are making it now or have made it formerly, all these will never return again, being once in possession of the transcendent true knowledge. They will be born in that Buddha country, have been born, or are being born now. Therefore, then, O Sariputra, mental prayer is to be made for that Buddha country by faithful sons and daughters of a family.

'And as I at present magnify here the inconceivable excellences of those blessed Buddhas, thus, O Sariputra, do those blessed Buddhas magnify my own inconceivable excellences.

'A very difficult work has been done by Syamuni, the sovereign of the Shakyas. Having obtained the transcendent true knowledge in this world, he taught the Law which all the world is reluctant to accept, during this corruption of the present kalpa, during this corruption of mankind, during this corruption of belief, during this corruption of life, during this corruption of passions.

'This is even for me, O Sariputra, an extremely difficult work that, having obtained the transcendent true knowledge in this world, I taught the Law which all the world is reluctant to accept, during this corruption of mankind, of belief, of passion of life, and of this present kalpa.'

Thus spoke Bhagavat joyful in his mind. And the honourable Sariputra, and the Bhikshus and Bodhisattvas, and the whole world with the gods, men, evil spirits and genii, applauded the speech of Bhagavat.

7

Mahaparinibbana Sutta

The Last Days and Teachings

Buddha at Rajagaha

Thus have I heard. The Blessed One was once dwelling in Rajagaha, on the hill called the Vulture's Peak. Now at that time Ajatasattu, the son of the queen-consort of Videha origin, the king of Magadha, was desirous of attacking the Vajjians; and he said to himself, 'I will root out these Vajjians, mighty and powerful though they be, I will destroy these Vajjians, I will bring these Vajjians to utter ruin!'

So he spake to the Brahmin Vassakara, the prime minister of Magadha, and said:

'Come now, O Brahmin, do you go to the Blessed One, and bow down in adoration at his feet on my behalf, and enquire in my name whether he is free from illness and suffering, and in the enjoyment of ease and comfort, and vigorous health. Then tell him that Ajatasattu, son of the Vedehi, the king of Magadha, in his eagerness to attack the Vajjians, has resolved, "I will root out these Vajjians, mighty and powerful though they be, I will destroy these Vajjians, I will bring these Vajjians to utter ruin!" And bear carefully in mind whatever the Blessed One may predict, and repeat it to me. For the Buddhas speak nothing untrue!'

Then the Brahmin Vassakara hearkened to the words

of the king, saying, 'Be it as you say.' And ordering a number of magnificent carriages to be made ready, he mounted one of them, left Rajagaha with his train, and went to the Vulture's Peak, riding as far as the ground was passable for carriages, and then alighting and proceeding on foot to the place where the Blessed One was. On arriving there he exchanged with the Blessed One the greetings and compliments of friendship and civility, sat down respectfully by his side and then delivered to him the message as the king had commanded.

Now at that time the venerable Ananda was standing behind the Blessed One, and fanning him. And the Blessed One said to him: 'Have you heard, Ananda, that the Vajjians hold full and frequent public assemblies?'

'Lord, so I have heard,' replied he.

'So long, Ananda,' rejoined the Blessed One, 'as the Vajjians hold these full and frequent public assemblies; so long may they be expected not to decline, but to prosper.'

And in like manner questioning Ananda, and receiving a similar reply, the Blessed One declared as follows the other conditions which would ensure the welfare of the Vajjian confederacy:

'So long, Ananda, as the Vajjians meet together in concord, and rise in concord, and carry out their undertakings in concord—so long as they enact nothing not already established, abrogate nothing that has been already enacted, and act in accordance with the ancient institutions of the Vajjians as established in former days—so long as they honour and esteem and revere and support the Vajjian elders, and hold it a point of duty to hearken to their words—so long as no women or girls belonging to their clans are detained among them by force or abduction—so long as they honour and esteem and revere and support the Vajjian shrines in town or country, and allow not the proper offerings and rites, as formerly given and performed, to fall into destitution—so long as the rightful protection, defence, and support shall be fully provided for the Arahats among them, so that Arahats from a distance may enter the realm, and the Arahats therein may live at ease—so long may the Vajjians be expected not to decline, but to prosper.'

Then the Blessed One addressed Vassakara the Brahmin, and said:

'When I was once staying, O Brahmin, at Vesali at the Sarandada Temple, I taught the Vajjians these conditions of welfare; and so long as those conditions shall continue to exist among the Vajjians, so long as the Vajjians shall be well instructed in those conditions, so long may we expect them not to decline, but to prosper.'

'We may expect then,' answered the Brahmin, 'the welfare and not the decline of the Vajjians when they are possessed of any one of these conditions of welfare, how much more so when they are possessed of all the seven. So, Gotama, the Vajjians cannot be overcome by the king of Magadha; that is, not in battle, without diplomacy or breaking up their alliance. And now, Gotama, we must go; we are busy, and have much to do.'

'Whatever you think most fitting, O Brahmin,' was the reply. And the Brahmin Vassakara, delighted and pleased with the words of the Blessed One, rose from his seat and went his way.

Conditions of Welfare

Now soon after he had gone the Blessed One addressed the venerable Ananda, and said: 'Go now, Ananda, and assemble in the Service Hall such of the brethren as live in the neighbourhood of Rajagaha.'

And he did so; and returned to the Blessed One, and informed him, saying:

'The company of the brethren, Lord, is assembled, let the Blessed One do as seemeth to him fit.'

And the Blessed One arose, and went to the Service Hall; and when he was seated, he addressed the brethren, and said:

'I will teach you, O mendicants, seven conditions of the

welfare of a community. Listen well and attend, and I will speak.'

'Even so, Lord,' said the brethren, in assent, to the Blessed One; and he spake as follows:

'So long, O mendicants, as the brethren meet together in full and frequent assemblies—so long as they meet together in concord, and rise in concord, and carry out in concord the duties of the order—so long as the brethren shall establish nothing that has not been already prescribed, and abrogate nothing that has been already established, and act in accordance with the rules of the order as now laid down—so long as the brethren honour and esteem and revere and support the elders of experience and long standing, the fathers and leaders of the order, and hold it a point of duty to hearken to their words—so long as the brethren fall not under the influence of that craving which, springing up within them, would give rise to renewed existence—so long as the brethren delight in a life of solitude—so long as the brethren so train their minds that good and holy men shall come to them, and those who have come shall dwell at ease—so long may the brethren be expected not to decline, but to prosper. So long as these seven conditions shall continue to exist among the brethren, so long as they are well-instructed in these conditions, so long may the brethren be expected not to decline, but to prosper.

'Other seven conditions of welfare will I teach you, O brethren. Listen well, and attend, and I will speak.'

And on their expressing their assent, he spake as follows:

'So long as the brethren shall not engage in, or be fond of, or be connected with business—so long as the brethren shall not be in the habit of, or be fond of, or be partakers in idle talk—so long as the brethren shall not be addicted to, or be fond of, or indulge in slothfulness—so long as the brethren shall not frequent, or be fond of, or indulge in society—so long as the brethren shall neither have, nor fall under the influence of, sinful desires—so long as the brethren shall not become the friends, companions, or intimates of sinners—so long as the brethren shall not come to a stop on their way to Nirvana because they have attained to any lesser thing—so long may the brethren be expected not to decline, but to prosper.'

'So long as these conditions shall continue to exist among the brethren, so long as they are instructed in these conditions, so long may the brethren be expected not to decline, but to prosper.'

'Other seven conditions of welfare will I teach you, O brethren. Listen well, and attend, and I will speak.'

And on their expressing their assent, he spake as follows:

'So long as the brethren shall be full of faith, modest in heart, afraid of sin, full of learning, strong in energy, active in mind, and full of wisdom, so long may the brethren be expected not to decline, but to prosper.'

'So long as these conditions shall continue to exist among the brethren, so long as they are instructed in these conditions, so long may the brethren be expected not to decline, but to prosper.'

'Other seven conditions of welfare will I teach you, O brethren. Listen well, and attend, and I will speak.'

And on their expressing their assent, he spake as follows:

'So long as the brethren shall exercise themselves in the sevenfold higher wisdom, that is to say, in mental activity, search after truth, energy, joy, peace, earnest contemplation, and equanimity of mind, so long may the brethren be expected not to decline, but to prosper.'

'So long as these conditions shall continue to exist among the brethren, so long as they are instructed in these conditions, so long may the brethren be expected not to decline, but to prosper.'

'Other seven conditions of welfare will I teach you, O brethren. Listen well, and attend, and I will speak.'

And on their expressing their assent, he spake as follows:

'So long as the brethren shall exercise themselves in the sevenfold perception due to earnest thought, that is to say, the perception of impermanency, of non-individuality, of corruption, of the danger of sin, of sanctification, of purity of heart, of Nirvana, so long may the brethren be expected not to decline, but to prosper.'

'So long as these conditions shall continue to exist among the brethren, so long as they are instructed in these conditons, so long may the brethren be expected not to decline, but to prosper.'

'Six conditions of welfare will I teach you, O brethren. Listen well, and attend, and I will speak.'

And on their expressing their assent, he spake as follows:

'So long as the brethren shall persevere in kindness of action, speech, and thought amongst the saints, both in public and in private—so long as they shall divide without partiality, and share in common with the upright and the holy, all such things as they receive in accordance with the just provisions of the order, down even to the mere contents of a begging bowl—so long as the brethren shall live among the saints in the practice, both in public and in private, of those virtues which, unbroken, intact, unspotted, unblemished, are productive of freedom, and praised by the wise; which are untarnished by the desire of future life, or by the belief in the efficacy of outward acts; and which are conducive to high and holy thoughts—so long as the brethren shall live among the saints, cherishing, both in public and in private, that noble and saving faith which leads to the complete destruction of the sorrow of him who acts according to it—so long may the brethren be expected not to decline, but to prosper.'

'So long as these six conditions shall continue to exist among the brethren, so long as they are instructed in these six conditions, so long may the brethren be expected not to decline, but to prosper.'

And whilst the Blessed One stayed there at Rajagaha on the Vulture's Peak he held that comprehensive religious talk with the brethren on the nature of upright conduct, and of earnest contemplation, and of intelligence. 'Great is the fruit, great the advantage of earnest contemplation when set round with upright conduct. Great is the fruit, great the advantage of intellect when set round with earnest contemplation. The mind set round with intelligence is freed from the great evils, that is to say, from sensuality, from individuality, from delusion, and from ignorance.'

Now when the Blessed One had sojourned at Rajagaha as long as he pleased, he addressed the venerable Ananda, and said: 'Come, Ananda, let us go to Ambalatthika.'

'So be it, Lord!' said Ananda in assent, and the Blessed One, with a large company of the brethren, proceeded to Ambalatthika.

There the Blessed One stayed in the king's house and held that comprehensive religious talk with the brethren on the nature of upright conduct, and of earnest contemplation, and of intelligence. 'Great is the fruit, great the advantage of earnest contemplation when set round with upright conduct. Great is the fruit, great the advantage of intellect when set round with earnest contemplation. The mind set round with intelligence is freed from the great evils, that is to say, from sensuality, from individuality, from delusion, and from ignorance.

With Sariputta at Nalanda

Now when the Blessed One had stayed as long as was convenient at Ambalatthika, he addressed the venerable Ananda, and said: 'Come, Ananda, let us go on to Nalanda.'

'So be it, Lord!' said Ananda, in assent, to the Blessed One.

Then the Blessed One proceeded, with a great company of the brethren, to Nalanda; and there, at Nalanda, the Blessed One stayed in the Pavarika mango grove.

Now the venerable Sariputta came to the place where the Blessed One was, and having saluted him, took his seat respectfully at his side and said: 'Lord! such faith have I in the Blessed One, that methinks there never has been, nor will there be, nor is there now any other, whether Samana or Brahman, who is greater and wiser than the Blessed One, that is to say, as regards the higher wisdom.'

'Grand and bold are the words of thy mouth, Sariputta: verily, thou hast burst forth into a song of ecstasy! of course then thou hast known all the Blessed Ones who in the long ages of the past have been Arahat Buddhas, comprehending their minds with yours, and aware what their conduct was, what their doctrine, what their wisdom, what their mode of life, and what salvation they attained to?'

'Not so, O Lord!'

'Of course then thou hast perceived all the Blessed Ones who in the long ages of the future shall be Arahat Buddhas comprehending in the same manner their whole minds with yours?'

'Not so, O Lord!"

'But at least then, O Sariputta, thou knowest me as the Arahat Buddha now alive, and hast penetrated my mind in the manner I have mentioned!'

'Not even that, O Lord!'

'You see then, Sariputta, that you know not the hearts of the Arahat Buddhas of the past and of the future. Why therefore are your words so grand and bold? Why do you burst forth into such a song of ecstasy?'

'O Lord! I have not the knowledge of the hearts of the Arahat Buddhas that have been, and are to come, and now are. I only know the lineage of the faith. Just, Lord, as a king might have a border city, strong in its foundations, strong in its ramparts and *toranas*, and with one gate alone; and the king might have a watchman there, clever, expert, and wise, to stop all strangers and admit only friends. And he, on going over the approaches all round the city, might not so observe all the joints and crevices in the ramparts of that city as to know where even a cat could get out. That might well be. Yet all living things of larger size that entered or left the city, would have to do so by that gate. Thus only is it, Lord, that I know the lineage of the faith. I know that the Arahat Buddhas of the past, putting away all lust, ill-will, sloth, pride, and doubt; knowing all those mental faults which make men weak; training their minds in the four kinds of mental activity; thoroughly exercising themselves in the sevenfold higher wisdom, received the full fruition of Enlightenment. And I know that the Arahat Buddhas of the times to come will do the same. And I know that the Blessed One, the Arahat Buddha of today, has done so now.'

There is the Pavarika mango grove the Blessed One held that comprehensive religious talk with the brethren on the nature of upright conduct, and of earnest contemplation, and of intelligence. 'Great is the fruit, great the advantage of earnest contemplation when set round with upright conduct. Great is the fruit, great the advantage of intellect when set round with earnest contemplation. The mind set round with intelligence is freed from the great evils, that is to say, from sensuality, from individuality, from delusion, and from ignorance.'

At Pataligama

'Now when the Blessed One had stayed as long as was convenient at Nalanda, he addressed the venerable Ananda, and said: 'Come, Ananda, let us go on to Pataligama.'

'So be it, Lord!' said Ananda, in assent, to the Blessed One.

Then the Blessed One proceeded, with a great company of the brethren, to Pataligama.

Now the disciples at Pataligama heard of his arrival there, and they went to the place where he was, took their seats respectfully beside him, and invited him to their village rest house. And the Blessed One signified, by silence, his consent.

Then the Pataligama disciples seeing that he had accepted the invitation, rose from their seats, and went away to the rest house, bowing to the Blessed One and keeping him on their right as they past him. On arriving there they made the rest house fit in every way for occupation, placed seats in it, set up a water-pot, and fixed an oil lamp. Then they returned to the Blessed One, and bowing, stood beside him, and said: 'All things are ready, Lord! It is time for you to do what you deem most fit.'

And the Blessed One robed himself, took his bowl and other things, went with the brethren to the rest house, washed his feet, entered the hall, and took his seat against the centre pillar, with his face towards the east. And the brethren also, after washing their feet, entered the hall, and took their seats round the Blessed One, against the western wall, and facing the east. And the Pataligama disciples too, after washing their feet, entered the hall, and took their seats opposite the Blessed One, against the eastern wall, and facing towards the west.

Then the Blessed One addressed the Pataligama disciples, and said: 'Fivefold, O householders, is the loss of the wrong-doer through his want of rectitude. In the first place the wrongdoer, devoid of rectitude, falls into great poverty through sloth; in the next place his evil repute gets noised abroad; thirdly, whatever society he enters—whether of Brahmins, nobles, heads of houses, or Samanas—he enters shyly and confused; fourthly, he is full of anxiety when he dies; and lastly, on the dissolution of the body, after death, he is reborn into some unhappy state of suffering or woe. This, O householders, is the fivefold loss of the evildoer!'

'Fivefold, O householders, is the gain of the welldoer through his practice of rectitude. In the first place the well-doer, strong in rectitude, acquires great wealth through his industry; in the next place, good reports of him are spread abroad; thirdly, whatever society he enters—whether of nobles, Brahmins, heads of houses, or members of the order—he enters confident and self-possessed; fourthly, he dies without anxiety; and lastly, on the dissolution of the body, after death, he is reborn into some happy state in heaven. This, O householders, is the fivefold gain of the welldoer.'

When the Blessed One had thus taught the disciples, and incited them, and roused them, and gladdened them, far into the right with religious discourse, he dismissed them, saying, 'The night is far spent, O householders. It is time for you to do what you deem most fit.' 'Even so, Lord!' answered the disciples of Pataligama, and they rose from their seats, and bowing to the Blessed One, and keepng him on their right hand as they passed him, they departed thence.

And the Blessed One, not long after the disciples of Pataligama had departed thence, entered into his private chamber.

At that time Sunidha and Vassakara, the chief ministers of Magadha, were building a fortress at Pataligama to repel the Vajjians, and there were a number of fairies who haunted in thousands the plots of ground there. Now, wherever ground is so occupied by powerful fairies, they bend the hearts of the most powerful kings and ministers to build dwelling places there, and fairies of middling and inferior power bend in a similar way the hearts of middling or inferior kings and ministers.

And the Blessed One, with his great and clear vision, surpassing that of ordinary men, saw thousands of those fairies haunting Pataligama. And he rose up very early in the morning, and said to Ananda: 'Who is it then, Ananda, who is building a fortress at Pataligama?'

'Sunidha and Vassakara, Lord, the chief ministers of Magadha, are building a fortress there to keep back the Vajjians.'

They act, Ananda, as if they had consulted with the Tavatimsa angels. And telling him of what he had seen, and of the influence such fairies had, he added: 'And among famous places of residence and haunts of busy men, this will become the chief, the city of Pataliputta, a centre for the interchange of all kinds of wares. But three dangers will hang over Pataliputta, that of fire, that of water, and that of dissension.'

Now Sunidha and Vassakara, the chief ministers of Magadha, proceeded to the place where the Blessed One was. And when they had come there they exchanged with the Blessed One the greetings and compliments of friendship and civility, and stood there respectfully on one side. And, so standing, Sunidha and Vassakara, the chief ministers of Magadha, spake thus to the Blessed One:

'May the Venerable Gotama do us the honour of taking his meal, together with the company of the brethren, at our house today.' And the Blessed One signified, by silence, his consent.

Then when Sunidha and Vassakara, the chief ministers of Magadha, perceived that he had given his consent, they returned to the place where they dwelt. And on arriving there, they prepared sweet dishes of boiled rice, and cakes; and informed the Blessed One, saying:

'The hour of food has come, O Gotama, and all is ready.'

And the Blessed One robed himself early, took his bowl with him and repaired with the brethren to the dwelling-place of Sunidha and Vassakara, and sat down on the seat prepared for him. And with their own hands they set the sweet rice and the cakes before the brethren with the Buddha at their head, and waited on them till they had had enough. And when the Blessed One had finished eating his meal, the ministers brought a low seat, and sat down respectfully at his side.

And when they were thus seated the Blessed One gave thanks in these verses:

Wheresoe'er the prudent man shall take up his abode.
Let him support there good and upright men of self-control.
Let him give gifts to all such deities as may be there.
Revered, they will revere him: honoured, they honour

him again;

Are gracious to him as a mother to her own, her only son.

And the man who has the grace of the gods, good fortune he beholds.'

And when he had thanked the ministers in these verses he rose from his seat and departed thence. And they followed him as he went, saying. 'The gate the Samana Gotama goes out by today shall be called Gotama's Gate, and the ferry at which he crosses the river shall be called Gotama's Ferry.' And the gate he went out at was called Gotama's Gate.

Swims across the Ganges

But the Blessed One went on to the river. And at that time the river Ganges was brimful and overflowing; and wishing to cross to the opposite bank, some began to seek for boats, some for rafts of wood, while some made rafts of basket-work. Then the Blessed One as instantaneously as a strong man would stretch forth his arm, or draw it back again when he had stretched it forth, vanished from this side of the river, and stood on the further bank with the company of the brethren.

And the Blessed One beheld the people looking for boats and rafts, and as he beheld them be brake forth at that time into this song:

'They who cross the ocean drear
Making a solid path across the pools—
Whilst the vain world ties its basket rafts—
These are the wise, these are the saved indeed!'

Now the Blessed One addressed the venerable Ananda, and said: 'Come, Ananda, let us go on to Kotigama.'

'So be it, Lord!' said Ananda, in assent, to the Blessed One.'

The Blessed One proceeded with a great company of the brethren to Kotigama: and there he stayed in the village itself.

And at that place the Blessed One addressed the brethren, and said: 'It is through not understanding and grasping four Noble Truths, O brethren, that we have had to run so long, to wander so long in this weary path of transmigration, both you and I!'

'And what are these four?'

'The Noble Truth about sorrow; the Noble truth about the cause of sorrows; the Noble Truth about the cessation of sorrow; and the Noble Truth about the path that leads to that cessation. But when these Noble truths are grasped and known the craving for existence is rooted out, that which leads to renewed existence is destroyed, and then there is no more birth!'

Thus spake the Blessed One; and when the Happy One had thus spoken, then again the Teacher said:

'By not seeing the four Noble Truths as they really are,
Long is the path that is traversed through many a birth;
When these are grasped, the cause of birth is then removed,
The root of sorrow rooted out, and there is no more birth.'

There too, while staying at Kotigama, the Blessed One held that comprehensive religious discourse with the brethren on the nature of upright conduct, and of earnest contemplation, and of intelligence. 'Great is the fruit, great the advantage of earnest contemplation when set round with upright conduct. Great is the fruit, great the advantage of intellect when set round with earnest contemplation. The mind set round with intelligance is freed from the great evils,—that is to say, from sensuality, from individuality, from delusion, and from ignorance.'

Now when the Blessed One had remained as long as was convenient at Kotigama, he addressed the venerable

Ananda, and said: 'Come, Ananda, let us go on to the villages of Nadika.'

'So be it, Lord!' said Ananda, in assent, to the Blessed One.

And the Blessed proceeded to the villages of Nadika with a great company of the brethren; and there, at Nadika, the Blessed One stayed at the Brick Hall.

And the venerable Ananda went to the Blessed One and paid him reverence and took his seat beside him. And when he was seated, he addressed the Blessed One, and said: 'The brother named Salha has died at Nadika, Lord. Where has he been reborn, and what is his destiny? The sister named Nanda has died, Lord, at Nadika. Where is she reborn, and what is her destiny?' And in the same terms he enquired concerning the devout Sudatta, and the devout lady Sugata, the devout Kakudha, and Kalinga, and Nikata, and Katissabha, and Tuttha, and Santuttha, and Bhadda, and Subhadda.

'The brother named Salha, Ananda, by the destruction of the great evils has by himself, and in this world, known and realised and attained to Arahatship, and to emancipation of heart and to emancipation of mind. The sister named Nanda, Ananda, has, by the complete destruction of the five bonds that bind people to this world, become an inheritor of the highest heavens, there to pass entirely away, thence never to return. The devout Sudatta, Ananda, by the complete destruction of the three bonds, and by the reduction to a minimum of lust, hatred, and delusion has become a Sakadagamin, who on his first return to this world will make an end of sorrow. The devout woman Sujata, Ananda, by the complete destruction of the three bonds, has become converted, is no longer liable to be reborn in a state of suffering, and is assured of final salvation. The devout Kakudha, Ananda, by the complete destruction of the five bonds that bind people to these lower worlds of lust, has become an inheritor of the highest heavens, there to pass entirely away, thence never to return. So also is the case with Kalinga,

Nikata, Katissabha, Tuttha, Santuttha, Bhadda, and Subhadda, and with more than fifty devout men of Nadika. More than ninety devout men of Nadika, who have died, Ananda, have by the complete destruction of the three bonds, and by the reduction of lust, hatred, and delusion, become Sakadagamins, who on their first return to this world will make an end of sorrow. More than five hundred devout men of Nadika who have died, Ananda, have by the complete destruction of the three bonds become converted, are no longer liable to be reborn in a state of suffering, and are assured of final salvation.'

'Now there is nothing strange in this, Ananda, that a human being should die, but that as each one does so you should come to the Buddha, and enquire about them in this manner, that is wearisome to the Buddha. I will, therefore, teach you a way of truth, called the Mirror of Truth, which if an elect disciple possess he may himself predict of himself, "Hell is destroyed for me, and rebirth as an animal, or a ghost, or in any place of woe. I am converted, I am no longer liable to be reborn in a state of suffering, and am assured of final salvation."

'What then, Ananda, is this Mirror of Truth? It is the consciousness that the elect disciple is in this world possessed of faith in the Buddha—believing the Blessed One to be the Holy One, the Fully-enlightened One, Wise, Upright, Happy, World-knowing, Supreme, the Bridler of men's wayward hearts, the Teacher of gods and men, the Blessed Buddha. And that he the disciple is possessed of faith in the Truth—believing the truth to have been proclaimed by the Blessed One, of advantage in this world, passing not away, welcoming all, leading to salvation, and to be attained to by the wise, each one for himself. And that he, the disciple, is possessed of faith in the Order—believing the multitude of the disciples of the Blessed One who are walking in the four stages of the noble eightfold path, the righteous, the upright, the just, the law-abiding—believing this church of the Buddha to be worthy of honour, of hospitality, of gifts, and of reverence; to be the supreme sowing ground of merit for the world; to be possessed of the virtues beloved by the good, virtues unbroken, intact, unspotted, unblemished virtues which make men truly free, virtues which are praised by the wise, are untarnished by the desire of future life or by the belief in the efficacy of outward acts, and are conducive to high and holy thought.'

'This, Ananda, is the way, the mirror of truth, which if an elect disciple possess he may himself predict of himself: "Hell is destroyed for me; and rebirth as an animal, or a ghost, or in any place of woe. I am converted; I am no longer liable to be reborn in a state of suffering, and am assured of final salvation." '

There, too, at the Brick Hall at Nadika the Blessed One addressed to the brethren that comprehensive religious discourse on the nature of upright conduct, and of earnest contemplation, and of intelligence.

'Great is the fruit, great the advantage of earnest contemplation when set round with upright conduct. Great is the fruit, great the advantage of intellect when set round with earnest contemplation. The mind set round with intelligence is freed from the great evils, that is to say, from sensuality, from individuality, from delusion, and from ignorance.'

Eats at Ambapali's

Now when the Blessed One had remained as long as he wished at Nadika, he addressed Ananda, and said: 'Come, Ananda, let us go on to Vesali.'

'So be it, Lord!' said Ananda, in assent, to the Blessed One.

Then the Blessed One proceeded, with a great company of the brethren, to Vesali; and there at Vesali the Blessed one stayed at Ambapali's grove.

Now there the Blessed One addressed the brethren, and said: 'Let a brother, O mendicants, be mindful and thoughtful;

this is our instruction to you.'

'And how does a brother become mindful?'

'Herein, O mendicants, let a brother, as he dwells in the body, so regard the body that he, being strenuous, thoughtful, and mindful, may, whilst in the world, overcome the grief which arises from bodily craving—while subject to sensations, let him continue so to regard the sensations that he, being strenuous, thoughtful, and mindful, may, whilst in the world, overcome the grief arising from the craving which follows our sensation—and so also as he thinks or reasons or feels let him overcome the grief which arises from the craving due to ideas, or reasoning, or feeling.'

'And how does a brother become thoughtful?'

''He acts, O mendicants, in full presence of mind whatever he may do, in going out and coming in, in looking and watching, in bending in his arm or stretching it forth, in wearing his robes or carrying his bowl, in eating and drinking, in consuming or tasting, in walking or standing or sitting, in sleeping or waking, in talking and in being silent.

'Thus let a brother, O mendicants, be mindful and thoughtful; this is our instruction to you.'

Ambapali invites to a meal

Now the courtesan Ambapali heard that the Blessed One had arrived at Vesali, and was staying at her mango grove. And ordering a number of magnificent vehicles to be made ready, she mounted one of them, and proceeded with her train towards her garden. She went in the carriage as far as the ground was passable for carriages; there she alighted; and she proceeded on foot to the place where the Blessed One was, and took her seat respectfully on one side. And when she was thus seated the Blessed One instructed, aroused, incited, and gladdened her with religious discourse.

Then she—instructed, aroused, incited, and gladdened with his words—addressed the Blessed One, and said:

'May the Blessed One do me the honour or taking his meal, together with the brethren, at my house tomorrow.'

And the Blessed One gave, by silence, his consent. Then when Ambapali the courtesan saw that the Blessed One had consented, she rose from her seat and bowed down before him, and keeping him on her right hand as she past him, she departed thence.

Now the Lichchhavis of Vesali heard that the Blessed One had arrived at Vesali, and was staying at Ambapali's grove. And ordering a number of magnificent carriages to be made ready, they mounted one of them and proceeded with their train to Vesali. Some of them were dark, dark in colour, and wearing dark clothes and ornaments: some of them were fair, fair in colour, and wearing light clothes and ornaments: some of them were red, ruddy in colour, and wearing red clothes and ornaments: some of them were white, pale in colour, and wearing white clothes and ornaments.

And Ambapali drove up against the young Lichchhavis, axle to axle, wheel to wheel, and yoke to yoke, and the Lichchhavis said to Ambapali the courtesan, 'How is it, Ambapali, that thou drivest up against us thus?'

'My Lords, I have just invited the Blessed One and his brethren for their morrow's meal,' said she.

'Ambapali! give up this meal to us for a hundred thousand,' said they.

'My Lords, were you to offer all Vesali with its subject territory, I would not give up so honourable a feast!'

Then the Lichchhavis cast up their hands, exclaiming, 'We are outdone by this mango girl! we are outreached by this mango girl!' and they went on to Ambapali's grove.

When the Blessed One saw the Lichchhavis approaching in the distance, he addressed the brethren, and said:

'O brethren, let those of the brethren who have never seen the Tavatimsa gods, gaze upon this company of the

Lichchhavis, behold this company of the Lichchhavis, compare this company of the Lichchhavis—even as a company of Tavatimsa gods.'

And when they had ridden as far as the ground was passable for carriages, the Lichchhavis alighted there, and then went on on foot to the place where the Blessed One was, and took their seats respectfully by his side. And when they were thus seated the Blessed One instructed and roused and incited and gladdened them with religious discourse.

Then they instructed and roused and incited and gladdened with his words, addressed the Blessed One, and said, 'May the Blessed One do us the honour of taking his meal, together with the brethren, at our house tomorrow.'

'O Lichchhavis, I have promised to dine tomorrow with Ambapali the courtesan,' was the reply.

Then the Lichchhavis cast up their hands, exclaiming, 'We are outdone by this mango girl! we are outreached by this mango girl!' And expressing their thanks and approval of the words of the Blessed One, they rose from their seats and bowed down before the Blessed One, and keeping him on their right hand as they past him, they departed thence.

And at the end of the night Ambapali the curtesan made ready in her mansion sweet rice and cakes, and announced the time to the Blessed One, saying, 'The hour, Lord, has come, and the meal is ready!''

And the Blessed One robed himself early in the morning, and took his bowl, and went with the brethren to the place where Ambapali's dwelling house was: and when he had come there he seated himself on the seat prepared for him. And Ambapali the courtesan set the sweet rice and cakes before the order, with the Buddha at their head, and waited upon them till they refused any more.

And when the Blessed One had quite finished his meal, the courtesan had a low stool brought, and sat down at his side, and addressed the Blessed One, and said: 'Lord, I present this mansion to the order of mendicants,

of which the Buddha is the chief.' And the Blessed One accepted the gift; and after instructing, and rousing, and inciting, and gladdening her with religious discourse, he rose from his seat and departed thence.

While at Ambapali's mango grove the Blessed One held that comprehensive religious discourse with the disciples on the nature of upright conduct, and of earnest contemplation, and of intelligence: 'Great is the fruit, great the advantage of earnest contemplation when set round with upright conduct. Great is the fruit, great the advantage of intellect when set round with earnest contemplation. The mind set round with intelligence is freed from the great evils, that is to say, from sensuality, from individuality, from delusion, and from ignorance.'

Now when the Blessed one had remained as long as he wished at Ambapali's grove, he addressed Ananda, and said: 'Come, Ananda, let us go on to Beluva.'

'So be it, Lord,' said Ananda, in assent, to the Blessed One.

Then the Blessed One proceeded, with a great company of the brethren, to Beluva, and there the Blessed One stayed in the village itself.

Now the Blessed one there addressed the brethren, and said: 'O mendicants, do you take up your abode round about Vesali, each according to the place where his friends, intimates, and close companions may live, for the rainy season of Vassa. I shall enter upon the rainy season here at Beluva.'

'So be it, Lord!' said those brethren, in assent to the Blessed One. And they entered upon the rainy season round about Vesali, each according to the place where his friends or intimates or close companions lived: whilst the Blessed One stayed even there at Beluva.

Buddha is Sick

Now when the Blessed One had thus entered upon the rainy season, there fell upon him a dire sickness, and sharp pains came upon him, even unto death. But the Blessed One, mindful and self-possessed, bore them without complaint.

Then this thought occurred to the Blessed One, 'It would not be right for me to pass away from existence without addressing the disciples, without taking leave of the Order. Let me now, by a strong effort of the will, bend this sickness down again, and keep my hold on life till the allotted time be come.'

And the Blessed One, by a strong effort of the will, bent that sickness down again, and kept his hold on life till the time he fixed upon should come. And the sickness abated upon him.

Now very soon after the Blessed One began to recover; when he had quite got rid of the sickness, he went out from the monastery, and sat down behind the monastery on a seat spread out there. And the venerable Ananda went to the place where the Blessed One was, and saluted him, and took a seat respectfully on one side, and addressed the Blessed One, and said: 'I have beheld, Lord, how the Blessed One was in health, and I have beheld how the Blessed One had to suffer. And though at the sight of the sickness of the Blessed One my body became weak as a creeper, and the horizon became dim to me, and my faculties were no longer clear, yet notwithstanding I took some little comfort from the thought that the Blessed One would not pass away from existence until at least he had left instructions as touching the order.'

'What, then, Ananda? Does the order expect that of me? I have preached the truth without making any distinction between exoteric and esoteric doctrine: for in respect of the truths, Ananda, the Tathagata has no such thing as the closed fist of a teacher, who keeps some things back. Surely, Ananda, should there be any one who harbours the thought, "It is I who will lead the brotherhood," or, "The order is dependent upon me," it is he who should lay down instructions in any matter concerning the order. Now the Tathagata, Ananda, thinks not that it is he who should lead the brotherhood, or that the order is dependent upon him. Why then should he leave instructions in any matter concerning the order? **I too, O Ananda, am now grown old, and full of years, my journey is drawing to its close, I have reached my sum of days, I am turning eighty years of age; and just as a worn-out cart, Ananda, can only with much additional care be made to move along, so, methinks, the body of the Tathagata can only be kept going with much additional care.** It is only, Ananda, when the Tathagata, ceasing to attend to any outward thing, or to experience any sensation, becomes plunged in that devout meditation of heart which is concerned with no material object—it is only then that the body of the Tathagata is at ease.

'Therefore, O Ananda, **be ye lamps unto yourselves. Be ye a refuge to yourselves. betake yourselves to no external refuge. Hold fast to the truth as a lamp. Hold fast as a refuge to the truth. Look not for refuge to any one besides yourselves.** And how, Ananda, is a brother to be a lamp unto himself, a refuge to himself, betaking himself to no external refuge, holding fast to the truth as a lamp, holding fast as a refuge to the truth, looking not for refuge to any one besides himself?

'Herein, O Ananda, let a brother, as he dwells in the body, so regard the body that he, being strenuous, thoughtful, and mindful, may, whilst in the world, overcome the grief which arises from bodily craving—while subject to sensations let him continue so to regard the sensations that he, being strenuous, thoughtful, and mindful, may whilst in the world, overcome the grief which arises from the sensations—and so, also, as he thinks, or reasons, or feels, let him overcome the grief which arises from the craving due to ideas, or to reasoning, or to feeling.

'And whosoever, Ananda, either now or after I am dead, shall be a lamp unto themselves, and a refuge unto themselves, shall betake themselves to no external refuge, but holding fast to the truth as their lamp, and holding fast as their refuge to the truth, shall look not for refuge to any one besides themselves—it is they, Ananda, among my bhikshus, who shall reach the very topmost height!—but they must be anxious to learn.'

Now the Blessed One robed himself early in the morning, and taking his bowl in the robe, went into Vesali for alms, and when he returned he sat down on the seat prepared for him, and after he had finished eating the rice he addressed the venerable Ananda, and said: 'Take up the mat, Ananda; I will go to spend the day at the Chapala Chetiya.'

'So be it, Lord!' said the venerable Ananda, in assent, to the Blessed One. And taking up the mat he followed step for step behind the Blessed One.

So the Blessed One proceeded to the Chapala Chetiya, and when he had come there he sat down on the mat spread out for him, and the venerable Ananda took his seat respectfully beside him. Then the Blessed One addrssed the venerable Ananda, and said: 'How delightful a spot, Ananda, is Vesali, and the Udena Chetiya, and the Gotamaka Chetiya, and the Sattambaka Chetiya, and the Bahuputta Chetiya, and the Sarandada Chetiya, and the Chapala Chetiya.

'Ananda! whosoever has thought out, developed, practised, accumulated, and ascended to the very heights of the four paths to Iddhi, and so mastered them as to be able to use them as a means of mental advancement, and as a basis for edification, he, should he desire it, could remain in the same birth for a kalpa, or for that portion of the kalpa which had yet to run. Now the Tathagata has thought them out, and thoroughly practised and developed them [in all respects as just more fully described], and he could, therefore, should he desire it, live on yet for a kalpa, or for that portion of the kalpa which has yet to run.'

But even though a suggestion so evident and a hint so clear were thus given by the Blessed One, the venerable

Ananda was incapable of comprehending them; and he besought not the Blessed One saying, 'Vouchsafe, Lord, to remain during the kalpa! Live on through the kalpa, O Blessed One! for the good and the happiness of the great multitudes, out of pity for the world, for the good and the gain and the weal of gods and men!' So far was his heart possessed by the Evil One.

A second and a third time did the Blessed One say the same thing, and a second and a third time was Ananda's heart thus hardened.

Now the Blessed One addressed the venerable Ananda, and said: 'You may leave me, Ananda, awhile, and do whatever seemeth to thee fit.'

'So be it, Lord!' said the venerable Ananda, in assent, to the Blessed One, and rising from his seat he saluted the Blessed One, and passing him on the right, sat down at the foot of a certain tree not far off thence.

'Pass away now'–says Mara

Now not long after the venerable Ananda had been gone, Mara, the Evil One, approached the Blessed One, and stood beside him. And so standing there, he addressed the Blessed One in these words:

'Pass away now, Lord, from existence; let the Blessed One now die. Now is the time for the Blessed One to pass away—even according to the word which the Blessed One spoke when he said: "I shall not die, O Evil One! until the brethren and sisters of the order, and until the lay-disciples of either sex shall have become true hearers, wise and well-trained, ready and learned, versed in the Scriptures, fulfilling all the greater and the lesser duties, correct in life, walking according to the precepts—until they, having thus themselves learned the doctrine, shall be able to tell others of it, preach it, make it known, establish it, open it, minutely explain it and make it clear—until they, when others start vain doctrine, shall be able by the truth to vanquish and refute it, and so to spread the wonder-working truth abroad!"

'And now, Lord, the brethren and sisters of the order and the lay-disciples of either sex have become all this, are able to do all this. Pass away now therefore, Lord, from existence; let the Blessed One now die! The time has come for the Blessed One to pass away—even according to the word which he spake when he said, "I shall not die, O Evil One! until this pure religion of mine shall have become successful, prosperous, widespread, and popular in all its full extent—until, in a word, it shall have been well proclaimed to men." And now, Lord, this pure religion of thine has become all this. Pass away now therefore, Lord, from existence; let the Blessed One now die! The time has come for the Blessed One to pass away!'

And when he had thus spoken, the Blessed One addressed Mara, the Evil One, and said: 'O Evil One! make thyself happy, the final extinction of the Tathagata shall take place before long. At the end of three months from this time the Tathagata will die!'

Thus the Blessed One while at the Chapala Chetiya deliberately and conscioulsy rejected the rest of his allotted sum of life. And on his so rejecting it there arose a mighty earthquake, awful and terrible, and the thunders of heaven burst forth. And when the Blessed One beheld this, he broke out at that time into this hymn of exultation:

'His sum of life the sage renounced,
The cause of life immeasurable or small;
With inward joy and calm, he broke,
Like coat of mail, his life's own cause!'

Now the following thought occurred to the venerable Ananda: 'Wonderful indeed and marvellous is it that this mighty earthquake should arise, awful and terrible, and that the thunders of heaven should burst forth! What may be the proximate, what the remote cause of the appearance of this earthquake?'

Then the venerable Ananda went up to the place where the Blessed One was, and did obeisance to the Blessed One, and seated himself respectfully at one side, and said: 'Wonderful indeed and marvellous is it that this mighty earthquake should arise, awful and terrible, and that the thunders of heaven should burst forth! What may be the proximate, what the remote cause of the appearance of his earthquake?'

'Eight are the proximate, eight the remote causes, Ananda, for the appearance of a mighty earthquake. What are the eight? This great earth, Ananda, is established on water, the water on wind, and the wind rests upon space. And at such a time, Ananda, as the mighty winds blow, the waters are skaken by the mighty winds as they blow, and by the moving water the earth is shaken. These are the first causes, proximate and remote, of the appearance of a mighty earthquake.

'Again, Ananda, a Samana or a Brahmin of great intellectual power, and who has the feelings of his heart well under his control; or a god or fairy of great might and power,—when such a one by intense meditation of the finite idea of earth or the infinte idea of water has succeeded in realising the comparative value of things he can make this earth move and tremble and be shaken violently. These are the second causes, proximate or remote, of the appearance of a mighty earthquake.

'Again, Ananda, when a Bodhisatta consciously and deliberately leaves his temporary form in the heaven of delight and descends into his mother' womb, then is this earth made to quake and tremble and is skaken violently. These are the third causes, proximate or remote, of the appearance of a mighty earthquake.

'Again, Ananda, when a Bodhisatta deliberately and consciously quits his mother's womb, then the earth quakes and trembles and is shaken violently. This is the fourth cause, proximate and remote, of the appearance of a mighty earthquake.

'Again, Ananda, when a Tathagata arrives at the supreme and perfect enlightenment, then this earth quakes and trembles and is shaken violently. This is the fifth cause, proximate and remote, of the appearance of a mighty earthquake.

"Again, Ananda, when a Tathagata founds the sublime kingdom of righteousness, then this earth quakes and trembles and is shaken violently. This is the sixth cause, proximate and remote, of the appearance of a mighty earthquake.

'Again, Ananda, when a Tathagata consciously and deliberately rejects the remainder of his life, then this earth quakes and trembles and is shaken violently. This is the seventh cause, proximate and remote, of the appearance of a mighty earthquake.

'Again, Ananda, when a Tathagata passes entirely away with that utter passing away in which nothing whatever is left behind, then this earth quakes and trembles and is shaken violently. This is the eighth cause, proximate and remote, of the appearance of a mighty earthquake.'

The Eight Kinds

'Now of eight kinds, Ananda, are these assemblies. Which are the eight? Assemblies of nobles, Brahmins, householders, and Samanas, and the angel hosts of the Guardian Angels, the Great Thirty-Three, Mara, and Brahma.

'Now I call to mind, Ananda, how when I used to enter into an assembly of many hundred nobles, before I had seated myself there or talked to them or started a conversation with them, I used to become in colour like unto their colour, and in voice like unto their voice. Then with religious discourse I used to instruct, incite, and quicken them, and fill them with gladness. But they knew me not when I spoke, and would say, "Who may this be who thus speaks? a man or a god?" Then having instructed, incited, quickened, and gladdened them with religious discourse I would vanish away.

But they knew me not even when I vanished away; and would say, "Who may this be who has thus vanished away? a man or a god?" '

And in the same words the Blessed One spake of how he had been used to enter into assemblies of each of the other of the eight kinds, and of how he had not been made known to them either in speaking or in vanishing away. 'Now these, Ananda, are the eight assemblies.'

'Now these, Ananda, are the eight positions of mastery over the delusion arising from the apparent permanence of external things. What are the eight?

'When a man having subjectively the idea of form sees externally forms which are finite, and pleasant or unpleasant to the sight, and having mastered them, is conscious that he knows and sees—this is the first position of mastery.

'When a man having subjectively the idea of form sees externally forms which are boundless, and pleasant or unpleasant to the sight, and having mastered them, is conscious that he knows and sees—this is the second position of mastery.

'When a man without the subjective idea of form sees externally forms which are finite, and pleasant or unpleasant to the sight, and having mastered them, is conscious that he knows and sees—this is the third position of mastery.

'When a man without the subjective idea of form sees externally forms which are boundless, and pleasant or unpleasant to the sight, and having mastered them, is conscious that he knows and sees—this is the fourth position of mastery.

'When a man without the subjective idea of form sees externally forms that are blue in colour, blue in appearance, and reflecting blue,—just, for instance, as the Umma flower is blue in colour, blue in appearance, and reflecting blue; or, again, as that fine muslin of Benares which, on whichever side you look at it, is blue in colour, blue in appearance, and reflecting blue,—when a man without the subjective idea of form sees externally forms which, just in that way, are blue, blue in colour, blue in appearance, and reflecting blue, and having mastered them, is conscious that he knows and sees—that is the fifth position of mastery.

'The sixth, seventh, and eight positions of mastery are explained in words identical with those used to explain the fifth; save that yellow, red, and white are respectively substituted throughout for blue; and the Kanikara flowers, the Bandhu-jivaka flower, and the morning star are respectively substituted for the Umma flower, as the first of the two objects given as examples.

'Now these stages of deliverance, Ananda, from the hindrance to thought arising from the sensations and ideas due to external forms, are eight in number. Which are the eight?

'A man possessed with the idea of form sees forms—this is the first stage of deliverance.

'Without the subjective idea of form, he sees forms externally—this is the second stage of deliverance.

'With the thought "it is well," he becomes intent upon what he sees—this is the third stage of deliverance.'

'By passing quite beyond all idea of form, by putting an end to all idea of resistance, by paying no attention to the idea of distinction, he, thinking "it is all infinite space," reaches mentally and remains in the state of mind in which the idea of the infinity of space is the only idea that is present—this is the fourth stage of deliverance.

'By passing quite beyond all idea of space being the infinite basis, he, thinking "it is all infinite reason," reaches mentally and remains in the state of mind to which the infinity of reason is alone present—this is the fifth stage of deliverance.

'By passing quite beyond the mere consciousness of the infinity of reason, he, thinking "nothing at all exists," reaches mentally and remains in the state of mind to which nothing at all is specially present—this is the sixth stage of deliverance.

'By passing quite beyond all idea of nothingness he reaches mentally and remains in the state of mind to which neither ideas nor the absence of ideas are specially present—this is the seventh stage of deliverance.

'By passing quite beyond the state of "neither ideas nor the absence of ideas" he reaches mentally and remains in the state of mind in which both sensations and ideas have ceased to be—this is the eighth stage of deliverance.

'Now these, Ananda, are the eight stages of deliverance.'

'I'll die after three months'

'On one occasion, Ananda, I was resting under the shepherd's Nigrodha tree on the bank of the river Neranjarna immediately after having reached the great enlightenment. Then Mara, the Evil One, came, Ananda, to the place where I was and standing beside me he addressed me in the words: "Pass away now, Lord, from existence! Let the Blessed One now die! Now is the time for the Blessed One to pass away!"

'And when he had thus spoken, Ananda, I addressed Mara, the Evil One and said: "I shall not die, O Evil One! until not only the brethren and sisters of the order, but also the lay-disciples of either sex shall have become true bearers, wise and well-trained, ready and learned, versed in the Scriptures, fulfilling all the greater and the lesser duties, correct in life, walking according to the precepts—until they, having thus themselves learned the doctrine, shall be able to tell others of it, preach it, make it known, establish it, open it, minutely explain it and make it clear—until they, when others start vain doctrine, shall be able by the truth to vanquish and refute it, and so to spread the wonder-working truth abroad!

' "I shall not die until this pure religion of mine shall have become successful, prosperous, widespread, and popular in all its full extent—until, in a word, it shall have been well proclaimed among men!"

'And now again today, Ananda, at the Chapala Chetiya, Mara, the Evil One, came to the place where I was, and standing beside me addressed me in the same words.

'And when he had thus spoken, Ananda, I answered him and said: "Make thyself happy, the final extinction of the Tathagata shall take place before long. At the end of three months from this time the Tathagata will die!'

'Thus, Ananda, the Tathagata has now today at the Chapala Chetiya consciously and deliberately rejected the rest of his allotted term of life.'

And when he had thus spoken the venerable Ananda addressed the Blessed One, and said: 'Vouchsafe, Lord, to remain during the kalpa! live on through the kalpa, O Blessed One! for the good and the happiness of the great multitudes, out of pity for the world, for the good and the gain and the weal of gods and men!'

'Enough now, Ananda, beseech not the Tathagata!' was the reply. 'The time for making such request is past.'

And again, the second time, the venerable Ananda besought the Bleessed One in the same words. And he received from the Blessed One the same reply.

And again, the third time, the venerable Ananda besought the Blessed One in the same words.

'Hast thou faith, Ananda, in the wisdom of the Tathagata?'

'Even so, Lord!'

'Now why, then, Ananda, dost thou trouble the Tathagata even until the third time?'

'From his own mouth have I heard from the Blessed One, from his own mouth have I received this saying, "Whosoever has thought out, Ananda, and developed, practised, accumulated, and ascended to the very heights of the four paths to saintship, and so mastered them as to be able to use them as a means of mental advancement, and as a basis for edification—he, should he desire it, could remain in the same birth for a kalpa, or for that portion of a kalpa which has yet to run." Now the Tathagata has thought out and thoroughly practised them in all respects as just now fully described, and might, should he desire it, remain alive, for a kalpa, or for that portion of a kalpa which has yet to run.

'Hast thou faith, Ananda?'

'Even so, Lord!'

'Then, O Ananda, thine is the fault, thine is the offence—in that when a suggestion so evident and a hint so clear were thus given thee by the Tathagata, thou wast yet incapable of comprehending them, and thou besoughtest not the Tathagata, saying, "Vouchsafe, Lord, to remain during the kalpa. Live on, O Blessed One! through the kalpa for the good and the happiness of the great multitudes, out of pity for the world, for the good and the gain and the weal of gods and men." If thou shouldst then have so besought the Tathagata, the Tathagata might have rejected the appeal even to the second time, but the third time he would have granted it. Thine, therefore, O Ananda, is the fault, thine is the offence!

'On one occasion, Ananda, I was dwelling at Rajagaha, on the hill called the Vulture's Peak. Now there, Ananda, I spoke to thee, and said: "How pleasant a spot, Ananda, is Rajagaha; how pleasant is this Vulture's Peak. Whosoever has thought out, Ananda, and developed, practised, accumulated, and ascended to the very heights of the four paths to saintship, and so mastered them as to be able to use them as a means of mental advancement, and so as basis for edification—he, should he desire it, could remain in the same birth for a kalpa, or for that portion of a kalpa which has yet to run. But even when a suggestion so evident and a hint so clear were thus given thee by the Tathagata, thou wast yet incapable of comprehending them, and thou besoughtest not the Tathagata, saying, "Vouchsafe, Lord, to remain during the kalpa. Live on, O Blessed One! through the kalpa for the good and the happiness of the great multitudes, out of pity for the world, for the good and the gain and the weal of gods and men." If thou shouldst then have so besought the Tathagata, the Tathagata might have rejected the appeal even to the second time, but the third time he would have granted it. Thine, therefore, O Ananda, is the fault, thine is the offence!

'On one occasion, Ananda, I was dwelling at that same Rajagaha in the Banyan Grove—on one occasion at that same

Rajagaha at the Robbers' Cliff—on one occasion at that same Rajagaha in the Sattapanni cave on the slope of Mount Vebhara—on one occasion at that same Rajagaha at the Black Rock on the slope of Mount Isigili—on one occasion at that same Rajagaha in the Sitavana Grove in the mountain cave Sappasondika—on one occasion at that same Rajagaha in the Tapoda Grove—on one occasion at that same Rajagaha in the Bambu Grove in the Squirrels' Feeding Ground—on one occasion at that same Rajagaha in Jivaka's Mango Grove—on one occasion at that same Rajagaha in the Deer Forest at Maddakuchchhi.

'Now there too, Ananda, I spoke to thee, and said: "How pleasnt, Ananda, is Rajagaha; how pleasant the Vulture's Peak; how pleasnt the Banyan tree of Gotama; how pleasant the Robbers' Cliff; how pleasant the Sattapanni cave on the slope of Mount Vebhara; how pleasant the Black Rock on the slope of Mount Isigili; how pleasant the mountain cave Sappasondika in the Sitavana Grove; how pleasant the Tapoda Grove; how pleasant the Squirrels' Feeding Ground in the Bambu Grove; how pleasant Jivaka's Mango Grove; how pleasant the Deer Forest at Maddakuchchhi!

' "Whosoever, Ananda, had thought out and developed, practised, accumulated, and ascended to the very heights of the four paths to saintship, and so mastered them as to be able to use them as a means of mental advancement and as a basis for edification—he, should he desire it, could remain in the same birth for a kalpa, or for that portion of a kalpa which has yet to run." Now the Tathagata has thought out and thoroughly practised them in all respects as just now fully described, and might, should he desire it, remain alive for a kalpa, or for that portion of a kalpa which has yet to run.

'On one occasion, Ananda, I was residing here at Vesali at the Udena Chetiya. And there too, Ananda, I spoke to thee, and said: "How pleasant, Ananda, is Vesali; how pleasant the Udena Chetiya. Whosoever, Ananda, has thought out and developed, practised, accumulated, and ascended to the very heights of the four paths to saintship, and so mastered them as to be able to use them as a means of mental advancement and as a basis for edification—he, should he desire it, could remain in the same birth for a kalpa, or for that portion of a kalpa which has yet to run." Now the Tathagata has thought out and thoroughly practised them and might, should he desire it, remain alive for a kalpa, or for that portion of a kalpa which has yet to run.

'On one occasion, Ananda, I was dwelling here at Vesali at the Gotamaka Chetiya—on one occasion here at Vesali at the Sattamba Chetiya—on one occasion here at Vesali at the Bahuputta Chetiya—on one occasion here at Vesali at the Sarandada Chetiya and on each occasion I spoke to thee, Ananda, in the same words.

'And now today, Ananda, at the Chapala Chetiya, I spoke to thee, and said: "How pleasant, Ananda, is Vesali; how pleasant the Udena Chetiya; how pleasant the Gotamaka Chetiya; how pleasant the Sattamba Chetiya; how pleasant the Bahuputta Chetiya; how pleasant the Sarandada Chetiya. Whosoever, Ananda, has thought out and developed, practised, accumulated, and ascended to the very heights of the four paths to saintship, and so mastered them as to be able to use them as a means of mental advancement, and as a basis for edification—he, should he desire it, could remain in the same birth for a kalpa, or for that portion of a kalpa which has yet to run. Now the Tathagata has thought and thoroughly practised them in all respects as just now fully descrbed, and might, should he desire it, remain alive for a kalpa, or for that portion of a kalpa which has yet to run." '

'But now, Ananda, have I not formerly declared to you that it is in the very nature of all things, near and dear unto us, that we must divide ourselves from them, leave them, sever ourselves from them? How then, Ananda, can this be possible—whereas anything whatever born, brought into being, and organised, contains within itself the inherent necessity of dissolution—how then can this be possible that such a being should not be dissolved? No such condition can exist! And this mortal being, Ananda, has been relinquished, cast away, renounced, rejected, and abandoned by the Tathagata. The remaining sum of life has been surrendered by him. Verily, the word has gone forth from the Tathagata, saying, "The final extinction of the Tathagata shall take place before long. At the end of three months from this time the Tathagata will die!" That the Tathagata for the sake of living should repent him again of that saying—this can no wise be!'

'Come, Ananda, let us go to the Kutagara Hall, to the Mahavana.'

'Even so, Lord!' said the venerable Ananda, in assent, to the Blessed One.

Then the Blessed One proceeded, with Ananda with him, to the Mahavana to the Kutagara Hall: and when he had arrived there he addressed the venerable Ananda, and said:

'Go now, Ananda, and assemble in the Service Hall such of the brethren as reside in the neighbourhood of Vesali.'

'Even so, Lord,' said the venerable Ananda, in assent, to the Blessed One. And when he had assembled in the Service Hall such of the brethren as resided in the neighbourhood of Vesali, he went to the Blessed One and saluted him and stood beside him. And standing beside him, he addressed the Blessed One, and said:

'Lord! the assembly of the brethren has met together. Let the Blessed One do even as seemeth to him fit.'

Then the Blessed One proceeded to the Service Hall, and sat down there on the mat spread out for him. And when he was seated the Blesed One addressed the brethren, and said:

'Therefore, O brethren—ye to whom the truths I have perceived have been made known by me—having thoroughly made yourselves masters of them, practise them, meditate upon them, and spread them abroad; in order that pure religion may last long and be perpetuated, in order that it may continue to be for the good and happiness of the great multitudes, out of pity for the world, to the good and the gain and the weal of gods and men!

'Which then, O brethren, are the truths which, when I had perceived, I made known to you, which, when you have mastered it behoves you to practise, meditate upon, and spread abroad, in order that pure religion may last long and be perpetuated, in order that it may continue to be for the good and the happiness of the great multitudes, out of pity for the world, to the good and the gain and the weal for gods and men?

'They are these:
The four earnest meditations.
The fourfold great struggle against sin.
The four roads to saintship.
The five moral powers.
The five organs of spiritual sense.
The seven kinds of wisdom, and
The noble eightfold path.

'These, O brethren, are the truth which, when I had perceived, I made known to you, which, when you have mastered it behoves you to practise, meditate upon, and spread abroad, in order that pure religion may last long and be perpetuated, in order that it may continue to be for the good and the happiness of the great multitudes, out of pity for the world, to the good and the gain and the weal of gods and men!'

And the Blessed One exhorted the brethren, and said:

'Behold now, O brethren, I exhort you, saying, "All component things must grow old. Work out your salvation with diligence. The final extinction of the Tathagata will take place before long. At the end of three months from this time the Tathagata will die!"

'My age is now full ripe, my life draws to its close:
I leave you, I depart, relying on myself alone!

Be earnest then, O brethren! holy, full of thought!
Be steadfast in resolve! Keep watch o'er your own hearts!
Who wearies not, but holds fast to this truth and law,
Shall cross this sea of life, shall make an end of grief.'

THE LAST DISCOURSES

Now the Blessed One early in the morning robed himself, and taking his bowl, entered Vesali for alms: and when he had passed through Vesali, and had eaten his meal and was returning from his alms-seeking he gazed at Vesali with an elephant look and addressed the venerable Ananda, and said: 'This will be the last time, Ananda, that the Tathagata will behold Vesali. Come, Ananda, let us go on to Bhandagama.'

'Even so, Lord!' said the venerable Ananda, in assent, to the Blessed One.

And the Blessed One proceeded with a great company of the brethren to Bhandagama; and there the Blessed One stayed in the village itself.

There the Blessed One addressed the brethren, and said: 'It is through not understanding and grasping four truths, O brethren, that we have had to run so long, to wander so long in this weary path of transmigration—both you and I.

'And what are these four? The noble conduct of life, the noble earnestness in meditation, the noble kind of wisdom and the noble salvation of freedom. But when noble conduct is realised and known, when noble meditation is realised and known, when noble wisdom is realised and known, when noble freedom is realised and known—then is the craving for existence rooted out, that which leads to renewed existence is destroyed, and there is no more birth.'

Thus spake the Blessed One; and when the Happy One had thus spoken, then again the teacher said:

'Righteousness, earnest thought, wisdom, and freedom sublime—

These are the truths realised by Gotama, far renowened.

Knowing them, he, the knower, proclaimed the truth to the brethren.

The master with eye divine, the quencher of griefs, must die!'

There too, while staying at Bhandagama, the Blessed One held that comprehensive religious discourse with the brethren on the nature of upright conduct, and of earnest contemplation, and of intelligence. 'Great is the fruit, great the advantage of earnest contemplation when set round with upright conduct. Great is the fruit, great the advantage of intellect when set round with earnest contemplation. The mind set round with intelligence is freed from the great evils—that is to say, from sensuality, from individuality, from delusion, and from ignorance.'

Now when the Blessed One had remained at Bhandagama as long as he desired, he addressed the venerable Ananda, and said: 'Come, Ananda, let us go on to Hatthigama.'

'Even so, Lord!' said Ananda, in assent, to the Blessed One.

Then the Blessed One proceeded with a great company of the brethren to Hatthigama.

And in similar words it is then related how the Blessed One went on to Ambagama, to Jambugama, and to Bhoganagara.

The Four Great References

Now there at Bhoganagara the Blessed One stayed at the Ananda Chetiya.

There the Blessed One addressed the brethren, and said: 'I will teach you, O brethren, these four Great References. Listen thereto, and give good heed, and I will speak.'

'Even so, Lord!' said the brethren, in assent, to the Blessed One, and the Blessed One spoke as follows:

'In the first place, brethren, a brother may say thus: "From the mouth of the Blessed One himself have I heard, from his own mouth have I received it. This is the truth, this the law, this the teaching of the Master." The word spoken, brethren, by that brother should neither be received with praise nor treated with scorn. Without praise and without scorn every word and syllable should be carefully understood, and then put beside the scripture and compared with the rules of the order. If when so compared they do not harmonise with the scripture, and do not fit in with the rules of the order, then you may come to the conclusion, "Verily, this is not the word of the Blessed One, and has been wrongly grasped by that brother?" Therefore, brethren, you should reject it. But if they harmonise with the scripture and fit in with the rules of the order, then you may come to the conclusion, "Verily, this is the word of the Blessed One, and has been well grasped by that brother." This, brethren, you should receive as the first Great Reference.

'Again, brethren, a brother may say thus: "In such and such a dwelling-place there is a company of the brethren with their elders and leaders. From the mouth of that company have I heard, face to face have I received it. This is the truth, this the law, this the teaching of the Master." The word spoken, brethren, by that brother should neither be received with praise nor treated with scorn. Without praise and without scorn every word and syllable should be carefully understood, and then put beside the scripture and compared with the rules of the order. If when so compared they do not harmonise with the scripture, and do not fit in with the rules of the order, then you may come to the conclusion, "Verily, this is not the word of the Blessed One, and has been wrongly grasped by that company of the brethren." Therefore, brethren, you should reject it. But if they harmonise with the scripture and fit in with the rules of the order, then you may come to the conclusion, "Verily, this is the word of the Blessed One, and has been well grasped by that company of the brethren." This, brethren, you should receive as the second Great Reference.

'Again, brethren, a brother may say thus: "In such and such a dwelling-place there are dwelling many elders of the order, Deeply read, holding the faith as handed down by tradition, versed in the truths, versed in the regulations of the order, versed in the summaries of the doctrines and the law. From the mouth of those elders have I heard, from their mouth have I received it. This is the truth, this the law, this the teaching of the Master." The word spoken, brethren, by that brother should neither be received with praise nor treated with scorn. Without praise and without scorn every word and syllable should be carefully understood, and then put beside the scripture and compared with the rules of the order. If when so compared they do not harmonise with the scripture, and do not fit in with the rules of the order, then you may come to the conclusion, "Verily, this is not the word of the Blessed One, and has been wrongly grasped by those elders." Therefore, brethren, you should reject it. But if they harmonise with the scripture and fit in with the rules of the order, then you may come to the conclusion, "Verily, this is the word of the Blessed One, and has been well grasped by those elders." This brethren, you should receive as the third Great Reference.

'Again, brethren, a brother may say, "In such and such a dwelling-place there is living a brother, deeply read, holding the faith as handed down by tradition, versed in the truths, versed in the regulations of the order, versed in the summaries of the doctrines and the law. From the mouth of that elder have I heard, from his mouth have I received it. This is the truth, this the law, this the teaching of the Master." The word spoken, brethren, by that brother should neither be received with praise nor treated with scorn. Without praise and without scorn every word and syllable should be carefully understood, and then put beside the scripture and compared with the rules of the order. If when so compared they do not harmonise with the scripture., and do not fit in with the rules of the order, then you may come to the conclusion, "Verily, this is not the word of the Blessed One, and has been wrongly grasped by the brother." Therefore, brethren, you should reject it. But if they harmonise with the scripture and fit in with the rules of the order, then you may come to the conclusion, "Verily, this is the word of the Blessed One, and has been well grasped by that brother." This, brethren, you should receive as the fourth Great Reference.

'These, brethren, are the Four Great References.'

There, too, the Blessed One held that comprehensive religious talk with the brethren on the nature of upright conduct, and of earnest contemplation, and of intelligence. 'Great is the fruit, great the advantage of earnest contemplation when set round with upright conduct. Great is the fruit, great the advantage of intellect when set round with earnest contemplation. The mind set round with intelligence is freed from the great evils—that is to say, from sensuality, from individuality, from delusion, and from ignorance.'

Now when the Blessed One had remained as long as he desired at Bhogagama, he addressed the venerable Ananda, and said: 'Come, Ananda, let us go on to Pava.'

'Even so, Lord!' said the venerable Ananda, in assent, to the Blessed One. And the Blessed One proceeded with a great company of the brethren to Pava.

And there at Pava the Blessed One stayed at the Mango Grove of Chunda, who was by family a smith.

Eats at the Smith's Home

Now Chunda, the worker in metals, heard that the Blessed One had come to Pava, and was staying there in his Mango Grove.

And Chunda, the worker in metals, went to the place where the Blessed One was, and saluting him took his seat respectufully on one side. And when he was thus seated, the Blessed One instructed, aroused, incited, and gladdened him with religious discourse.

Then he, instructed, aroused, incited, and gladdened by the religious discourse, addressed the Blessed One, and said: 'May the Blessed One do me the honour of taking his meal, together with the brethren, at my house tomorrow.'

And the Blessed One signified, by silence, his consent.

Then seeing that the Blessed One had consented, Chunda, the worker in metals, rose from his seat and bowed down before the Blessed One, and keeping him on his right hand as he past him, departed thence.

Now at the end of the night, Chunda, the worker in metals, made ready in his dwelling-place sweet rice and cakes, and a quantity of dried boar's flesh. And he announced the hour to the Blessed One, saying, 'The hour, Lord, has come, and the meal is ready.'

And the Blessed One robed himself early in the morning, and taking his bowl, went with the brethren to the dwelling-place of Chunda, the worker in metals. When he had come thither he seated himself on the seat prepared for him. And when he was seated he addressed Chunda, the worker in metals, and said: 'As to the dried boar's flesh you have made ready, serve me with it, Chunda; and as to the other food, the sweet rice and cakes, serve the brethren with it.'

'Even so, Lord!' said Chunda, the worker in metals, in assent, to tbe Blessed One. And the dried boar's flesh he had made ready he served to the Blessed one; whilst the other food, the sweet rice and cakes, he served to the members of the order.

Now the Blessed One addressed Chunda, the worker in metals, and said: 'Whatever dried boar's flesh, Chunda, is left over to thee, bury that in a hole. I see no one, Chunda, on earth nor in Mara's heaven, nor in Brahma's heaven, no one among Samanas and Brahmins, among gods and men, by whom, when he has eaten it, that food can be assimilated, save by the Tathagata.'

'Even so, Lord!' said Chunda, the worker in metals, in assent, to the Blessed One. And whatever dried boar's flesh remained over, that he buried in a hole.

And he went to the place where the Blessed One was; and when he had come there, took his seat respectfully on one side. And when he was seated, the Blessed One instructed and aroused and incited and gladdened Chunda, the worker in metals, with religious discourse. And the Blessed One then rose from his seat and departed thence.

Now when the Blessed One had eaten the food prepared by Chunda, the worker in metal, there fell upon him a dire sickness, the disease of dysentery, and sharp pain came upon him, even unto death. But the Blessed One, mindful and self-possessed, bore it without camplaint.

And the Blessed One addressed the venerable Ananda, and said: 'Come, Ananda, let us go on to Kusinara.'

'Even so, Lord!' said the venerable Ananda, in assent, to the Blessed One.

When he had eaten Chunda's food,
The coppersmith's—thus have I heard—
He bore with fortitude the pain,
The sharp pain even unto death!
And from the dried flesh of the boar,
as soon as he had eaten it,
There fell upon the teacher sickness dire,
Then after nature was relieved the Blessed One
announed and said:
'I am now going on to Kusinara.'

'I'm thirsty, Ananda'

Now the Blessed One went aside from the path to the foot of a certain tree; and when he had come there he addressed the venerable Ananda, and said: 'Fold, I pray you, Ananda, the robe; and spread it out for me. I am weary, Ananda, and must rest awhile!'

'Even so, Lord!' said the venerable Ananda, in assent,

to the Blessed One, and spread out the robe folded fourfold.

And the Blessed One seated himself on the seat prepared for him; and when he was seated, he addressed the venerable Ananda, and said: 'Fetch me, I pray you, Ananda, some water. I am thirsty, Ananda, and would drink.'

When he had thus spoken, the venerable Ananda said to the Blessed One: 'But just now, Lord, about five hundred carts have gone over. That water stirred up by the wheels has become shallow and flows fouled and turbid. This river Kakuttha, Lord, not far off, is clear and pleasant, cool and transparent, easy to get down into, and delightful. There the Blessed One may both drink the water, and cool his limbs.'

Again the second time the Blessed One addressed the venerable Ananda, and said: 'Fetch me, I pray you, Ananda, some water. I am thirsty, Ananda, and would drink.'

And again the second time the venerable Ananda said to the Blessed One: 'But just now, Lord, about five hundred carts have gone over. That water stirred up by the wheels has become shallow and flows fouled and turbid. This river Kakuttha, Lord, not far off, is clear and pleasant, cool and transparent, easy to get down into, and delightful. There the Blessed One may both drink the water, and cool his limbs.'

Again the third time the Blessed One addressed the venerable Ananda, and said: 'Fetch me, I pray you, Ananda, some water. I am thirsty, Ananda, and would drink.'

'Even so, Lord!' said the venerable Ananda, in assent, to the Blessed One; and taking a bowl he went down to the streamlet. And lo! the streamlet which, stirred up by the wheels, was but just now become shallow, and was flowing fouled and turbid, had begun, when the venerable Ananda came up to it, to flow clear and bright and free from all turbidity.

Then Ananda thought: 'How wonderful, how marvellous is the great might and power of the Tathagata! For this streamlet which, stirred up by the wheels, was but just now become shallow and flowing foul and turbid, now, as I come up to it, is flowing clear and bright and free from all turbidity.'

And taking water in the bowl he returned towards the Blessed One; and when he had come where the Blessed One was, he said to him: 'How wonderful, how marvellous is the great might and power of the Tathagata! For this streamlet which, stirred up by the wheels, was but just now become shallow and flowing foul and turbid, now, as I come up to it, is flowing clear and bright and free from all turbidity. Let the Blessed One drink the water! Let the Happy One drink the water!'

Then the Blessed One drank of the water.

'Make me your disciple, sir'

Now at that time a man named Pukkusa, a young Mallian, a disciple of Alara Kalama's, was passing along the high road from Kusinara to Pava.

And Pukkusa, the young Mallian, saw the Blessed One seated at the foot of a tree. On seeing him, he went up to the place where the Blessed One was, and when he had come there he saluated the Blessed One, and took his rest respectfully on one side. And when he was seated Pukkusa, the young Mallian, said to the Blessed One: 'How wonderful a thing is it, Lord! and how marvellous, that those who have gone forth out of the world should pass their time in a state of mind so calm!

'Formerly, Lord, Alara Kalama was once walking along the high road; and leaving the road he sat himself down under a certain tree to rest during the heat of the day. Now, Lord, five hundred carts passed by one after the other, each close to Alara Kalama. And a certain man, who was following close behind that caravan of carts, went up to the place where Alara Kalama was, and when he was come there he spake as follows to Alara Kalama:

' "But, Lord did you see those five hundred carts go by?"'

' "No, indeed, sir, I saw them not." '

' "But, Lord, did you hear the sound of them?"

' "No, indeed, sir, I heard not their sound."

' "But, Lord, were you then asleep?" '

' "No, sir, I was not asleep." '

' "But, Lord, were you then conscious?" '

' "Yes, I was conscious, sir." '

' "So that you, Lord, though you were both conscious and awake, neither saw, nor heard the sound of five hundred carts passing by, one after the other, and each close to you. Why, Lord, even your robe was sprinkled over with the dust of them!" '

' "It is even so, sir."

'Then thought that man: "How wonderful a thing is it, and how marvellous, that those who have gone forth out of the world should pass their time in a state of mind so calm! So much so that a man though being both conscious and awake, neither sees, nor hears the sound of five hundred carts passing by, one after the other, and each close to him."

'And after giving utterance to his deep faith in Alara Kalama, he departed thence.'

'Now what think you, Pukkusa, which is the more difficult thing either to do or to meet with—that a man being conscious and awake should neither see, nor hear the sound of five hundred carts passing by, one after the other, close to him,—or that a man, being conscious and awake, should neither see, nor hear the sound thereof when the falling rain goes on beating and splashing, and the lightnings are flashing forth, and the thunderbolts are crashing?'

'What in comparison, Lord, can these five hundred carts do, or six or seven or eight or nine or ten hundred, yea, even hundreds and thousands of carts. That certainly is more difficult, both to do and to meet with, that a man being conscious and awake should neither see, nor hear the sound thereof when the falling rain goes on beating and splashing, and the lightnings are flashing forth, and the thunderbolts are crashing.'

'Now on one occasion, Pukkusa, I was dwelling at Atuma, and was at the Threshing-floor. And at that time the falling rain begun to beat and to splash, and the lightnings to flash forth, and the thunderbolts to crash; and two peasants, brothers, and four oxen were killed. Then, Pukkusa, a great multitude of people went forth from Atuma, and went up to the place where the two peasants, brothers, and the four oxen, lay killed.

'Now at that time, Pukkusa, I had gone forth from the Threshing-floor, and was walking up and down thinking at the entrance to the Threshing-floor. And a certain man came, Pukkusa, out of that great multitude of people, up to the place where I was; and when he came up he saluted me, and took his place respectfully on one side.

'And as he stood there, Pukkusa, I said to the man: "Why then, sir, is this great multitude of people assembled together?"

' "But just now, the falling rain began to beat and to splash, and the lightnings to flash forth, and the thunderbolts to crash; and two peasants, brothers, were killed, and four oxen. Therefore is this great multitude of people gathered together. But where, Lord, were you?"

' "I, sir, have been here all the while." '

' "But, Lord, did you see it?" '

' "I, sir, saw nothing." '

' "But, Lord, did you hear it?" '

' "I, sir, heard nothing." '

' "Were you then, Lord, asleep?" '

' "I, sir, was not asleep." '

' "Were you then conscious, Lord?" '

' "Even so, sir." '

' "So that you, Lord, being conscious and awake, neither saw, nor heard the sound thereof when the falling rain went on beating and splashing, and the lightnings were flashing forth, and the thunderbolts were crashing." '

' "That is so, sir." '

'Then, Pukkusa, the thought occurred to that man: "How wonderful a thing is it, and marvellous that those who have gone forth out of the world should pass their time in a state of mind so calm!—so that a man being conscious and awake neither sees nor hears the sound thereof when the falling rain is beating and splashing, and the thunderbolts are crashing." And after giving utterance to his deep faith in me, he departed from me with the customary demonstrations of respect.'

And when he had thus spoken Pukkusa, the young Mallian, addressed the Blessed One in these words: 'Now I, Lord, as to the faith that I had in Alara Kalama, that I winnow away as in a mighty wind, and wash it away as in a swiftly running stream. Most excellent, Lord, are the words of thy mouth, most excellent! Just as if a man were to set up that which is thrown down, or were to reveal that which is hidden away, or were to point out the right road to him who has gone astray, or were to bring a lamp into the darkness, so that those who have eyes can see external forms—just even so, Lord, has the truth been made known to me, in many a figure, by the Blessed One. And I, even I, betake myself, Lord, to the Blessed One as my refuge, to the Truth, and to the Brotherhood. May the Blessed One accept me as a disciple, as a true believer, from this day forth, as long as life endures!'

Now Pukkusa, the young Mallian, addressed a certain man, and said: 'Fetch me, I pray you, my good man, a pair of robes of cloth of gold, burnished and ready for wear.'

'So be it, sir!' said that man, in assent, to Pukkusa, the young Mallian; and he brought a pair of robes of cloth of gold, burnished and ready for wear.

And the Mallian Pukkusa presented the pair of robes of cloth of gold, burnished and ready for wear, to the Blessed One, saying, 'Lord, this pair of robes of burnished cloth of gold is ready for wear. May the Blessed One show me favour and accept it at my hands!'

'In that case, Pukkusa, robe me in one, and Ananda in one.'

'Even so, Lord!' said Pukkusa, in assent, to the Blessed One; and in one he robed the Blessed One, and in one, Ananda.

Then the Blessed One instructed and aroused and incited

and gladdened Pukkusa, the young Mallian, with religious discourse. And Pakkusa, the young Mallian, when he had been instructed and aroused and incited and gladdened by the Blessed One with religious discourse, arose from his seat, and bowed down before the Blessed One; and keeping him on his right hand as he past him, departed thence.

Now not long after the Mallian Pukkusa had gone, the venerable Ananda placed that pair of robes of cloth of gold, burnished and ready for wear, on the body of the Blessed One, and when it was so placed on the body of the Blessed One it appeared to have lost its splendour!

And the venerable Ananda said to the Blessed One: 'How wonderful a thing is it, Lord, and how marvellous, that the colour of the skin of the Blessed One should be so clear, so exceeding bright! For when I placed even this pair of robes of burnished cloth of gold and ready for wear on the body of the Blessed One, lo! it seemed as if it had lost its splendour!'

'It is even so, Ananda, there are two occasions on which the colour of the skin of a Tathagata becomes clear and exceeding bright. What are the two?

'On the night, Ananda, on which a Tathagata attains to the supreme and perfect insight, and on the night in which he passes finally away in that utter passing away which leaves nothing whatever to remain—on these two occasions the colour of the skin of the Tathagata becomes clear and exceeding bright.

'And now this day, Ananda, at the third watch of the night, in the Upavattana of Kusinara, in the Sala Grove of the Mallians, between the twin Sala trees, the utter passing away of the Tathagata will take place. Come, Ananda! let us go on to the river Kukuttha.'

'Even so, Lord!' said the venerable Ananda, in assent, to the Blessed One.

The pair of robes of cloth of gold,
All burnished, Pukkusa had brought,

Clad on with them the Master then
Shone forth in colour like to gold!

Now the Blessed One with a great company of the brethren went on to the river Kuakuttha; and when he had come there, he went down into the water, and bathed, and drank. And coming up out again on the other side he went on to the Mango Grove.

And when he was come there he addressed the venerable Chundaka, and said: 'Fold, I pray you, Chundaka, a robe in four and spread it out. I am weary, Chundaka, and would lie down.'

'Even so, Lord!' said the venerable Chundaka, in assent, to the Blessed One. And he folded a robe in four, and spread it out.

And the Blessed One laid himself down on his right side, with one foot resting on the other; and calm and self-possessed, he meditated on the idea of rising up again in due time. And the venerable Chundaka seated himself there in front of the Blessed One.

The Buddha to Kakuttha's river came,
Whose clear and pleasant waters limpid flow,
He plunged beneath the stream wearied and worn,
The Buddha without equal in the world!
When he had bathed and drunk, the teacher then
Crossed o'er, the brethren thronging round his steps;
The Blessed Master, preaching the while the truth,
The Mighty Sage came to the Mango Grove.

There spake he to the brother Chundaka:
'Spread me the fourfold robe out as a couch.'
Cheered by the Holy One, he quickly spread
The fourfold robe in order on the ground.
The Master laid him down, wearied and worn;
And there, before him, Chunda took his seat.

And the Blessed One addressed the venerable Ananda, and said: 'Now it may happen, Ananda, that some one should stir up remorse in Chunda the smith, by saying, "This is evil to thee, Chunda, and loss to thee in that when the Tathagata had eaten his last meal from thy provision, then he died." Any such remorse, Ananda, in Chunda the smith should be checked by saying, "This is good to thee, Chunda, and gain to thee, in that when the Tathagata had eaten his last meal from thy provision, then he died. From the very mouth of the Blessed One, Chunda, have I heard, from his own mouth have I received this saying, 'These two offerings of food are of equal fruit, and of equal profit, and of much greater fruit and much greater profit than any other—and which are the two? The offering of food which, when a Tathagata has eaten, he attains to supreme and perfect insight; and the offering of food which, when a Tathagata has eaten, he passes away by that utter passing away in which nothing whatever remains behind—these two offerings of food are of equal fruit and of equal profit, and of much greater fruit and much greater profit than any others. There has been laid up by Chunda the smith a karma redounding to length of life, redounding to good birth, redounding to good fortune, redounding to good fame, redounding to the inheritance of heaven, and of sovereign power.' " In this way, Ananda, should be checked any remorse in Chunda the smith.'

Then the Blessed One perceiving how the matter stood, uttered, even at that time, this hymn of exultation:

The him who gives shall virtue be increased;
In him who curbs himself, no anger can arise;
The righteous man casts off all sinfulness,
And by the rooting out of lust, and bitterness,
And all delusion, doth to Nirvana reach!

Prepares to Pass Away

Now the Blessed One addressed the venerable Ananda, and said: 'Come, Ananda, let us go on to the Sala Grove of the Mallas, the Upavattana of Kusinara, on the further side of the river Hiranyavati.'

'Even so, Lord!' said the venerable Ananda, in assent, to the Blessed One.

And the Blessed One proceeded with a great company of the brethren to the Sala Grove of the Mallas, the Upavattana of Kusinara, on the further side of the river Hiranyavati: and when he had come there he addressed the venerable Ananda, and said:

'Spread over for me, I pray you, Ananda, the couch with its head to the north, between the twin Sala trees. I am weary, Ananda, and would lie down.'

'Even so, Lord!' said the venerable Ananda, in assent, to the Blessed One. And he spread a covering over the couch with its head to the north, between the twin Sala trees. And the Blessed One laid himself down on his right side, with one leg resting on the other; and he was mindful and self-possessed.

Now at that time the twin Sala trees were all one mass of bloom with flowers out of season; and all over the body of the Tathagata these dropped and sprinkled and scattered themselves, out of reverence for the successor of the Buddhas of old. And heavenly Mandarava flowers, too, and heavenly sandal-wood powder came falling from the sky, and all over the body of the Tathagata they descended and sprinkled and scattered themselves, out of reverence for the successor of the Buddhas of old. And heavenly music was sounded in the sky, out of reverence for the successor of the Buddhas of old. And heavenly songs came wafted from the skies, out of reverence for the successor of the Buddhas of old!

Then the Blessed One addressed the venerable Ananda, and said: 'The twin Sala trees are all one mass of bloom with flowers out of season; all over the body of the Tathagata these drop and sprinkle and scatter themselves, out of reverence for the successor of the Buddhas of old. And heavenly Mandarava flowers, too, and heavenly sandalwood powder come falling from the sky, and all over the body of the Tathagata they descend and sprinkle and scatter themselves, out of reverence for the successor of the Buddhas of old. And heavenly music sounds in the sky, out of reverence for the successor of the Buddhas of old. And heavenly songs come wafted from the skies, out of reverence for the successor of the Buddhas of old!'

'Now it is not thus, Ananda, that the Tathagata is rightly honoured, reverenced, venerated, held sacred or revered. But the brother or the sister, the devout man or the devout woman, who continually fulfils all the greater and the lesser duties, who is correct in life, walking according to the precepts—it is he who rightly honours, reverences; venerates, holds sacred, and reveres the Tathagata with the worthiest homage. Therefore, O Ananda, be ye constant in the fulfilment of the greater and of the lesser duties, and be ye correct in life, walking according to the precepts; and thus, Ananda, should it be taught.'

Now at that time the venerable Upavana was standing in front of the Blessed One, fanning him. And the Blessed One was not pleased with Upavana, and he said to him : 'Stand aside, O brother, stand not in front of me!'

Then this thought sprung up in the mind of the venerable Ananda: 'The venerable Upavana has long been in close personal attendance and service on the Blessed One. And now, at the last moment, the Blessed One is not pleased with Upavana, and has said to him, "Stand aside, O brother, stand not in front of me!" What may be the cause and what the reason that the Blessed One is not pleased with Upavana, and speaks thus with him?'

And the venerable Ananda said to the Blessed One: 'The venerable Upavana has long been in close personal attendance and service on the Blessed One. And now, at the last moment, the Blessed One is not pleased with Upavana, and has said to him, "Stand aside, O brother, stand not in front of me!" What may be the cause and what the reason that the Blessed One is not pleased with Upavana, and speaks thus with him?'

'Spirits want to see me passing away'

'In great numbers, Ananda, are the gods of the ten world-systems assembled together to behold the Tathagata. For twelve leagues, Ananda, around the Sala Grove of the Mallas, the Upavattana of Kusinara, there is no spot in size even as the pricking of the point of the tip of a hair which is not pervaded by powerful spirits. And the spirits, Ananda, are murmuring, and say, "From afar have we come to behold the Tathagata. Few and far between are the Tathagatas, the Arahat Buddhas who appear in the world: and now today, in the last watch of the night, the death of a Tathagata will take place; and this eminent brother stands in front of the Tathagata, concealing him, and in his last hour we are prevented from beholding the Tathagata;" thus, Ananda, do the spirits murmur.'

'But of what kind of spirits is the Blessed One thinking?'

'There are spirits, Ananda, in the sky, but of worldly mind, who dishevel their hair and weep, who stretch forth their arms and weep, who fall prostrate on the ground, and roll to and fro in anguish at the thought: "Too soon will the Blessed One die! Too soon will the Happy One pass away! Full soon will the Light of the world vanish away!"

'There are spirits, too, Ananda, on the earth, and of worldly mind, who tear their hair and weep, who stretch forth their arms and weep, who fall prostrate on the ground, and roll to and fro in anguish at the thought: "Too soon will the Blessed One die! Too soon will the Happy One pass away! Full soon will the Eye of the world disappear from sight!" '

'But the spirits who are free from passion bear it, calm

and self-possessed, mindful of the saying which begins, "Impermanent indeed are all component things. How then is it possible whereas anything whatever, when born, brought into being, and organised, contains within itself the inherent necessity of dissolution—how then is it possible that such a being should not be dissolved? No such condition can exist!" '

'In times past, Lord, the brethren, when they had spent the rainy season in different districts, used to come to see the Tathagata, and we used to receive those very reverend brethren to audience, and to wait upon the Blessed One. But, Lord, after the end of the Blessed One, we shall not be able to receive those very reverend brethren to audience, and to wait upon the Blessed One.'

The Four Places

'There are these four places, Ananda, which the believing man should visit with feelings of reverence and awe. Which are the four?

'The place, Ananda, at which the believing man can say, "Here the Tathagata was born!" is a spot to be visited with feelings of reverence and awe.

'The place, Ananda, at which the believing man can say, "Here the Tathagata attained to the supreme and perfect insight!" is a spot to be visited with feelings of reverence and awe.

'The place, Ananda, at which the believing man can say, "Here was the kingdom of righteousness set on foot by the Tathagata!" is a spot to be visited with feelings of reverence and awe.

'The place, Ananda, at which the believing man can say, "Here the Tathagata passed finally away in that utter passing away which leaves nothing whatever to remain behind!" is a spot to be visited with feelings of reverence and awe.

'And there will come, Ananda, to such spots, believers,

brethren and sisters of the order, or devout men and devout women, and will say, "Here was the Tathagata born!" or, "Here did the Tathagata attain to the supreme and perfect insight!" or, "Here was the kingdom of rightesouness set on foot by the Tathagata!" or, "Here the Tathagata passed away in that utter passing away which leaves nothing whatever to remain behind!"

'And they, Ananda, who shall die while they, with believing heart, are journeying on soul pilgrimage, shall be reborn after death, when the body shall dissolve, in the happy realms of heaven.'

'How are we to conduct overselves, Lord, with regard to womankind?'

'Don't see them, Ananda.'

'But if we should see them, what are we to do?'

'Abstain from speech, Ananda.'

'But if they should speak to us, Lord, what are we to do?'

'Keep wide awake, Ananda.'

About the Remains

'What are we to do, Lord, with the remains of the Tathagata?'

'Hinder not yourselves, Ananda, by honourng the remains of the Tathagata. Be zealous, I beseech you, Ananda, in your own behalf! Devote yourselves to your own good! Be earnest, be zealous, be intent on your own good! There are wise men, Ananda, among the nobles, among the Brahmins, among the heads of houses, who are firm believers in the Tathagata; and they will do due honour to the remains of the Tathagata.'

'What should be done, Lord, with the remains of the Tathagata?'

'As men treat the remains of a king of kings, so, Ananda, should they treat the remains of a Tathagata.'

'And how, Lord, do they treat the remains of a king of kings?'

'They wrap the body of a king of kings, Ananda, in

new cloth. When that is done they wrap it in carded cotton wool. When that is done they warp it in a new cloth,—and so on till they have wrapped the body in five hundred successive layers of both kinds. Then they place the body in an oil vessel of iron, and cover that close up with another oil vessel of iron. They then build a funeral pile of all kinds of perfumes, and burn the body of the king of kings. And then at the four cross roads they erect a dagaba to the king of kings. This, Ananda, is the way in which they treat the remains of a king of kings.

'And as they treat the remains of a king of kings, so Ananda, should they treat the remans of the Tathagata. At the four cross roads a dagaba should be erected to the Tathagata. And whosoever shall there place garlands or perfumes or paint, or make salutation there, or become in its presence calm in heart—that shall long be to them for a profit and a joy.

'These men, Ananda, worthy of a dagaba, are four in number. Which are the four?

'A Tathagata, or Arahat-Buddha, is worthy of a dagaba. A Pachcheka-Buddha is worthy of a dagaba. A true hearer of the Tathagata is worthy of dagaba. A king of kings is worthy of a dagaba.'

'And on account of what circumstance, Ananda, is a Tathagata, an Arahat-Buddha, worthly of a dagaba?'

'At the thought, Ananda, "This is the dagaba of that Blessed One, of that Arahat-Buddha," the hearts of many shall be made calm and happy; and since they there had calmed and satisfied their hearts they will be reborn after death, when the body has dissolved, in the happy realms of heaven. It is on account of this circumstance, Ananda, that a Tathagata, an Arahat-Buddha, is worthy of a dagaba.'

'And on account of what circumstance, Ananda, is a Pachcheka-Buddha worthy of a dagaba?'

'At the thought, Ananda, "This is the dagaba of that Blessed One, of that Pachcheka-Buddha," the hearts of many shall be made calm and happy; and since they there had clamed and satisfied their hearts they will be reborn after death, when the body has dissolved, in the happy realms of heaven. It is on account of this circumstance, Ananda, that a Pachcheka-Buddha is worthy of a dagaba.'

'And on account of what circumstance, Ananda, is a true hearer of the Blessed One, the Arahat-Buddha, worthy of a dagaba?'

'At the thought, Ananda, "This is the dagaba of that true hearer of the Blessed Arahat-Buddha," the hearts of many shall be made calm and happy; and since they there had calmed and satisfied their hearts they will be reborn after death, when the body has dissolved, in the happy realms of heaven. It is on account of this circumstance, Ananda, that a true hearer of the Blessed One, the Arahat-Buddha, is worthy of a dagaba.'

'And on account of what circumstance, Ananda, is a king of kings worthy of a dagaba?'

'At the thought, Ananda, "This is the dagaba of that righteous king who ruled in righteousness," the hearts of many shall be made calm and happy; and since they there had calmed and satisfied their hearts they will be reborn after death, when the body has dissolved, in the happy realms of heaven. It is on account of this circumstance, Ananda, that a king of kings is worthy of a dagaba.

'These four, Ananda, are the persons worthy of a dagaba.'

Ananda Weeps

'Now the venerable Ananda went into the Vihara, and stood leaning against the lintel of the door, and weeping at the thought: "Alas! I remain still but a learner, one who has yet to work out his own perfection. And the Master is about to pass away from me—he who is so kind!" '

Now the Blessed One called the brethren, and said: 'Where, then, brethren, is Ananda?'

The venerable Ananda, Lord, has gone into the Vihara, and stands leaning against the lintel of the door, and weeping at the thought: 'Alas! I remain still but a learner, one who has yet to work out his own perfection. And the Master is about to pass away from me—he who is so kind!'

And the Blessed One called a certain brother, and said: 'Go now, brother, and call Ananda in my name, and say, "brother Ananda, the Master calls for thee." '

'Even so, Lord!' said that brother, in assent, to the Blessed One. And he went up to the place where the Blessed One was; and when he had come there, he sad to the venerable Ananda: 'Brother Ananda, the Master calls for thee.'

'Very well, brother,' said the venerable Ananda, in assent, to that brother. And he went up to the place where the Blessed One was, and when he had come there, he bowed down before the Blessed One, and took his seat respectfully on one side.

Then the Blessed One said to the venerable Ananda, as he sat there by his side: 'Enough Ananda! Do not let yourself be troubled; do not weep! Have I not already, on former occasions, told you that it is in the very nature of all things most near and dear unto us that we must divide ourselves from them, leave them, sever ourselves from them? How, then, Ananda, can this be possible—whereas anything whatever born, brought into being, and organised, contains within itself the inherent necessity of dissolution—how, then, can this be possible, that such a being should not be dissolved? No such condition can exists! For a long time Ananda, have you been very near to me by acts of love, kind and good, that never varies, and is beyond all measure. For a long time, Ananda, have you been very near to me by words of love, kind and good, that never varies, and is beyond all measure. Fopr a long time, Ananda, have you been very near to me by thoughts of love, kind and good, that never varies, and is beyond all measure. You have done well, Ananda! Be earnest in effort, and you too shall soon be free from the great evils—from sensuality, from individuality, from delusion, and from ignorance!'

The Qualities of Ananda

Then the Blessed One addressed the brethren, and said: 'Whosoever, brethren, have been Arahat-Buddhas through the long ages of the past, there were servitors just as devoted to those Blessed Ones as Ananda has been to me. And whosoever, brethren, shall be Arahat-Buddhas in the long ages of the future, there shall be servitors, just as devoted to those Blessed Ones as Ananda has been to me.

'He is a wise man, brethren,—is Ananda. He knows when it is the right time for him to come and visit the Tathagata, and when it is the right time for the brethren and sisters of the order, for devout men and devout women, for a king, or for a king's ministers, for other teachers of their disciples, to come and visit the Tathagata.

'Brethren, there are these four wonderful and marvellous qualities in Ananda. Which are the four?

'If, brethren, a number of the brethren of the order should come to visit Ananda, they are filled with joy on beholding him; and if Ananda should then preach the truth to them, they are filled with joy at the discourse; while the company of brethren is ill at ease, brethren, when Ananda is silent.

'If, brethren, a number of the sisters of the order, or of devout men, or of devout women, should come to visit Ananda, they are filled with joy on beholding him; and if Ananda should then preach the truth to them, they are filled with joy at the discourse; while the company of sisters is ill at ease, brethren, when Ananda is silent.

'Brethren, there are these four wonderful and marvellous qualities in a king of kings. What are the four?'

'If, brethren, a number of nobles, or Brahmins, or heads of houses, or Samanas should come to visit a king of kings, they are filled with joy on beholding him; and if the king of kings should then speak, they are filled with joy at what is said; while they are ill at ease, brethren, when the king of kings is silent.

'Just so, brethren, are the four wonderful and marvellous

qualities in Ananda.'

'If, brethren, a number of the brethren of the order, or the sisters of the order, or of devout men, or of devout women, should come to visit Ananda, they are filled with joy on beholding him; and if Ananda should then preach the truth to them, they are filled with joy at the discourse; while the company of brethren is ill at ease, brethren, when Ananda is silent.

'Now these, brethren, are the four wonderful and marvellous qualities that are in Ananda.'

When he had thus spoken, the venerable Ananda said to the Blessed One:

'Let not the Blessed One die in this little wattel and daub town, in this town in the midst of the jungle, in this branch township. For, Lord, there are other great cities, such as Champa, Rajagaha, Savatthi, Saketa, Kosambi, and Benares. Let the Blessed One die in one of them. There are many wealthy nobles and Brahmans and heads of houses, believers in the Tathagata, who will pay due honour to the remains of the Tathagata.'

'Say not so, Ananda! Say not so, Anands, that this is but a small wattel and daub town, a town in the midst of the jungle, a branch township. Long ago, Ananda, there was a king, by name Maha-Sudassana, a king of kings, a righteous man who ruled in righteousness, Lord of the four quarters of the earth, conqueror, the protector of his people, possessor of the seven royal treasures. This Kusinara, Ananda, was the royal city of king Maha-Sudassana, under the name of Kusavati, and on the east and on the west it was twelve leagues in length, and on the north and on the south it was seven leagues in breadth.

'That royal city Kusavati, Ananda, was mighty, and prosperous, and full of people, crowded with men, and provided with the things for food. Just, Ananda, as the royal city of the gods. Alakananda by name is mighty, prosperous, and full of people, crowded with the gods, and provided with all kinds of food, so, Ananda, was the royal city Kusavati mighty and prosperous, full of people, crowded with men, and provided with all kinds of food.

'Both by day and by night, Ananda, the royal city Kusavati resounded with the ten cries; that is to say, the nose of elephants, and the noise of horses, and the noise of chariots; the sounds of the drum, of the tabor, and of the lute; the sound of singing, and the sounds of the cymbal and of the gong; and lastly, with the cry, "Eat, drink, and be merry!"

'Go now, Ananda, and enter into Kusinara, and inform the Mallas of Kusinara, saying, "This day, O Vasetthas, in the last watch of the night, the final passing away of the Tathagata will take place. Be favourable herein, O Vasetthas, be favourable. Give no occassion to reproach yourselves hereafter, saying, "In our own village did the death of our Tathagata take place, and we took not the opportunity of visiting the Tathagata in his last hours." '

'Even so, Lord,' said the venerable Ananda, in assent, to the Blessed One; and he robed himself, and taking his bowl, entered into Kusinara attended by another member of the order.

Ananda Goes to Kusinara

Now at that time the Mallas of Kusinara were assembled in the council hall on some public affair.

And the venerable Ananda went to the council hall of the Mallas of Kusinara; and when he had arrived there, he informed them, saying, 'This day, O Vasetthas, in the last watch of the night, the final passing away of the Tathagata will take place. Be favourable herein, O Vasetthas, be favourable. Give no occasion to reproach yourselves hereafter, saying, "In our own village did the death of our Tathagata take place, and we took not the opportunity of visiting the Tathagata in his last hours." '

And when they had heard this saying of the venerable

Ananda, the Mallas with their young men and maidens and their wives were grieved, and sad, and afflicted at heart. And some of them wept, dishevelling their hair, and stretched forth their arms and wept, fell prostrate on the ground, and rolled to and fro in anguish at the thought: 'Too soon will the Blessed One die! Too soon will the Happy One pass away! Full soon will the Light of the world vanish away!'

Then the Mallas, with their young men and maidens and their wives, being grieved and sad and afflicted at heart, went to the Sala Grove of the Mallas, to the Upavattana, and to the place where the venerable Ananda was.

Then the venerable Ananda thought: 'If I allow the Mallas of Kusinara, one by one, to pay their respect to the Blessed One, the whole of the Mallas of Kusinara will not have been presented to the Blessed One until this night brightens up into the dawn. Let me, now, cause the Mallas of Kusinara to stand in groups, each family in a group, and so present them to the Blessed One, saying, "Lord! a Malla of such and such a name, with his children, his wives, his retinue, and his friends, humbly bows down at the feet of the Blessed One." '

And the venerable Ananda caused the Mallas of Kusinara to stand in groups, each family in a group, and so presented them to the Blessed One, and said: 'Lord! a Malla of such and such a name, with his children, his wives, his retinue, and his friends, humbly bow down at the feet of the Blessed One.'

And after this manner the venerable Ananda presented all the Mallas of Kusinara to the Blessed One in the first watch of the night.

Now at that time a mendicant named Subhadda, who was not a believer, was dwelling at Kusinara. And the mendicant Subhadda heard the news: 'This very day, they say, in the third watch of the night, will take place the final passing away of the Samana Gotama.'

Then thought the mendicant Subhadda: 'This have I

heard from fellow mendicants of mine, old and well stricken in years, teachers and disciples, when they said: "Sometimes and full seldom do Tathagatas appear in the world, the Arahat-Buddhas." Yet this day, in the last watch of the night, the final passing away of the Samana Gotama will take place. Now a certain feeling of uncertainty has sprung up in my mind; and this faith have I in the Samana Gotama, that he, methinks, is able so to present the truth that I may get rid of this feeling of uncertainty.'

Then the mendicant Subhadda went to the Sala Grove of the Mallas, to the Upavattana of Kusinara, to the place where the venerable Ananda was.

And when he had come there he said to the venerable Ananda: 'Thus have I heard from fellow mendicants of mine, old and well stricken in years, teachers and disciples, when they said: "Sometimes and full seldom do Tathagatas appear in the world, the Arahat-Buddhas." Yet this day, in the last watch of the night, the final passing away of the Samana Gotama will take place. Now a certain feeling of uncertainty has sprung up in my mind; and this faith have I in the Samana Gotama, that he, methinks, is able so to present the truth that I may get rid of this feeling of uncertainty. O that I, even I, Ananda, might be allowed to see the Samana Gotama!'

And when he had thus spoken the venerable Ananda said to the mendicant Subhadda: 'Enough! friend Subhadda. Trouble not the Tathagata. The Blessed One is weary.'

And again the mendicant Subhadda made the same request in the same words, and received the same reply; and the third time the mendicant Subhadda made the same request in the same words, and received the same reply.

Now the Blessed One overheard this conversation of the venerable Ananda with the mendicant Subhadda. And the Blessed One called the venerable Ananda, and said: 'It is enough, Ananda! Do not keep out Subhadda. Subhadda, Ananda, may be allowed to see the Tathagata. Whatever Subhadda may ask of me, he will ask from a desire for knowledge, and not to annoy me. And whatever I may say in answer to his questions, that he will quickly understand.'

Then the venerable Ananda said to Subhadda, the mendicant: 'Enter in, friend Subhadda; for the Blessed One gives you leave.'

Subhadda Becomes the Last Disciple

Then Subhadda, the mendicant, went in to the place where the Blessed One was, and saluted him courteously, and after exchanging with him the compliments of esteem and of civility, he took his seat on one side. And when he was thus seated, Subhadda, the mendicant, said to the Blessed One: 'The Brahmins by saintliness of life, Gotama, who are heads of companies of disciples and students, teachers of students, well known, renowned, founders of schools of doctrine, esteemed as good men by the multitude—to wit, Purana Kassapa, Makkhali of the cattle-pen, Ajita of the garments of hair, Kachchayana of the Pakudha tree, Sanjaya the son of the Belatthi slave-girl, and Nigantha of the Natha clan—have they all, according to their own assertion, thoroughly understood things? or have they not? or are there some of them who have understood, and some who have not?'

'Enough, Subhadda! Let this matter rest whether, they, according to their own assertion, have thoroughly understood things, or whether they have not, or whether some of them have understood and some have not! The truth, Ananda, will I teach you. Listen well to that, and give ear attentively, and I will speak.'

'Even so, Lord!' said the mendicant Subhadda, in assent, to the Blessed One.'

And the Blessed one spake: 'In whatsoever doctrine and discipline, Subhadda, the noble eightfold path is not found, neither in it is there found a man of true saintliness of the first or of the second or of the third or of the fourth degrees. And in whatsoever doctrine and discipline, Subhadda, the noble eightfold path is found, is found the man of true saintliness of the first and the second and the third and the fourth degree. Now in this doctrine and discipline, Subhadda, is found the noble eightfold path, and in it alone, Subhadda, is the man of true saintliness. Void are the systems of other teachers—void of true saints. And in this one, Subhadda, may the brethren live the Life that's Right, so that the world be not bereft of Arahats.

But twenty-nine was I when I renounced
The world, Subhadda, seeking after good.
For fifty years and one year more, Subhadda,
Since I went out, a pilgrim have I been
Through the wide realms of virtue and of truth,
And outside these no really "saint" can be!

'Yea, not of the first, nor of the second, nor of the third, nor of the fourth degree. Void are the systems of other teachers—void of true saints. But in this one Subhadda, may the brethren live the perfect life, that the world be not bereft of those who have reached the highest fruit.'

And when he had thus spoken, Subhadda, the mendicant, said to the Blessed One: 'Most excellent, Lord, are the words of they mouth, most excellent! Just as if a man were to set up that which is thrown down, or were to reveal that which is hidden away, or were to point out the right road to him who has gone astray, or were to bring a lamp into the darkness, so that those who have eyes can see external forms;—just even so, Lord, has the truth been made known to me, in many a figure, by the Blessed One. And I, even, I betake myself, Lord, to the Blessed One as my refuge, to the truth, and to the order. May the Blessed One accept me as a disciple, as a true believer, from this day forth, as long as life endures!'

'Whosoever, Subhadda, that has formerly been a follower of another doctrine and then desires to be received into the higher or the lower grade in this doctrine and discipline, he remains on probation for the space of four months; and at the end of the four months the brethren, exalted in spirit, receive him into the lower or into the higher grade of the order. Nevertheless in this case I acknowledge the difference in persons.'

'If, Lord, whosoever that has formerly been a follower of another doctrine and then desires to be received into the higher or the lower grade in ths doctrine and discipline,—if, in that case, such a person remains on probation for the space of four months; and at the end of the four months, the brethren, exalted in spirit, receive him into the lower or into the higher grade of the order—I too, then, will remain on probation for the space of four months; and at the end of the four months let the brethren, exalted in spirit, receive me into the lower or into the higher grade of the order!'

But the Blessed One called the venerable Ananda, and said: 'As it is, Ananda, receive Subhadda into the order!'

'Even so, Lord!' said the venerable Ananda, in assent, to the Blessed One.

And Subhadda, the mendicant, said to the venerable Ananda: 'Great is your gain, friend Ananda, great is your good fortune, friend Ananda, that you all have been sprinkled with the sprinkling of discipleship in this brotherhood at the hands of the Master himself!'

So Subhadda, the mendicant, was received into the higher grade of the order under the Blessed One; and from immediately after his ordination the venerable Subhadda remained along and separate, earnest, zealous, and resolved. And e'er long he attained to that supreme goal of the higher life for the sake of which men go out from all and every household gain and comfort to become houseless wanderers—yea, that supreme goal did he, by himself, and while yet in this visible world, bring himself to the knowledge, of, and continue to realise, and to see face to face! And he become conscious that birth was at an end, that the higher life had been fulfilled, that all that should be done had been accomplished, and that after this present life there would be no beyond!

So the venerable Subhadda became yet another among the Arahats; and he was the last disciple whom the Blessed One himself converted.

Passes into Nirvana

Now the Blessed One addressed the venerable Ananda, and said: 'It may be, Ananda, that in some of you the thought may arise, "The word of the Master is ended, we have no teacher more!" But it is not thus, Ananda, that you should regard it. The truths and the rules of the order which I have set forth and laid down for you all, let them, after I am gone, be the Teacher to you.

'Ananda! when I am gone address not one another in the way in which the brethren have heretofore addressed each other—with the epithet, that is, of "Avuso" (Friend). A younger brother may be addressed by an elder with his name, or his family name, or the title "Friend." But an elder should be addressed by a younger brother as "Lord" or as "Venerable Sir."

'When I am gone, Ananda, let the order, if it should so which, abolish all the lesser and minor precepts.

'When I am gone, Ananda, let the higher penalty be imposed on brother Channa.

'But what, Lord, is the higher penalty?'

'Let Channa say whatever he may like, Ananda, the brethren should neither speak to him, nor exhort him, nor admonish him.'

'Enquire freely'

Then the Blessed One addressed the brethren, and said: 'It may be, brethren, that there may be doubt or misgiving in the mind of some brother as to the Buddha, or the truth, or the path, or the way. Enquire, brethren, freely. Do not have to reproach yourselves afterwards with the thought "Our teacher was face to face with us, and we could not bring ourselves to enquire of the Blessed One when we were face to face with him." '

And when he had thus spoken the brethren were silent.

And again the second and the third time the Blessed One addressed the brethren, and said: 'It may be, brethren, that there may be doubt or misgiving in the mind of some brother as to the Buddha, or the truth, or the path, or the way. Enquire, brethren, freely. Do not have to reproach yourselves afterwards with the thought, "Our teacher was face to face with us, and we could not bring ourselves to enquire of the Blessed One when we were face to face with him." '

And even the third time the brethren were silent.

Then the Blessed One addressed the brethren, and said: 'It may be, brethren, that you put no questions out of reverence for the teacher. Let one friend communicate to another.'

And when he had thus spoken the brethren were silent.

And the venerable Ananda said to the Blessed One: 'How wonderful a thing is it, Lord, and how marvellous! Verily, I believe that in this whole assembly of the brethren there is not one brother who has any doubt or misgiving as to the Buddha, or the truth, or the path, or the way!'

'It is out of the fulness of faith that thou hast spoken, Ananda! But, Ananda, the Tathagata knows for certain that in this whole assembly of the brethren there is not one brother who has any doubt or misgiving as to the Buddha, or the truth, or the path, or the way! For even the most backward, Ananda, of all these five hundred brethren has become converted, and is no longer liable to be born in a state of suffering, and is assured of final salvation.'

The Last Word

Then the Blessed One addressed the brethren, and said, 'Behold now, brethren, I exhort you, saying, "Decay is inherent in all component things! Work out your salvation with diligence!" '

This was the last word of the Tathagata!

Passing into Infinity

Then the blessed One entered into the first stage of deep meditation. And rising out of the first stage he passed into the second. And rising out of the second he passed into the third. And rising out of the third stage he passed into the fourth. And rising out of the fourth stage of deep meditation be entered into the state of mind to which the infinity of space is also present. And passing out of the mere consciousness of the infinity of space he entered into the state of mind to which the infinity of thought is alone present. And passing out of the mere consciousness of the infinity of thought he entered into a state of mind to which nothing at all was specialy present. And passing out of the consciousness of no special object he fell into a state between consciousness and unconsciousness. And passing out of the state between consciousness and unconsciousness he fell into a state in which the consciousness both of sensations and of ideas had wholly passed away.

Then the venerable Ananda said to the venerable Anuruddha: 'O my Lord, O Anuruddha, the Blessed One is dead!'

'Nay! brother Ananda, the Blessed One is not dead. He has entered into that state in which both sensations and ideas have ceased to be!'

Then the Blessed One passing out of the state in which both sensations and ideas have ceased to be, entered into the state between consciousness and unconsciousness. And passing out of the state between consciousness and unconsciousness he entered into the state of mind to which nothing at all is specially present. And passing out of the consciousness of no special object he entered into the state of mind to which the infinity of thought is alone present. And passing out of the mere consciousness of the infinity of thought he entered into the state of mind to which the infinity of space is alone present. And passing out of the mere consciousness of the infinity of space he entered into the fourth stage of deep meditation. And passing out of the fourth stage he entered into the third. And passing out of the third stage he entered into the second. And passing out of the second he entered into the first. And passing out of the first stage of deep meditation he entered into the second. And passing out of the second stage he entered into the third. And passing out of the third stage he entered into the fourth stage of deep meditation. And passing out of the last stage of deep meditation he immediately expired.

An Earthquake

When the Blessed one died there arose, at the moment of his passing out of existence, a mighty earthquake, terrible and awe-inspiring: and the thunders of heaven burst forth.

When the Blessed One died, Brahma Sahamapati, at the moment of this passing away from Existence, uttered this stanza:

'They all, all being that have life, shall lay
Aside their complex form—that aggregation
Of mental and material qualities,
That gives them, or in heaven or on earth,
Their fleeting individuality!
E'en as the teacher—being such a one,
Unequalled among all the men that are,'Successor of the prophets of old time,
Mighty by wisdom, and in insight clear—

Hath died!'

When the Blessed One died, Sakka, the king of the gods, at the moment of his passing away from existence, uttered this stanza:

'They're transient all, each being's parts and powers,
Growth is their nature, and decay.
They are produced, they are dissolved again:
And then is best, when they have sunk to rest!'

When the Blessed One died, the venerable Aniruddha, at the moment of his passing away from existence, uttered these stanzas:

'When he who from all craving want was free,
Who to Nirvana's tranquil state had reached,
When the great sage finished his span of life,
No gasping struggle vexed that steadfast heart!

'All resolute, and with unshaken mind,
He calmly triumphed o'er the pain of death.
E'en as a bright flame dies away, so was
His last deliverance from the bonds of life!'

When the Blessed One died, the venerable Ananda, at the moment of his passing away from existence, uttered this stanza:

'Then was there terror!
Then stood the hair on end!
Whe he endowed with every grace—
The supreme Buddha—died!'

When the Blessed One died, of those of the brethren who were not yet free from the passions, some stretched out their arms and wept, and some fell headlong on the ground, rolling to and fro in anguish at the thought: 'Too soon has the Blessed One died! Too soon has the Happy One passed away from existence! Too soon has the Light gone out in the world!'

But those of the brethren who were free from the passions, the Arahats, bore their grief collected and composed at the thought: 'Impermanent are all component things! How is it possible that they should not be dissolved?

'Weep not, neither lament'

Then the venerable Aniruddha exhorted the brethren, and said: 'Enough, my brethren! Weep not, neither lament! Has not the Blessed One formerly declared this to us, that it is in the very nature of all things near and dear unto us, that we must divide ourselves from them, leave them, sever ourselves from them? How then, brethren, can this be possible—that whereas anything whatever born, brought into being, and organised, contains within itself the inherent necessity of dissolution—how then can this be possible that such a being should not be dissolved? No such condition can exist! Even the spirits, brethren, will reproach us.'

'But of what kind of spirit is the Lord, the venerable Aniruddha, thinking?'

'There are spirits, brother Ananda, in the sky, but of worldly mind, who dishevel their hair and weep, and stretch forth their arms and weep, fall prostrate on the ground, and roll to and fro in anguish at the thought: "Too soon has the Blessed One died! Too soon has the Happy One passed away! Too soon has the Light gone out in the world!" '

'There are spirits, too, Ananda, on the earth, and of wordly mind, who tear their hair and weep, and stretch forth their arms and weep, fall prostrate on the ground, and roll to and fro in anguish at the thought: "Too soon has the Blessed One died! Too soon has the Happy One passed away! Too soon has the Light gone out in the world!" '

'But the spirits who are free from passion bear it, calm and self-possessed, mindful of the saying which begins, "Impermanent indeed are all component things. How then is it possible that such a being should not be dissolved?" '

Afterward

Now the venerable Aniruddha and the venerable Ananda spent the rest of that night in religious discourse. Then the venerable Aniruddha said to the venerable Ananda: 'Go now, brother Ananda, into Kusinara and inform the Mallas of Kusinara, saying, "The Blessed One, O Vasetthas, is dead: do, then, whatever seemeth to you fit!"

'Even so, Lord!' said the venerable Ananda, in assent, to the venerable Aniruddha. And having robed himself early in the morning, he took his bowl, and went into Kusinara with one of the brethren as an attendant.

Now at that time the Mallas of Kusinara were assembled in the council hall concerning that very matter.

And the venerable Ananda went to the council hall of the Mallas of Kusinara; and when he had arrived there, he informed them, saying, 'The Blessed One, O Vasetthas, is dead; do, then, whatever seemeth to you fit!'

And when they had heard this saying of the venerable Ananda, the Mallas, with their young men and their maidens and their wives, were grieved, and sad, and afflicted at heart. And some of them wept, dishevelling their hair, and some stretched forth their arms and wept, and some fell prostrate on the ground, and some reeled to and fro in anguish at the thought: 'Too soon has the Blessed One died! Too soon has the Happy One passed away! Too soon has the Light gone out in the world!'

Then the Mallas of Kusinara gave orders to their attendants, saying, 'Gather together perfumes and garland, and all the music in Kusinara!'

And the Mallas of Kusinara took the perfumes and

garlands, and all the musical instruments, and five hundred suits of apparel, and went to the Upavattana, to the Sala Grove of the Mallas, where the body of the Blessed One lay. There they past the day in paying honour, reverence, respect, and homage to the remains of the Blessed One with dancing, and hymns, and music, and with garlands and perfumes; and in making canopies of their garments, and preparing decoration wreaths to hang thereon.

Then the Mallas of Kusinara thought:

'It is much too late to burn the body of the Blessed One today. Let us now perform the cremation tomorrow.' And in paying honour, reverence, respect, and homage to the remains of the Blessed One with dancing, and hymns, and music, and with garlands, and perfumes; and in making canopies of their garments, and preparing decoration wreaths to hang thereon, they past the second day too, and then the third day, and the fourth, and the fifth, and the sixth day also.

Then on the seventh day the Mallas of Kusinara thought:

'Let us carryy the body of the Blessed One, by the south and outside, to a spot on the south, and outside of the city,—paying it honour, and reverence, and respect, and homage, with dance and song and music, with garlands and perfumes,—and there, to the south of the city, let us perform the cremation ceremony!'

And thereupon eight chieftains among the Mallas bathed their heads, and clad themselves in new garments with the intention of bearing the body of the Blessed One. But, behold, they could not lift it up!

Then the Mallas of Kusinara said to the venerable Anuruddha: 'What, Lord, can be the reason, what can be the cause that eight chieftains of the Mallas who have bathed their heads, and clad themselves in new garments with the intention of bearing the body of the Blessed One, are unable to lift it up?'

'It is because you, O Vasetthas, have one purpose, and the spirits have another purpose.'

'But what, Lord, is the purpose of the spirits?'

'Your purpose, O Vasetthas, is this, Let us carry the body of the Blessed One, by the south and outside, to a spot on the south, and outside of the city,—paying it honour, and reverence, and respect, and homage, with dance and song and music, with garlands and perfumes,—and there, to the south of the city, let us perform the cremation ceremony. But the purpose of the spirits, Vasetthas, is this, Let us carry the body of the Blessed One by the north to the north of the city, and entering the city by the north gate, let us bring it through the midst of the city into the midst thereof. And going out again by the eastern gate,—paying honour, and reverence, and respect, and homage to the body of the Blessed One, with heavenly dance, and song, and music, and garlands, and perfumes,—let us carry it to the shrine of the Mallas called Makuta-bandhana, to the east of the city, and there let us perform the cremation ceremony.'

'Even according to the purpose of the spirits, so, Lord, let it be!'

Then immediately all Kusinara down even to the dust bins and rubbish heaps became strewn knee-deep with Mandarava flowers from heaven! and while both the spirits from the skies, and the Mallas of Kusinara upon earth, paid honour, and reverence, and respect, and homage to the body of the Blessed One, with dance and song and music, with garlands and with perfumes, they carried the body by the north to the north of the city; and entering the city by the north gate they carried it through the midst of the city into the midst thereof; and going out again by the eastern gate they carried it to the shrine of the Mallas, called Makuta-bandhana; and there, to the east of the city, they laid down the body of the Blessed One.

Then the Mallas of Kusinara said to the venerable Ananda: 'What should be done, Lord, with the remains of the Tathagata?'

'As men treat the remains of a king of kings, so, Vasetthas, should they treat the remains of a Tathagata.'

'And how, Lord, do they treat the remains of a king of kings?'

'They wrap the body of a king of kings, Vasetthas, in a new cloth. When that is done they wrap it in cotton wool. When that is done they wrap it in a new cloth,—and so on till they have wrapped the body in five hundred successive layers of both kinds. They they place the body in an oil vessel of iron, and cover that close up with another oil vessel of iron. They then build a funeral pile of all kinds of perfumes, and burn the body of the king of kings. And then at the four cross roads they erect a dagaba to the king of kings. This, Vasetthas, is the way in which they treat the remains of a king of kings.'

'And as they treat the remains of king of kings, so, Vasetthas, should they treat the remains of the Tathagata. At the four cross roads a dagaba should be erected to the Tathagata. And whosoever shall there place garlands or perfumes or paint, or make salutation there, or become in its presence calm in heart—that shall long be to them for a profit and a joy.'

Therefore, the Mallas gave orders to their attendants, saying, 'Gather together all the carded cotton wool of the Mallas!'

Then the Mallas of Kusinara wrapped the body of the Blessed One in a new cloth. And when that was done, they wrapped it in cotton wool. And when that was done, they wrapped it in a new cloth,—and so on till they had wrapped the body of the Blessed One in five hundred layers of both kinds. And then they placed the body in an oil vessel of iron, and covered that close up with another oil vessel of iron. And then built a furneral pile of all kinds of perfumes, and upon it they placed the body of the Blessed One.

Now at that time the venerable Maha Kassapa was journeying along the high road from Pava to Kusinara with a great company of the brethren, with about five hundred of the brethren. And the venerbale Maha Kassapa left the high road, and sat himself down at the foot of a certain tree.

Just at that time a certain naked ascetic who had picked up a Mandarava flower in Kusinara was coming along the high road to Pava.

And the venerable Maha Kassapa saw the naked ascetic coming in the distance; and when he had seen him he said to the naked ascetic:

'O friend! surely thou knowest our master?'

'Yea, friend! I know him. This day the Samana Gotama has been dead a week! That is how I obtained this Mandarava flower.'

And immediately of those of the brethren who were not yet free from the passion, some stretched out their arms and wept, and some fell headlong on the ground, and some reeled to and fro in anguish at the thought: 'Too soon has the Blessed One died! Too soon has the Happy One passed away from existence! Too soon has the Light gone out in the world!'

But those of the brethren who were free from the passion, the Arahats, bore their grief collected and composed at the thought: 'Impermanent are all component things! How is it possible that they should not be dissolved?'

Now at that time a brother named Subhadda, who had been received into the order in his old age, was seated there in their company.

And Subhadda the old addressed the brethren, and said: 'Enough, brethren! Weep not, neither lament! We are well rid of the great Samana. We used to be annoyed by being told, "This beseems you, this beseems you not." But now we shall be able to do whatever we like; and what we do not like, that we shall not have to do!'

But the venerable Maha Kassapa addressed the brethren, and said: 'Enough, my brethren! Weep not, neither lament! Has not the Blessed One formerly declared this to us, that it is in the very nature of all things, near and dear unto us, that we must divide ourselves from them, leave them sever ourselves from them? How then, brethren, can this be possible—that whereas anything whatever born brought into being, and organised contains within itself the inherent necessity of dissolution—how then can this be possible that such a being should not be dissolved? No such condition can exist!'

The Funeral

Now just at that time four chieftains of the Mallas had bathed their heads and clad themselves in new garments with the intention of setting on fire the funeral pile of the Blessed One. But, behold, they were unable to set it alight!

Then the Mallas of Kusinara said to the venerable Aniruddha : 'What, Lord, can be the reason, and what the cause, that four chieftains of the Mallas who have bathed their heads, and clad themselves in new garments, with the intention of setting on fire the funeral pile of the Blessed One, are unable to set it on fire?'

'It is because you, O Vasetthas, have one purpose, and the spirits have another purpose.'

'But what, Lord, is the purpose of the spirits?'

'The purpose of the spirits, O Vasetthas, is this : That venerable brother Maha Kassapa is now journeying along the high road from Pava to Kusinara with a great company of the brethren, with five hundred of the brethren. The funeral pile of the Blessed one shall not catch fire, until the venerable Maha Kassapa shall have been able reverently to salute the sacred feet of the Blessed One.'

'Even according to the purpose of the spirits, so, Lord, let it be!'

Then the venerable Maha Kassapa went on to Makuta-bandhana of Kusinara, to the shrine of the Mallas, to the place where the funeral pile of the Blessed One was. And when he had come up to it, he arranged his robe on one shoulder; and bowing down with clasped hands he thrice walked reverently round the pile; and then, uncovering the feet, he bowed down in reverence at the feet of the Blessed One.

And those five hundred brethren arranged their robes on one shoulder; and bowing down with clasped hands, they thrice walked reverently round the pile, and then bowed down in reverence at the feet of the Blessed One.

And when the homage of the venerable Maha Kassapa and of those five hundred brethren was ended, the funeral pile of the Blessed One caught fire of itself.

Now as the body of the Blessed One burned itself away, from the skin and the integument, and the flesh, and the nerves, and the fluid of the joints, neither soot nor ash was seen: and only the bones remained behind.

Just as one sees no soot or ash when glue or oil is burned; so, as the body of the Blessed One burned itself away, from the skin and the integument, and the flesh, and the nerves,and the fluid of the joints, neither soot nor ash was seen: and only the bones remained behind. And of those five hundred pieces of raiment the very innermost and outermost were both consumed.

And when the body of the Blessed One had been burnt up, there came down streams of water from the sky and extinguished the furnearl pile of the Blessed One; and there burst forth streams of water from the storehouse of the waters (beneath the earth), and extinguished the funeral pile of the Blessed One. The Mallas of Kusinara also brought water scented with all kinds of perfumes, and extinguished the funeral pile of the Blessed One.

Then the Mallas of Kusinara surrounded the bones of the Blessed One in their council hall with a lattice work of spears, and with a rampart of bows; and there for seven days they paid honour and reverence and respect and homage to them with dance and song and music, and with garlands and perfumes.

The Relics

Now the king od Magadha, Ajatasattu, the son of the queen of the Videha clan, heard the news that the Blessed One had died at Kusinara.

Then the king of Magadha, Ajatasattu, the son of the queen of the Videha clan, sent a messenger to the Mallas, saying, 'The Blessed One belonged to the soldier caste, and I too am of the soldier caste. I am worthy to receive a portion of the relics of the Blessed One. Over the remains of the Blessed one will I put up a sacred cairn, and in their honour will I celebrate a feast!'

And the Lichchavis of Vesali heard the news that the Blessed One had died at Kusinara. And the Lichchavis of Vesali sent a messenger to the Mallas, saying, 'The Blessed One belonged to the soldier caste, and we too are of the soldier caste. We are worthy to receive a portion of the relics of the Blessed One. Over the remains of the Blessed One will we put up a sacred cairn, and in their honour will we celebrate a feast!'

And the Sakiyas of Kapilavatthu heard the news than the Blessed One had died at Kusinara. And the Sakiyas of Kapilavatthu sent a messenger to the Mallas, saying, 'The Blessed One was the pride of our race. We are worthy to receive a portion of the relics of the Blessed One. Over the remains of the Blessed One will we put up a sacred cairn, and in their honour will we celebrate a feast!'

And the Bulis of Allakappa heard the news that the Blessed One had died at Kusinara. And the Bulis of Allakappa sent a messenger to the Mallas, saying, 'The Blessed One belonged to the soldier caste, and we too are of the soldier caste. We are worthy to receive a portion of the relics of the Blessed One. Over the remains of the Blessed One will we put up a sacred cairn, and in their honour will we celebrate a feast!'

And the Koliyas of Ramagama heard the news that the Blessed One had died at Kusinara. And the Koliyas of

Ramagama sent a messenger to the Mallas, saying, 'The Blessed One belonged to the soldier caste,and we too are of the soldier caste. We are worthy to receive a portion of the relics of the Blessed One. Over the remains of the Blessed One will we put up a sacred cairn, and in their honour will we celebrate a feast!'

And the Brahmin of Vethadipa heard the news that the Blessed One had died at Kusinara. And the Brahmin of Vethadipa sent a messenger to the Mallas, saying, 'The Blessed One belonged to the soldier caste, and I am a brahmin. I am worthy to receive a portion of the relics of the Blessed One. Over the remains of the Blessed One will I put up a sacred cairn, and in their honour will I celebrate a feast!'

And the Mallas of Pava heard the news that the Blessed One had died at Kusinara. Then the Mallas of Pava sent a messenger to the Mallas, saying, 'The Blessed One belonged to the soldier caste, and we too are of the soldier caste. We are worthy to receive a portion of the relics of the Blessed One. Over the remains of the Blessed One will we put up a sacred cairn, and in their honour will we celebrate a feast!'

When they heard these things the Mallas of Kusinara spoke to the assembled brethren, saying, 'The Blessed One died in our village domain. We will not give away any part of the remains of the Blessed One!'

When they had thus spoken, Dona the Brahman addressed the assembled brethren, and said:

'Hear, reverend sirs, one single word from me.
Forbearance was our Buddha wont to teach.
Unseemly is it that over the division
Of the remains of him who was the best of beings
Strife should arise, and wounds, and war!

Let us all, sirs, with one accord unite
In friendly harmony to make eight portions.

Wide spread let Thupas rise in every land
That in the Englightened One mankind may trust!'

'Do thou then, O Brahmin, thyself divide the remains of the Blessed One equally into eight parts, with fair division.'

'Be it so, sir!' said Dona, in assent, to the assembled brethren. And he divided the remains of the Blessed One equally into eight parts, with fair division. And he said to them: 'Give me, sirs, this vessel and I will set up over it a sacred cairn, and in its honour will I estabish a feast.'

And they gave the vessel to Dona the Brahmin.

And the Moriyas of Pipphalivana heard the news that the Blessed One had died at Kusinara.

Then the Moriyas of Pipphalivana sent a messenger to the Mallas, saying, 'The Blessed One belonged to the soldier caste, and we too are of the soldier caste. We are worthy to receive a portion of the relics of the Blessed One. Over the remains of the Blessed One will we put up a sacred cairn, and in their honour will we celebrate a feast!'

And when they heard the answer, saying, 'There is no portion of the remains of the Blessed One left over. The remains of the Blessed One are all distributed,' then they took away the embers.

Then the king of Magadha, Ajatasattu, the son of the queen of the Videha clan, made a mound in Rajagaha over the remains of the Blessed One, and held a feast.

And the Lichchavis of Vesali made a mound in Vesali over the remains of the Blessed One, and held a feast.

And the Bulis of Allakappa made a mound in Allakappa over the remains of the Blessed One, and held a feast.

And the Koliyas of Ramagama made a mound in Ramagama over the remains of the Blessed One, and held a feast.

And Vethadipaka the Brahman made a mound in Vethadipa over the remains of the Blessed One, and held a feast.

And the Mallas of Pava made a mound in Pava over the remains of the Blessed One, and held a feast.

And the Mallas of Kusinara made a mound in Kusinara over the remains of the Blessed One, and held a feast.

And Dona the Brahmin made a mound over the vessel in which the body had been burnt, and held a feast.

And the Moriyas of Pipphalivana made a mound over the embers, and held a feast.

Thus were there eight mounds, Thupas, for the remains, and one for the vessel, and one for the embers. This was how it used to be.

Eight measures of relics there were of him of the far-seeing eye,
Of the best of the best of men. In India seven are worshipped,
And one measures in Ramagama, by the kings of the serpent race.
One tooth, too, is honoured in heaven, and one in Gandhara's city.
One in the Kalinga realm, and one more by the Naga race.

Through their glory the bountiful earth is made bright with offerings painless—

For with such are the Great Teacher's relics best honoured by those who are honoured,

By gods and by Nagas and kinds, yea, thus by the noblest of monarchs—

Bow down with clasped hands!

Hard, hard is a Buddha to meet with through hundreds of ages!

• • •